THE NEW
LEXINGTON
PRESS

FROM HERESY TO DOGMA

ADVANCE PRAISE FOR *FROM HERESY TO DOGMA*

"A timely review of the sea change that has taken place in American corporations in the past thirty-five years. Hoffman's history offers an intriguing perspective of the external drivers and the internal workings of a firm as it wrestles with ever-increasing demands for environmental protection. It gives the reader a rich history, engaging analyses, and provocative conclusions."—WILLIAM D. RUCKELSHAUS, *former administrator, U.S. Environmental Protection Agency, and current chairman and CEO, Browning Ferris Industries*

"In delving into the corporate psyche, Hoffman manages to treat a usually highly charged subject dispassionately, apolitically, and with thorough research and remarkable balance. An interesting and rewarding analysis of the magnitude and reality of the change which public concern about environmental issues has brought about in corporate and political/regulatory life."—ROBERT D. KENNEDY, *retired chairman and CEO, Union Carbide Corporation*

"By tracing the historical evolution of corporate responses to the environmental movement, Hoffman tells an important story about how and why corporations change, one that offers important lessons for environmental advocates."—FRED KRUPP, *executive director, Environmental Defense Fund*

"Hoffman's work presents a new perspective on the environmental issue. It combines a historical perspective of the environmental movement with an analysis of the parallel corporate management structures that evolved. Both the experienced observer and the novice will find that it contributes to their understanding of the ever-changing issue of environmental responsibility."—ROBERT H. CAMPBELL, *chairman and CEO, Sun Company, Inc.*

"You've got a winner here, one that will be of broad appeal to multiple audiences: academic environmentalists, corporate environmental managers, business historians, organization theorists, government regulators, and environmental activists. Hoffman's book fills a huge void in the literature of environmentalism."—THOMAS N. GLADWIN, *professor and director, Global Environment Program, Leonard N. Stern School of Business, New York University*

"This is an extraordinary story and analysis, combining the research of an incisive organization theorist with fascinating observations of an important chapter in our nation's recent political history. *From Heresy to Dogma* is a major contribution on all counts."—PAUL HIRSCH, *professor of organization behavior, J. L. Kellogg Graduate School of Management, Northwestern University*

FROM HERESY TO DOGMA

An Institutional History of Corporate Environmentalism

Andrew J. Hoffman

•

The New Lexington Press
San Francisco

BKO 1447 - 9|3

GIFT
11/7/97

For sales outside the United States, please contact your local Simon &
Schuster International Office.

Manufactured in the United States of America on Lyons Falls
TCF Turin Book. This paper is acid-free and 100 percent totally chlo-
rine-free.

Library of Congress Cataloging-in-Publication Data

Hoffman, Andrew J.,
    From heresy to dogma : an institutional history of corporate envi-
ronmentalism / Andrew J. Hoffman.
        p. cm. — (The New Lexington Press management series)
    Includes bibliographical references and index.
    ISBN 0-7879-0819-3 (alk. paper). — ISBN 0-7879-0820-7 (pbk. :
alk. paper)
    1. Industrial management—Environmental aspects—United
States. 2. Social responsibility of business—United States.
    3. Environmental policy—United States. I. Title. II. Series.
HD30.255.H64 1997
658.4'08—dc21   97-3694

FIRST EDITION

HB Printing 10 9 8 7 6 5 4 3 2 1

PB Printing 10 9 8 7 6 5 4 3 2 1

The New Lexington Press Management Series

CONTENTS

PART ONE:
Heresy Becomes Dogma

PART TWO:
An Institutional History of Corporate Environmentalism

PART THREE:
The Sum of Institutional Change

LIST OF FIGURES AND TABLES

FIGURES

TABLES

In memory of Hank Thaler (1943–1996)

PREFACE

heresy   n., *1.* religious opinion or doctrine at variance with the orthodox or accepted doctrine. *2.* any belief or theory that is strongly at variance with established beliefs, mores, etc.

dogma   n., *1.* a system of principles or tenets, as of a church. *2.* a settled or established opinion, belief, or principle.[1]

On February 9, 1993, the Amoco Corporation held its worldwide senior management meeting in Houston, Texas. Three hundred fifty managers from the corporation's oil, chemical, and exploration subsidiaries questioned senior executives for two hours. When it came his turn to speak, Vice Chairman Lawrie Thomas carefully laid out the corporation's strategic framework for the coming decade. Integral to that framework was the company's goal of becoming an environmental leader. "It must be kept in mind," he explained, "that environmental costs will place an increasing burden on the industry cost structure as developing countries expand legislation. For an environmentally progressive company like Amoco, this trend may represent a competitive advantage." As the vice chairman concluded his remarks, the deputy managing director of United Kingdom operations leaned over to Walter Quanstrom, the corporate vice president for environmental health and safety (EH&S), and asked, "How does it feel to hear your heresy become dogma?"

I love that metaphor. With succinct clarity, it captures much of what this book is about. As its transition from heresy to dogma suggests, corporate environmentalism has come a long way in the past three decades. But the words *heresy* and *dogma* suggest something deeper, invoking images of symbolic language, formal ceremony, cultural norms, and religious values. Much like parishioners following an overarching set of theological tenets, firms have followed an encompassing set of industry rules, norms, perceptions, and beliefs as their environmental policies have evolved. But rather than originating within a single body, these *institutions,* as they are called, originate within each firm's business, economic, political, and social networks, what is called the firm's *organizational field.* And as one would expect in any such social change, compliance with industry dogma may be either substantive or symbolic in nature. Yet even though the depth of the conversion varies from firm to firm, adoption of the accepted practices of the day becomes universal.

Developing such an argument would not be possible through traditional analyses of corporate environmentalism, based on law or economics. It emerges through the lens of organizational behavior, an area of academic research notably absent from the debate over this socially important issue. This absence has not gone without criticism within academia. My inspiration to write this book comes from both the empirical and the theoretical ends of the academic spectrum. First, in 1993, Tom Gladwin[2] made a plea for an application of organizational theory to the study of corporate environmental management. He wrote that "sociological theory pertaining to organizations holds the greatest promise for improving our understanding of how greening works."[3] Second, in the keynote speech at the 1996 Stanford Conference on Organization Research,[4] Stephen Barley[5] challenged the field of organizational behavior to produce more work of broad social relevance. He argued that most academic contributions to contemporary social issues such as the environment, health care, international relations, and labor trends presently come from economists and lawyers. While they have much to offer, these disciplines focus narrowly on the coercive mechanisms of policy and law for explaining and solving societal problems. They neglect the systemic organizational contexts in which these mechanisms are based. To respond to both Dr. Barley's and Dr. Gladwin's calls to action, the challenge is to apply theoretical models in explaining practical social problems.

In my view, socially relevant research lies in the middle ground between theory and practice. To stray too far to one extreme or the other leads the researcher away from a direct contribution to addressing societal or managerial issues. On the one hand, empirical analysis without a theoretical grounding risks becoming purely editorial, lacking explanatory credibility beyond that of the author's observations. On the other hand, theoretical analysis without an empirical application risks becoming impotent, awaiting another author to remove the theory from the confines of its academic ivory tower and give it relevance by applying it to the "real" world. To offer something of lasting value to audiences beyond those who already share your views (as in the former case) or to those within a small and select academic universe (as in the latter case), a bridge between the theoretical and the empirical must be built.

This book attempts to build that bridge. I have three objectives in writing this book. First, I want to tell the history of corporate environmentalism. Second, I want to tell why it happened as it did. Underlying both of these objectives is a third, that of forecasting where corporate environmentalism is going. The first goal began in 1993, when I spent two months poring over thirty-four years of trade journals in the basement of the campus library at MIT. Finding the same desk, day after day, in the dark and dusty carrels, I scanned volume after volume to uncover the vein of corporate environmentalism woven into the market reports, technology reviews, and strategy assessments. Lying within this vein was a history I had never before seen; it was like opening a time capsule after years of neglect.

I read about how the chemical industry had fervently rejected the conclusions of Rachel Carson's *Silent Spring* in 1962,[6] denouncing her personally and parodying her book with a version produced by the chemical company Monsanto called *The Desolate Year*. I read how the oil industry had denied the environmental effects of the 1969 Santa Barbara oil spill and the health effects of lead, arguing at one point that politically inspired air pollution regulations would put the automobile out of the reach of the average American. But the story I read was not one of an industry out of touch; rather, it was a story of an industry facing dramatic societal change. These industries were composed of proud people who believed that they were taming nature for the good of humankind; they were a remnant of what Samuel Florman[7] called the "Golden Age of Engineering." At first they regarded as a personal affront the aggressive claims that their actions were misguided and that they were, in fact, harming those they believed they were helping.

Over time, as societal perspectives changed, so did perspectives within industry. As I continued to read, the tone and focus of corporate environmentalism evolved. Environmentalism, at first seen as a threat from the fringes of society, became a central component of businesses' competitive strategy. The original environmental priorities of clean water and clean air gave way to safe hazardous waste disposal and cleanup of abandoned waste sites, which were replaced in turn by waste minimization, pollution prevention, and product stewardship. Paradoxically, the evolution came full circle in the 1990s, as the oil industry held up the Santa Barbara oil spill as a psychological turning point in U.S. environmentalism and as the chemical industry traced its environmental roots back to the publication of *Silent Spring*. I couldn't have asked for a better education in corporate environmentalism, and having learned it, I feel better able to understand both how much things have changed and where they are going. I am compelled to share this valuable education, both with those seeking to satisfy their curiosity about environmentalism and with those searching for historical models around which to conduct further investigations and analyses.

It is for this latter group that I maintain my second objective, to explain why this historical evolution took place. My goal is to offer something more than simply an entertaining account with no explanatory value beyond this particular context. The history of corporate environmentalism is a story of corporate change. Environmentalism has profoundly altered the form and function of the corporate enterprise. But in this case, the origins of change lie predominantly outside the firm. To properly capture this phenomenon, the analytic lens must look beyond the individual organization and consider also the social, political, and market context in which it exists. To that end, I have broadened this history to consider how both the internal structure of firms and their external environment have evolved over time. Both of these histories are constructed within a theoretical framework that reveals the interconnections between them. As a result, this framework can be applied to contexts other than environmentalism.

To satisfy both the historical and the theoretical objectives is a daunting challenge. Those drawn to this book by the words *history of corporate environmentalism* may feel intimidated by the theoretical content. Those seeking an "institutional" analysis may lament that the theoretical model does not take center stage. I challenge each reader to consider the value of the whole, for my goal is to create a story out of the building blocks of history and theory that, in the end, is greater in its explanatory power than the sum of its parts.

My model for this goal is Graham Allison's *Essence of Decision.*[8] Allison's book occupies a prominent space on my bookshelf; it is a classic in its ability to provide a history that is inseparable from the theoretical models used to explain it. In reviewing the Cuban missile crisis, Allison applies three different models to provide three different analyses. Viewing the crisis through the lens of the "rational actor model," one might conclude that "since nuclear war between the United States and Soviet Union would be mutual suicide, neither nation would choose nuclear war, and nuclear war [was] therefore not a serious possibility."[9] However, through the lens of the "organizational process model," the story becomes more compelling. Allison shows that the United States and Soviet Union were not monoliths but rather were large bureaucracies—organizations through which information is developed, interpreted, disseminated, and translated. Conclusions from this model suggest that the chances of war were much greater. Organizational dynamics alter rational expectations. He concludes that "nuclear crises between machines as large as the United States and Soviet governments are inherently chancy. The information and estimates available to leaders about the situation will reflect organizational goals and routines as well as facts."[10] Not ending there, Allison applies his third model, the "bureaucratic politics model," to reveal conclusions that are even more tenuous. The responses advocated by leaders of the U.S. government ranged from doing nothing to inflicting a full air strike. The ultimate decision to impose a blockade emerged from many uncertain political factors. Had President Kennedy proved his mettle in the earlier Bay of Pigs confrontation, the diplomatic track might have prevailed. Had earlier events surrounding Cuba not brought the tempering voices of Robert Kennedy and Theodore Sorenson into the discussion, an air strike would probably have been ordered. In the end, "the interaction of internal games" and "the mix of personality, expertise, influence and temperament that allows a group to clarify alternatives even while it pulls and hauls for separate preferences" could indeed have yielded nuclear war as an outcome.[11]

In each case, the analytical model Allison applies tells something different about the same history. His point is not that one model is right while the others are wrong, but rather that each tells a different part of the whole. At the same time, he shows that the history explains something important about the applicability of each model. In the end, neither the history nor the theory takes center stage. Their combination is greater than the sum of both parts, providing a rich and convincing explanation both of a seminal event in our country's history and of the internal dynamics of the organization of government. In the same way, I believe there is a need for the book you are now holding. It fills a vacuum in the literature of corporate environmentalism and contributes to the literature of organizational change.

Many good books have been written on the history of environmentalism in the United States,[12] but none have written about this history from the corporate point of view. They focus predominantly on the evolution of environmental ideology, political activism, public opinion, or government regulation, neglecting what is perhaps the central objective of many of these movements—corporate change. Furthermore, while many good books have been written about corporate environmental practice,[13] few address the issue in either a historical fashion or through the lens of a theoretical model. Rather, most are built on case studies that depict management practice in a positivist fashion, outlining a normative prescription for how "leading" companies are acting and how others ought to follow. But by combining theory and history, convincing conclusions can be drawn that allow credible projections of the future. These are based neither on my own values nor on those of a hidden environmental agenda, but instead on established models and theory in the organizational and management literature.

For the management literature, this book offers a powerful account of a unique organizational phenomenon, providing new insights into the behavior of firms and the theories used to explain that behavior. Over the past three decades, environmentalism has been a dramatic and encompassing force for social change. Thirty years ago, the billowing smokestack signified economic progress and jobs. Today, it represents wasted resources, damage to the environment, and a threat to the health of the community. Thirty years ago, environmental affairs were handled as an adjunct to the engineering department. Today, they are handled by a large and sophisticated environmental health and safety (EH&S) department, with support from core functions such as law, public relations, marketing, finance, accounting, and even the board of directors. Environmentalism has transformed product markets, process designs, organizational structures, and, ultimately, corporate objectives. All told, its uniqueness lies in its holistic impact, allowing interdisciplinary analysis in both the technical and the social sciences. The focus of this book is organizational behavior, but it would be impossible to leave out the strands of engineering, chemistry, economics, political science, and sociology that affect that behavior. Thus in providing one slice of this complex story, I fully expect to expose other avenues of research for other researchers to explore.

The book's structure is consistent with my theoretical and historical objectives. Following a brief introduction in Chapter One, Chapter Two sets the stage for the history of corporate environmentalism provided in Chapters Three through Six. Chapter Two explains both the theoretical tools used in this book and the industrial context within which they are applied. Like all the chapters in this book, it is written in a fashion that should be accessible to both the lay reader and the scholar. Chapters Three through Six present the history of corporate environmentalism, broken into four general stages. These chapters represent the bulk of my research work and should satisfy those searching for the historical component of corporate environmentalism. In Chapter Seven, I bring the historical and the theoretical together in an encompassing analysis, offering an overarching framework for understanding this dramatic progression of organizational change. Finally, in Chapter Eight, I test and expand the model and history to consider implications for the future.

Although my goal is to present this analysis in as orderly and complete a fashion as possible, the ultimate power in the writer-reader relationship lies with the reader. It is the reader who chooses how to interpret what is written and whether or not to read the work at all. So, in this brief moment I would like to dissuade you from exercising your reader's prerogative and selectively reading portions of this book. While the history could be read in isolation to provide some understanding of how corporate norms and structures have evolved, and the theory could be read alone to provide an overview of the institutional model, without reading both and making the necessary connections, the story and lessons this book presents will be incomplete. Because I wish to combine the historical and the theoretical, my explanation evolves through both.

ACKNOWLEDGMENTS

A central theme of this book is that the external social environment has directed much concerning how the corporate organization has developed with respect to environmentalism. Motivations for change and corporate conceptions of that change have originated outside firms. To be consistent, I must also acknowledge how much my own external social environment has influenced the ideas developed in this book. In the final analysis, every personal endeavor is, in large part, the product of a collective. With this in mind, I give credit and thanks to those around me with whom I have discussed my ideas and expectations.

The foundation of this work began as a doctoral dissertation at the Massachusetts Institute of Technology, where it was guided by a group of professors from both the management and engineering schools. Physicist Alan Lightman divides scientists into two camps, "theorists or experimentalists and abstractionists or tinkerers";[14] this committee of six professors represented both. The resulting support and conflict kept me true to the challenge of providing both theoretical rigor and practical relevance. Since my talents lie more in the application than the creation of theory, I would place myself more in the experimentalist category. As such, I found comforting support with my practical thinking reviewers: Fred Moavenzadeh, John Ehrenfeld, Bill Pounds, and David Marks. However, my forays into the world of abstract theory would not have been possible without the assistance of many wonderful tutors, two of whom were on my committee: Willie Ocasio and Bob Thomas.

After leaving MIT, I joined the Organization Behavior Department at Northwestern's J. L. Kellogg School of Management. Here my thoughts and arguments have been further developed through the support of both the faculty and students. I must particularly acknowledge the private tutelage of Marc Ventresca, Paul Hirsch, and Lex Donaldson, without whom this book would likely not have been written.

I must also acknowledge those on whom I have been able to test my ideas. The master of management students in my first environmental strategy class (though not necessarily with their direct knowledge) gave me a forum in which to test and refine the articulation of my arguments. Also, several individuals graciously gave their time to review an early draft of this manuscript: Jackie Prince Roberts, Gwen Ruta, Mary Beth Tuohy, Marc Ventresca, Max Bazerman, Claire Buisseret, and Bill Hicks. My thanks also go to the executives at the Amoco Corporation who provided such generous support by participating in this research: Wally Quanstrom, Jerry Houren, Bob Batch, and Larry Heidemann.

This list of acknowledgments would not be complete without mentioning the family of which I am a product. I am the fifth of seven industrious children raised by parents who stressed the importance of both character and education in life. While I am proud to have earned a Ph.D., this honor is tempered both by the fact that I am the third in my family to do so and by the realization that the importance of this accomplishment is secondary to the goals and objectives to which I apply it in my life's work.

Evanston, Illinois   ANDREW J. HOFFMAN
March 1997

THE AUTHOR

Andrew J. Hoffman is professor of organization behavior at the J. L. Kellogg Graduate School of Management at Northwestern University. He earned a bachelor's degree (1983) from the Department of Chemical Engineering at the University of Massachusetts at Amherst, a master's degree (1991) from the Department of Civil and Environmental Engineering at MIT, and an interdepartmental doctoral degree (1995) from the Sloan School of Management and the Department of Civil and Environmental Engineering at MIT. Before earning his Ph.D., he was a compliance engineer for the Environmental Protection Agency, a consultant for Metcalf & Eddy, Inc., and an analyst for the Amoco Oil Corporation.

Hoffman's main research activities focus on the managerial and technical aspects of corporate environmentalism. In particular, he applies organizational behavior theory to his empirical research in order to understand how and why corporations adopt environmental practices and procedures. He has published articles on this work in leading academic, professional, and popular journals.

From 1995 until 1997, Hoffman was awarded the Environmental Council Post-Doctoral Fellowship at Northwestern University and was also the recipient of the 1995 Klegerman Award for Environmental Excellence at MIT. He is a member of the Academy of Management, the Society of Environmental Journalists, and Tau Beta Pi.

FROM HERESY TO DOGMA

PART ONE

HERESY BECOMES DOGMA

I

A ROAD MAP OF CORPORATE ENVIRONMENTALISM

IN 1970, University of Chicago economist Milton Friedman wrote in the *New York Times Magazine* that any company making pollution control expenditures beyond what was "required by law in order to contribute to the social objective of improving the environment" was practicing "pure and unadulterated socialism."[1] Consistent with Friedman's dim view of proactive environmental management, a 1974 Conference Board survey found that the majority of companies treated environmental management as a "threat." The survey noted "a widespread tendency in most of industry to treat pollution control expenditures as non-recoverable investments."[2] Even President Nixon's decision to form the Environmental Protection Agency (EPA) in December 1970 was more the result of the president's need to deflate the growing environmental strength of his political opponent, Senator Edmund Muskie, than an indication of his belief in the validity of the emerging social movement of environmentalism. Nixon associated the environmental movement with the antiwar movement, both of which he saw as reflecting weaknesses in the American character.[3] The consensus at the time was that environmental protection was at best a necessary evil and at worst a temporary nuisance. Over the next two decades, however, much changed.

In 1995, Harvard strategy professor Michael Porter wrote in the *Harvard Business Review* that environmental protection was not a threat to the corporate enterprise but rather an opportunity, one that could increase its competitive advantage in the marketplace.[4] Put another way, he was arguing that any company that made pollution control expenditures beyond what was required by law was now practicing *pure and unadulterated capitalism*. Consistent with this shift in mindset, a 1991

3

survey by the Conference Board found that 77 percent of U.S. companies had a formal system in place for proactively identifying key environmental issues.[5] And executives from corporations such as Dow,[6] Monsanto,[7] DuPont,[8] and Union Carbide[9] were actively espousing the benefits of proactive environmental management while instituting programs for community relations, product stewardship, pollution prevention, and environmental leadership, all in the name of increasing corporate competitiveness and shareholder returns.

Such a dramatic transformation in so short a period of time—but what kind of transformation has it been? While many see this as indicative of a shift in the industrial mindset, a signal that environmentalism has been "internalized" into firms' core objectives, skeptics see a mere rhetorical shift, an acquiescence to the current vogue, without any substantive foundation. What is really happening here? Providing an explanation is the goal of this book. In particular, I will seek to answer two questions:

1. How did industry move from a posture of vehement resistance to environmentalism to one of proactive environmental management?

2. Why has this transformation occurred?

Answering the first question involves an historical account; the second requires a theoretical model. In actuality, however, these objectives are not separate and distinct. I want to tell the story of how corporations have evolved with regard to environmentalism, but I want also to explain the underlying dynamics of organizational change. Thus I frame the story in terms of organizational behavior. History and theory are intertwined to offer an explanation that reveals more than either could reveal on its own. The book not only explains history in hindsight but also provides a framework for understanding how history has and will play out. In so doing, it provides an analysis of what the transformation in corporate environmentalism means. How deep is this transformation entrenched? What are its implications for the corporate executive, the policy analyst, or the environmental activist in affecting organizational change? And what possible future events may either sustain or alter the direction history has taken thus far?

This book is not aimed at the environmentalist, although environmentalists should find its conclusions provoking. In fact, you need not even believe that environmental degradation is occurring to find this book useful. What lies in the following chapters is not a treatise on the impact of the corporation on the environment, nor is it a projection of environmental values on the corporation. I am not pushing any political agenda. I am chronicling how industry's views have evolved on a particular issue. In so doing, I draw on management theory, not to tell managers what they must do, but rather to present a compelling analysis of what they have historically done and, in the process, present a model of what they can do in the future. In this way, we can look at the broader implications of this account of organizational change. By employing historical facts, the account reveals where we are going based on where we have been. It is an analysis of how the business environment has been altered by environmentalism and what have been the ramifications of this change for the corporate enterprise. That is what makes this book distinctive among "environmental" anthologies.

Many have written about "the environmental movement," but in reality, each account has covered only one particular aspect of what is a multifaceted movement. For example, in their books *Forcing the Spring: The Transformation of the American Environmental Movement* and *Losing Ground: American Environmentalism at the Close of the Twentieth Century*, Robert Gottlieb and Mark Dowie provide analyses focused on political activism.[10] In his book *Public Policies for Environmental Protection*, Paul Portney chronicles the evolution of environmental regulation.[11] In *The Shaping of Environmentalism in America*, Victor Scheffer writes about the evolution of environmental problems and the ideologies they have spawned.[12] And rounding out this list of noteworthy authors, Anthony Downs and Riley Dunlap write about the evolution of public opinion.[13] Although each is presented as an analysis of "the environmental movement," each is actually a solid analysis of one particular aspect of it.

This book is no exception. It focuses on one aspect of the overall environmental movement, that of corporate environmentalism. In particular, it focuses on the transformation that has taken place within the U.S. chemical and petroleum industries. That is not to say that other aspects of the environmental movement will not be considered. Since components of the movement overlap and intertwine, this story cannot be told without an account of the influences of political activism, environmental regulation, environmental ideology, and public opinion. But in each case these components will be reviewed as they are perceived from this book's central frame of reference, that of industry. Thus this is not a stylized interpretation of environmental events and pressures but rather a careful analysis of how the chemical and petroleum industries have viewed those events and pressures. And more important, it is about how and why the members of each industry have responded as they did. It is this perspective that is this book's unique contribution.

THE INSTITUTIONAL HISTORY OF CORPORATE ENVIRONMENTALISM

Let us begin with an overview of the origins of corporate environmentalism and then focus more tightly on the specifics.

The General Argument

Why has industrial and environmental history evolved as it has? How can one conceptualize the history of corporate change related to environmentalism? The answer lies in a complex analysis of the social dynamics of organizational behavior. To proceed, an important distinction regarding corporate action in response to environmentalism must be noted. In some arenas of business management, firms have great latitude to exercise control over corporate strategy. Actions are motivated largely by internal objectives. In other arenas, however, that flexibility of action is quite limited. The firm is pushed along by external forces over which it has limited control. For the past three decades, corporate environmental management has fallen into this latter category.

The fact that corporate environmental expenditures have increased at a steady rate of $250 million per year since 1973[14] is indicative not of industry's being motivated to act but of its being forced to react. But beyond mandated increases in environmental expenditures, the environmental history of the past thirty-five years reflects an evolution in what environmentalism "means" to the corporation—how it is conceptualized and what is seen as the proper role and response of the corporation in responding to it. This meaning is not for the corporation alone to decide. Many other actors have a stake and a voice in deciding how it is framed. And over the course of time, this group of actors has expanded greatly. It is through this group that the perception and framing of what business activities mean have steadily evolved. How corporate activities were perceived in the 1960s, 1970s, 1980s, and 1990s is a subjective reflection of the historical context in which they were observed. In point of fact, no corporate activity is objectively defined. Whether it is a smokestack, an environmental accident, or a corporate environmental strategy, each action or issue is conceptualized based on the context at its inception.

For this reason, the impartial observer cannot judge the behavior of the 1960s as primitive or naive when viewing it from the context of the 1990s. When looking across history, the observer is never impartial. Every observer reflects the cultural norms of his or her period, much in the same way as the observed reflect the norms of theirs. The beliefs and ideas of the business manager of the 1960s were representative of the mindset of the time. Similarly, business managers of the 1990s reflect the contemporary mindset in developing business strategy. They cannot base their strategy on the conceptions of ten, five, or even one year ago. Environmentalism has been evolving much too quickly. Things that were considered unthinkable just a few years ago are now standard business practice. This is not the result of individual firms' getting smarter, nor does it suggest that firms were dumb to begin with. It suggests that how a firm behaves is a reflection of how accepted conceptions of corporate behavior are defined. And this definition has been steadily evolving.

Central to this point is the notion that context and history are dependent on more than the individual firm. A core theme of this book is how corporations identify an issue as important and how that issue subsequently becomes framed. In all business matters, particularly areas as rapidly changing as environmental protection, issues are not objectively defined by individual firms but are socially defined by firms' external environment—the collection of organizations that are influential in the formation and alteration of industrial norms. The boundaries between a firm and its business environment are never clear or distinct. They shift and disappear; they are arbitrarily drawn and are quite blurred.[15] How the issue of environmental protection is defined within the organization is dependent on how it is defined outside the organization. This is not to suggest that corporate actions are determined completely externally. Rather, it is a statement of how internal decisions are influenced by the structures of the external environment. Firms can choose from a variety of possible actions, but the range of that choice is limited by the external environment.

Therefore, to study the history of corporate environmentalism, the firm cannot be viewed in isolation from its environment. Thus the history presented in this book addresses the institutional evolution of corporate environmentalism by means of a three-tiered analysis. On the first level, it presents the evolution of the actors that make up the firm's social environment, or what is termed the *organizational field*. It is from this group of organizations that dominant conceptions of environmental management emerge. As the membership of the organizational field evolves, the resultant rules, norms, and beliefs concurrently evolve to reflect their combined interests.

The second level of analysis tracks the evolution of the dominant industry perspectives and norms. While the corporate executive can take some credit for the cultural changes within his or her organization, that organization's culture reflects the dominant conceptions of environmental management within the organizational field. The framing, perspectives, and level of importance applied to environmentalism are a direct reflection of the coercive rules, normative standards, and cognitive values of the organizational field, or what are referred to as its *institutions*. In much the same way that people refer to the "institution of marriage," institutions in this sense of the word apply to dominant beliefs and conceptions of behavior.

The third and deepest level of this analysis addresses the *internal structure and culture* of the corporate organization. How have the firm's environmental affairs been structured? How has it rewarded and promoted its employees? Who has been assigned particular responsibilities? Has the corporation established environmental goals, and were these goals supported by executive management? These are but a few of the questions that lead to an assessment of the firm's culture. And it is the culture that reveals the organizational motivation for addressing environmental affairs. While environmental expenditures or aggregate emission levels may reveal a vague snapshot of the environmental posture of a firm relative to other firms, organizational structure and culture are a measure of the firm's environmental commitment over the long term.

Analyzing corporate environmentalism in terms of these organizational variables also represents a relatively untouched area of research. Reviewing the journals dealing with environmental management yields a variety of titles focused primarily on three areas: technology, covered in such journals as *Environmental Science & Technology, Environmental Progress*, and the *Journal of Environmental Engineering;* economics and policy, covered in such journals as the *EPA Journal, the Environmental Forum,* and *Ecology Law Quarterly;* and activism, covered in such journals as *Audubon, Sierra,* the *Ecologist,* and *E Magazine.* Likewise, the environmental course offerings at most colleges and universities fall into similar categories. But the organizational aspects of environmentalism remain wide open, creating both a challenge for the researcher, in that there is little foundational work on which to draw, and an opportunity for this book, in that it fills a critical void.

So important is organizational behavior to the field of environmentalism that in 1993 the EPA for the first time mandated management changes as part of an enforcement action. On August 19, the Region 1 office of the EPA fined the United Technologies Corporation (UTC) a record $5,301,910 for violations of federal and state hazardous waste and water pollution laws. And as part of the settlement, UTC was required to implement an extensive multimedia environmental audit of all twenty-six of its New England facilities. The company was forced to hire a management consultant to make recommendations on developing management improvement strategies to achieve compliance with every major environmental law at all of its facilities. According to an EPA press release, it was "one of the most extensive environmental audits ever agreed to in an enforcement action. . . . By this settlement we have not only corrected past problems, but have also acted to assure future violations will be deterred."

In the end, whether it is shaped by explicit coercive pressure or through more implicit normative or cognitive pressures, the internal structure and culture of the firm is a reflection of the dominant institutions of the organizational field. This is not an argument about stakeholder interests. The members of the organizational field need not be in direct contact with a firm in order to affect its structure and strategy. This is an explanation of how social forces define accepted practices and drive corporations to adopt them. The influence of these forces is on industry broadly, not just on each firm individually. When insurance companies began withholding coverage for nonsudden environmental liabilities in the mid 1980s, the norms of environmental risk management changed for all firms, not just for those with affected policies. Likewise, in the wake of Occidental Chemical's 1978 Love Canal disaster, Union Carbide's 1984 Bhopal disaster, and Exxon's 1989 *Valdez* disaster, it was not strictly those companies that were affected. The norms regarding hazardous waste disposal, corporate disclosure, and oil transport, respectively, were altered throughout industry.

In sum, organizational change is the product of institutional change. In the field of organizational behavior there is a debate much like the "nature versus nurture" controversy in the study of individual behavior—that of "structure versus agency." Is the firm a completely autonomous unit, free to define itself and its actions in any fashion it sees fit (agency)? Or is the firm the product of its social surroundings, bound by the mindsets of its social environment (structure)? In terms of corporate environmentalism, this book leans toward the latter view. However, it does not argue total external determinism. The firm cannot be viewed in isolation, free from the influence of its external environment; but conversely, it is not totally powerless in influencing the state of that environment. Its internal structure and environmental practices are a reflection of the prevailing institutions of the organizational field, but the firm can act with a degree of self-interest in affecting the development of these institutions. Understanding the evolution of the institutional environment reveals a great deal about the evolution of the firms within it. And in analyzing this evolution, individual actors emerge who play prominent roles in initiating institutional shifts and in influencing the resulting rules and norms that guide the actions of others.

The Specific Argument

This book deals specifically with the U.S. petroleum and chemical industries. This analytical frame was not chosen at random, nor is it peripheral to the environmental movement as a whole. Both industries have been central to the environmental debate taking place in this country since the early 1960s. Their products are of central importance to various prominent environmental issues, and their waste streams contribute disproportionately to environmental problems. As shown in Figure 1.1, the EPA ranked the chemical and oil industries as the first and seventh most polluting industries, respectively, in 1990.

But it was not for their impact on the environment that these industries were chosen for this study. Rather, it was for the impact of the environment on them. Both industries have been singled out by the general public as significant environmental threats, from the 1970s[17] through the 1990s.[18] Beginning with the Clean Air Act of 1970, many regulations have been written to target the activities of these industries specifically. By 1992, the chemical and petroleum industries each were spending nearly 10 percent of their capital expenditure budgets on environmental projects.[19] As a result of this legacy of pressure and scrutiny, environmental concerns related to these two industries emerged earlier and developed with more intensity than those involving other, less controversial industries. It would be reasonable to expect, therefore, that the environmental movement surrounding these industries would be richer and more developed than other industry-related environmental movements.

The time frame chosen for this study was 1960 through 1993. Although corporate environmental problems can be traced back to the industrial revolution and beyond, clear identification of these problems and development of institutional solutions to them began only in the mid to late 1960s. Thus this study, which covers what is often termed the "modern" environmental movement, begins in 1960 so as to chronicle its emergence. In the ensuing thirty-five years, the movement has progressed through four loosely defined stages, driven by the emergence of critical and formative events that include the publication of *Silent Spring* (1962), the Santa Barbara oil spill (1969), the first Earth Day (1970), the formation of the EPA (1970), the termination of Ann Burford Gorsuch as EPA administrator (1983), the Bhopal disaster (1984), and the *Exxon Valdez* oil spill (1989).

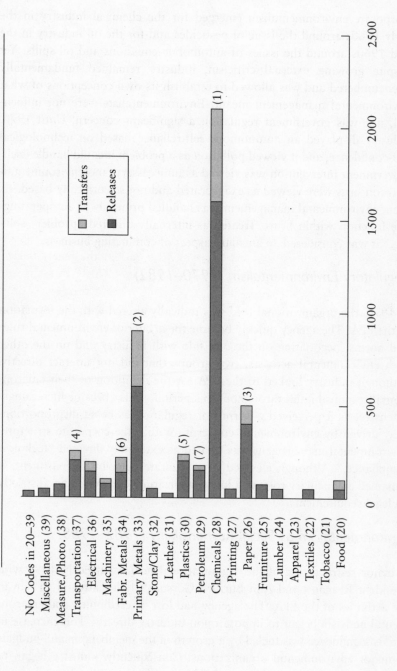

Figure 1.1. 1990 Toxic Release Inventory Data (Millions of Pounds).[16]

Industrial Environmentalism (1960–1970)

Corporate environmentalism emerged for the chemical industry in the early 1960s around the issue of pesticides and for the oil industry in the mid 1960s around the issues of automobile emissions and oil spills. Yet despite growing external criticism, industry remained fundamentally unencumbered and was allowed to establish its own conceptions of what environmental management meant. Environmentalists were not influential, nor was government regulation a significant concern. Until 1970, industry displayed an autonomous self-reliance based on technological self-confidence, and it viewed pollution as a problem it could handle itself. Government intervention was viewed as unnecessary, and environmentalists' concerns were viewed as exaggerated and not scientifically based. As such, environmental management was handled primarily as an operating-line function within firms. Treated as internally directed "problem solving," it was considered an ancillary aspect of conducting business.

Regulatory Environmentalism (1970–1982)

In 1970, the organizational field was radically altered with the formation of the EPA. The agency quickly became the arbiter of environmental rules and norms, negotiating on the one side with industry and on the other with environmental activists, two groups that did not interact directly. Although industry looked to the EPA for the definition of their environmental responsibilities throughout this period, it also became increasingly defensive, as it perceived government regulation as being disproportionately driven by environmental concerns. Within the corporate structure, environmental management was treated as externally directed "technical compliance." Although elevated to a separate corporate department, it remained an ancillary role with low organizational power, focused strictly on legal requirements.

Environmentalism as Social Responsibility (1982–1988)

A major restructuring of the organizational field occurred in 1982 with President Reagan's and Ann Burford Gorsuch's failed attempt to rein in the activities of the EPA. The agency had lost its credibility, and environmental activists began to impose upon industry directly. This increase in activists' influence was fueled by a growth in the membership and budgets of major environmental organizations. Consequently, industry began to take a more prominent role in establishing environmental rules and norms as a signal of its social responsibility. Throughout this period, industry adopted an increasingly cooperative stance toward government, as it once again saw itself as part of the solution, not part of the problem. Within the firm, environmental management evolved to internally directed "managerial compliance." Moving beyond merely technical responses, managerial structures were developed to achieve emissions compliance, while environmental responsibilities began to diffuse throughout the organization.

Strategic Environmentalism (1988–1993)

Beginning in 1988, the organizational field witnessed the introduction of three new and influential groups of actors: investors, insurers, and competitors. Furthermore, the power balance between industry, the government, and activists began to equalize. As a result, industry moved to a proactive stance on environmental protection, and it once again saw the problem as one it could handle itself. However, in this instance, unlike the period from 1960 to 1970, autonomy was not part of the corporate perception of the solution. Instead, solutions were seen as emerging from the organizational field in its then expanded form. For the firm, organizational boundaries began to blur, allowing direct influence by these external constituents. Environmental management became redefined as "proactive management." The corporate environmental department reached new levels of organizational power, while environmental considerations began to be pushed back down into the line operations and integrated into both process and product decisions.

IMPLICATIONS

This analysis expands the focus of corporate environmentalism from organizational change on the individual level to include institutional change on the field level. Such a shift in emphasis has powerful implications for understanding the process of organizational change. Institutional theory illustrates more complex channels through which this change occurs. The firm is a socially based organization, seeking the subjective goals of survival and legitimacy rather than the supposedly objective goals of efficiency and profit maximization. There is nothing terribly revolutionary about this; it merely acknowledges that the firm is neither monolithic nor singularly rational. In other words, it is dynamic and complex and subject to social influences. Organizational dynamics both inside and outside the firm affect internal corporate perceptions and actions. In the end, the firm is a reflection of the society of which it is a part—not directly, but as mediated and filtered through its institutional environment.

This institutional environment has been in steady flux, and the definition of corporate environmental management has thus been equally dynamic. The upshot it that there is no such thing as "a green company." The best one can do is describe the progression of how companies are "going green." In this progression, common trends of corporate action become visible. While believing that they are acting autonomously, firms are in fact behaving in a clannish fashion. Whether one considers the focus on regulatory compliance of the 1970s, the creation of pollution prevention or waste minimization programs in the 1980s, the establishment of environmental vice presidents in the mid 1980s, or the formation of board-level environmental management committees and the publication of environmental annual reports in the 1990s, it is clear that firms have been moving in relative unison in both strategy and structure.

The trajectory of this history represents an evolution of institutional forces that strike progressively deeper into the institutional framework driving corporate action. From 1970 until 1982, the dominant institutions were "regulative." Organizations were being coerced into adopting an accepted mode of behavior. From 1982 until 1988, dominant institutions reached deeper, becoming "normative" in nature. While continuing to be supported by a coercive regulatory structure, environmental management became a matter of good business practice and proper social responsibility. Finally, beginning in 1988, environmental management institutions became even more deeply seated, beginning to develop at the "cognitive" level. While continuing to exist within the normative and regulative levels, certain aspects of corporate environmental management began to become taken-for-granted aspects of corporate behavior. The implications of environmentalism's reaching the cognitive level significantly alters notions about how to deal with the issue in the future.

As environmental management institutions reach the cognitive level, it becomes imperative that firms project an image of environmental responsibility. They become trapped into incorporating a public relations component into their environmental strategies. For some this reflects actual internal change. For others it amounts to *greenwashing,* the merely symbolic adoption of standard practices and procedures. As the word *dogma* implies, firms may adopt environmental management structures purely as a matter of social obligation. It becomes a necessary aspect of remaining consistent with existing institutional expectations. To risk contradicting the accepted norms of the day could force social censure in one of many possible forms—legal penalties, public protests, inability to gain liability coverage, and so on.

Companies can also find it difficult to incorporate cognitive institutions, as multiple institutional demands create conflicting expectations. Not all companies face uniform institutional demands. Neither the firm nor the field is monolithic. Firms exist within multiple fields and respond to them with different levels of attention. As a result, one division of an organization could adopt proactive environmental management while another lobbies Congress to relax environmental standards.

Moving beyond the dynamics of this history of organizational change, the trajectory of this change yields important implications for the business manager, environmental activist, and policy analyst. First, business managers cannot remain fixated on trends in public opinion or shifts in political agendas in establishing environmental strategy. As the organizational field becomes increasingly complex, they will find that such measures inaccurately reflect the demands on their environmental performance. Regulatory shifts are but a part of the evolving organizational field that includes activists, investors, insurance companies, competitors, and others (including the media, the local community, financial institutions, and consultants). It is these interests that must be understood if the firm hopes to gain control of its environmental affairs.

Moving from the external to the internal, the institutional model provides additional insights. Given that corporate environmentalism is defined largely at the field level, the evolving field creates an evolving definition of corporate environmental management that reflects the interests of its constituency. In effect, environmental management is becoming less an environmental issue and more an issue of investor relations, insurance liability, process design, competitive strategy, and so on. For the corporate organization, this means that there will be less of a need for a dedicated environmental affairs department. While some sort of department will always be necessary as long as regulations continue to be written, more of the responsibility for carrying out corporate environmental activities will fall to the core functions of the firm, which are better equipped to handle these issues. As a result, corporations will look less for environmental specialists and more for environmental generalists. An individual seeking a job in corporate environmental affairs will find it best to position himself or herself as a marketing manager or a human resources specialist who knows the environmental implications of the job, not as an environmental specialist who knows the implications of environmental management on marketing and human resources.

For the policy analyst, the implications of the institutional model suggest a redirection of policy efforts to promote indirect systemwide institutional change rather than direct individual corporate change. Blunt regulatory pressures in the 1970s yielded blunt compliance responses from organizations. But more recent pressures from strategic institutional constituents have triggered responses from functions more central to the organizational core. This suggests a challenge to the efficacy of new market incentive schemes. Regulations should instead focus on changing institutions directly through cooperative industrywide efforts and indirectly through the empowerment of new institutional actors such as financial institutions or consumers.

Finally, the institutional model reveals a new juncture for the environmental activist. In driving institutional change, two roles become visible. Activists can either offer support services to the corporations they are trying to change (acting as *consultants*) or remain outside the field in an attempt to develop new institutional norms and beliefs (acting as *militants*). In the former case, environmentalists can develop alliances with powerful organizations within the field and facilitate institutional shifts that force less powerful firms to follow. Or they can ally themselves with new institutional actors (such as health care providers or investment capital providers), creating additional pressures on individual firms and increasing consistency of action within the institutional environment. Pitfalls to this route include reduced flexibility and tacit co-optation. Some environmentalists, therefore, must act as militants, remaining outside the institutional field to develop independent conceptions of newly emerging environmental issues.

The next emerging issue appears to be that of *sustainable development*. Yet at present the term is quite ambiguous. The institutional model provides a useful lens through which to assess how it will materialize. To understand how it will be defined, one must assess the state of the field defining it. Much like the industrial environmentalism of the 1960s, that field is presently dominated by industry. Yet on the fringe of the field, alternative definitions are emerging from environmentalists, academics, and international regimes. The merging of these diverse perspectives will come when a critical mass coupled with a formative event forces them into institutional "war," out of which will precipitate a new set of institutional conceptions of environmental management that include considerations for sustainability.

WHY THIS PARTICULAR HISTORY?

Before closing this introductory chapter, a final question should be considered—what makes environmentalism such a unique consideration for the management of corporate concerns? Why is this particular history interesting? What makes the environment different? Identifying its uniqueness is an issue often ignored by both proponents and critics of corporate environmental concerns. While its implications for the corporation are clear in terms of fiscal and operational impact, the questions remain, what is different about this particular issue, and what unique considerations are required for managing corporate environmental strategy?

To answer these thorny questions, I return to the source of this book's metaphorical title—an interview I conducted with Amoco's EH&S vice president, Walter Quanstrom, in 1994. His professional career is one that mirrors the history told in this book. He joined Amoco in 1974, when environmental management had only six employees. Today he oversees an independent department that numbers over three hundred. In 1974, he was a staff ecologist for a department with reporting responsibilities to research and development. Today, he is a vice president, counseling the board of directors on the environmental implications of the company's strategic objectives. The idea that environmental protection could represent a strategic opportunity to the company was heresy when he first presented it over ten years ago. At that time, the entire oil industry, Amoco included, generally agreed with the chairman of Getty Oil, who publicly proclaimed that "the EPA is the worst enemy the oil industry has."[20] Today, demonstrating a completely different tack, the company has been lauded for a recently completed collaborative research project with the EPA at its Yorktown refinery.

When Quanstrom was asked how it felt to have his heresy become dogma, his answer reflected a pace of change that has been both rapid and profound. He replied, "It scares me to death. It's hard when your dreams are not only met but exceeded. What do you do then? Do you simply set new dreams? It's not that easy. I think I might be on my third or fourth plateau. The first may have been the establishment of the Environmental Health and Safety Coordinating Committee in 1982. The second may have been the creation of the Environmental Health and Safety Council in 1989. The revised Environmental Health and Safety Policy in 1991 may be yet another."

As at other firms, environmental considerations have been difficult to keep up with at Amoco. Societal perceptions of and expectations toward environmentalism have grown at a rate unmatched in other arenas of corporate affairs. Beyond the pace of corporate change Quanstrom described, his selection of critical moments in the company's environmental evolution is equally revealing. Rather than highlighting the company's technical accomplishments, such as the development of Amoco Ultimate gasoline, which contains less polynuclear aromatic compounds and therefore produces less polluting emissions (and, incidentally, is clear), or the company's hazardous waste reduction program, which has decreased the production of hazardous waste by over 95 percent since 1983, he highlighted key developments in the company's organizational evolution. In his choices is an acknowledgment that the true measure of the degree to which environmentalism has been integrated into this corporation lies less in its technical accomplishments and more in changes in its organizational structure and strategy. These represent the fundamentals of how a company gets things done, and they reveal the depth and permanence of any change for guiding future strategy. Environmentalism is unique in its ability to transcend purely technological considerations and cut across multidisciplinary departments (and industries, for that matter). Environmentalism diffuses throughout a firm, affecting all facets of its organizational structure.

But as the words *heresy* and *dogma* imply, the environmental transformation is not simply structural. It also involves a shift in the way the company views both the world and its place in it. It places organizational action on a different plane. Explained Dr. Quanstrom,[21] "The only thing that makes environment different from other parts of the company is that it has a moral, ethical side to it. From a management systems standpoint, it is no different. Cash management, for instance, has no moral implications." After a short pause, however, he continued: "Well, maybe there is one other factor that makes environment different. Things like finance have only facts. But in environment there are 'facts' and there are 'gut facts.' For example, on the fact side, it is true that carbon dioxide levels are going up. On the gut-fact side, 64 percent of Americans believe global warming is happening."

He has seen the significance of this for his own company:

> Companies like Amoco are very digital and deductive. What's amazing about this company is not what it does wrong but what it does right. The process of getting oil out of the ground, transporting it, refining it, marketing it, and selling it is truly amazing. You have to ask how do we do these things right. It's because Amoco has a digital way of doing things that adds individual pieces up and makes the whole. But environmental issues aren't entirely digital. They are also analog. The political world is wired completely the opposite way. They are an analog system. In the deductive world, we say if you don't agree with me, I'll get more data and convince you. In the political-analog world, they say that there is no idea that they can't sell, regardless of the data.

This is an important consideration for the engineers that manage Amoco's operations. No longer able to focus simply on the end results of engineering calculations, they must now understand the social, political, economic, and cultural context of their tasks. Environmentalism signifies a redefinition of both technology and the engineer's role in developing it.

So, whether it involves the "moral-ethical" or the "digital-analog" implications of the issue, responding to environmentalism has initiated a completely new viewpoint, from which Amoco has had to deal with its external environment, both the physical and the social. New concepts such as waste minimization, pollution prevention, and product stewardship are finding their way into all aspects of operations, from gasoline reformulation to process design and implementation.

In the fabric of Dr. Quanstrom's words are the threads with which to weave the layout of this book. The issue of environmentalism represents a blending of the physical ("facts") with the social ("gut facts") aspects of corporate reality. Adapting to this dual-faceted reality requires a completely new concept of the firm's purpose and how it is achieved (shifting from "digital" to "analog"). But its complexity as a corporate issue lies also in the "moral-ethical" component applied to the issue. This creates a minefield of problems for corporations that attempt to undertake independent action.

So, in summing up what makes environmental management different from other corporate concerns, several answers emerge:

1. *Pace.* It represents a phenomenon of rapid social change, one whose growth is unmatched in other arenas of corporate affairs.

2. *A moral component.* It has a moral-ethical side to it that differentiates it from other strategic concerns (but makes it similar to other social issues, such as civil rights).

3. *Multidisciplinary scope.* Unlike other social issues, environmental management has a strategic aspect, cutting across departmental lines to alter product, process, and management considerations within the firm.

4. *Challenge to corporate autonomy.* The certainty of scientific data is no longer absolute. Organizational activities are interpreted by external determinants of legitimacy.

What is common about each of these considerations is the emerging perception that the corporation is not separate and isolated from either its physical or its social environment. The mindset of the pre–1960s corporation was one of privacy and autonomy. No one had the "right" to peer over the plant boundary and direct how corporate activities should be undertaken. But today, responding effectively to environmental concerns involves more systems-based thinking, acknowledging the interconnections of corporate activities with both the social and the physical environment.

So, how did this change take place? What has driven a major petrochemical company like Amoco to undertake such a fundamental transition? Was it internal leadership and foresight? Was it the demands of others outside the firm? Was it a response to external events? Was it the costs of environmental compliance? Through successive questions, Dr. Quanstrom slowly revealed the complexity of what this book presents as the underlying answer.

Initially, he cited internal leadership and regulatory compliance:

> In 1970, the start of the environmental health and safety [EH&S] function was due to the development of NEPA [National Environmental Policy Act] and the requirement for environmental impact statements. We started to have to build and maintain pollution control plants. These were mostly water treatment plants. Around 1979, there was a change of heart within the EPA, from looking at environment as a "bugs and slugs" issue to an issue of human health. It was no longer an animal issue. This was accompanied by a focus on occupational medicine and air pollution control. The centralization and growth that Amoco experienced in the late 1970s was not an attempt to follow what other companies were doing. We're too stubborn for that. It was an attempt to respond to this shift within EPA.

His response suggested a completely self-directed company attempting to comply with federal and state environmental laws. But did external events have any impact? I asked him about the corporate effect of the 1978 *Amoco Cadiz* shipwreck off the coast of Brittany, France. At this, he acknowledged some external influence: "the *Amoco Cadiz* disaster was coincidental in its timing with the growth in EH&S in the early 1980s. It did have its effect, though. It forced people to reconsider the implications of environmental [mishaps]. It taught us that if you [have an accident], it can cause much pain. The consequences can be expensive, both financially and in terms of the company reputation. It was a real wake-up call." Quick to add the positive, he added, "There was another major event at that time that you are missing. The other wake-up call was the construction of the Cooper River plant. It started in 1978 and won a national award for best environmental development. This was around the same time that Dow was having its troubles siting its plant in California. This taught us that if you do the right thing, there can be great benefits."

If external events can effect corporate change, then it stands to reason that external interpretations of those events is also influential. I asked him what caused the company's explicitly stated shift in 1989 from compliance focus to proactive management in its 10–K and internal reports. Was it his and his department's ability to cause Amoco to change, or was Amoco simply following along with the changing times? At this point, he finally acknowledged the role of external players: "I've always felt strongly about being proactive. My ability to cause the organization to think like that has grown. I'm not sure what the factors were that allowed me to do that. Many of them were probably external. But I look at it like football. Other people can make you an opening, but you still have to guide the football through it. Incidentally, that may hold true for the EPA as well. They may have to follow the times. But then again, the EPA is also the referee. They can call back the play, and often do."

Reflecting on the evolution of the external environment, he saw that

> In the last ten years, environment has been driven by an owner's movement placing pressure on companies for greater environmental performance. I think Joan Bavaria [founder of the Coalition for Environmentally Responsible Economies (CERES) and coauthor of the Valdez Principles] sensed the owner's movement and acted on it. CERES represented a piece of what was fundamentally going on, owners of corporations trying to effect change in corporate governance of environmental issues. Without CERES, things could have happened as they did, but perhaps later. It was part of a whole owner's movement. I believe that the next ten years will be driven by customers. Just look at what is happening in Europe with things like the green seals program.

Integrating Dr. Quanstrom's words with the framework in this book, the essence of how environmentalism changes the corporate enterprise lies not primarily in its technical adjustments but, more important, in its *structural, strategic,* and *cultural* transformation. This transformation is driven by decisions made internally but within the bounds of the institutions defined by the external social environment in which the organization exists, or the organizational field. As Dr. Quanstrom puts it, his ability to direct change within Amoco was both internally and externally empowered. External interests made the opening, but he and the EH&S Department got the ball through it. Events play a critical role in facilitating the evolution of this organizational field. Whether they are events specifically directed at the individual firm and to which it can extend its own interpretations (such as the *Amoco Cadiz* spill and the construction of the Cooper River plant) or events that affect the entire industry through one firm (such as Dow's problems siting a plant in California in the mid 1970s), both the organizational field and the internal structure of the firm is altered. This alteration of the organizational field is marked by the empowerment of new institutional interests, such as what Dr.

Quanstrom calls the owner's or the customer's movements, which, in turn, push corporate management to initiate creation of new organizational forms and strategies.

His assessment that CERES is as much a product of the organizational field as it is a change agent acting on that field acknowledges the circular nature of this entire process. All institutional members—industry, external interests, and the government—both affect and are affected by the organizational field. Corporate strategy and structures emerge in response to institutional demands, and strategy and structures, in turn, cause changes within the organizational field. The process continually drives toward convergence, until external events disrupt the emerging status quo and start the process again. However, events are time- and context-specific. It is not simply their emergence that causes change; it is their social interpretation as well. Who makes up the organizational field that will form that social interpretation becomes as important as the event itself.

In the end, to look at the environmental transformation of American industry, one cannot isolate the individual firm as the sole unit of analysis. Corporate environmentalism must be viewed less as a purely internal process and more as a social interaction in which external interests and actions empower an internal transformation. As those external interests change in both makeup and power balances, so too will the internal structure and strategy of the firm. In other words, the firm changes within the context of an economic, political, and social system that is itself also changing. To profess, as many today do, that industry is finally seeing the light is to argue that the light has always been there to see. In fact it has not. How companies define their responsibility toward the environment is a direct reflection of how we, as a society, view the environmental issue and the role of business in responding to it. *l)*

A ROAD MAP

The remainder of this book is divided into three sections. Chapter Two continues this introduction, laying out the theoretical model that is used to explain this model of corporate environmental history. It presents the basic concepts and constructs of a branch of organizational literature known as *institutional theory* and explains the methodology used to build this history. Part Two is divided into four chapters. Chapters Three through Six present four general periods in the history of corporate environmentalism. Each chapter contains a discussion constructed around the three levels of analysis: the organizational field, the dominant institutions, and corporate structure and strategy. Part Three concludes with two chapters. Chapter Seven pulls everything together to develop an overarching model and answer the question, "How did we get here?" Chapter Eight closes the book by addressing the prognosis for the future. It discusses where this model suggests we are going and offers predictions for future directions in corporate environmental management.

2

A FRAMEWORK FOR ANALYZING
INSTITUTIONAL PROCESSES

WHAT CAN EXPLAIN the dramatic transformation in corporate environmentalism that has occurred over the past quarter century? Why have firms adopted new structures and practices for protecting the environment? One might reasonably argue that as regulation and costs have continued to rise, recent corporate pronouncements of proactive environmental ethics are an attempt to preempt further regulation and regain control of capital and operating expenditures. Facts would seem to support such a reasonable thesis. As shown in Figures 2.1 and 2.2, both the number of environmental health and safety laws and the amount of industrial environmental expenditures have been growing steadily since the early 1970s.[1] The threat of fiscal, legal, and punitive damages would certainly suggest a motivation for corporate change. But is that all that is happening? While such an explanation appears quite reasonable, it is only accurate in hindsight. The history of corporate environmentalism is, in fact, marked by shifts and characteristics that bear little relation to the trajectory of costs or regulation.

Where do the motivations for corporate environmentalism originate? Consider that a firm exists within an "open system."[4] That is, the firm's activities are inescapably influenced by its external environment. No organization can function in complete isolation, insulated from external interaction and control. On the most basic level, firms rely on their external environment for resources such as raw materials, labor, and energy. This is the firm's *technical* environment—where products and services are exchanged through a market such that the organization is rewarded for effective and efficient control of the work process.[5] Environmental expenditures and regulatory penalties are a drain on technical resources.

Figure 2.1.   U.S. Federal Environmental Health and Safety Laws.[2]

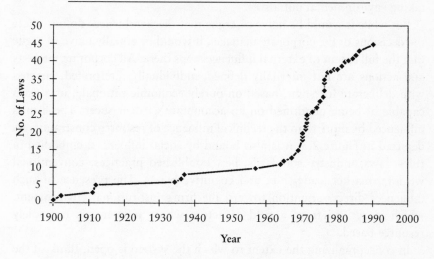

Figure 2.2.   Industrial Environmental Expenditures, 1973–1992.[3]

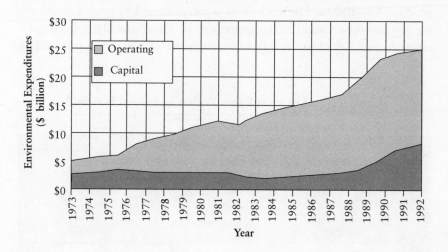

Therefore, firms would be expected to respond to such stimuli in undertaking environmental initiatives.

But while it would be naive to argue that these influences do not affect the decisions of the corporate manager, it would be equally naive to argue that the full extent of external influence stops there. All corporate interests and actions are not internally defined, individually interpreted, enacted with deliberate foresight, based on purely economic rationale, or always capable of being quantified on an accountant's ledger sheet. The firm is influenced by more than the technical influence of resource constraints. As depicted in Figure 2.3, it is also bound by social influences, embodied in rules, laws, industry standards, best established practices, conventional wisdom, market leadership, and cognitive biases. The presence of such influences directs attention toward the firm's institutional environment, which is derived from a field of actors whose influence is not solely resource-based.

In conceptualizing the extent to which the system is open, think of the firm as relying on constituents in its external environment for both technical resources and corporate conceptions of the outside world. Customers, suppliers, labor unions, and the government each provide technical resources on which the firm depends. But these constituents and others (such as social activists, the local community, and the general public) also interpret the external environment for the firm. What is considered a valid product, how it should be made, how workers should be treated, and how the environment should be protected are all institutionally defined concepts. In fact, as illustrated by the placement of the input and output

Figure 2.3.   The Firm Exists Within an "Open System."

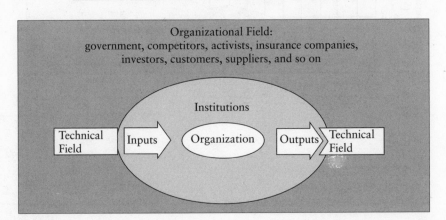

arrows in Figure 2.3, even what constitutes a technical resource is defined by the institutional environment. The presence and purpose of all technical constraints are mediated by cultural and contextual influences.

For example, one might consider that the corporate investor holds considerable resource control over the firm in the form of investment capital. But such an assumption is based on a particular perception of what a resource is. This, in fact, has not been consistently perceived over time. In the 1960s, corporate boards and CEOs paid little heed to the demands of stockholders in annual meetings. In other words, investor concerns were conceived as posing no resource constraints on the firm, both by the firm and by investors. Summing up the mood of the time, one CEO was recorded as stating, "I don't a give damn about the annual meeting. I'd like to see the whole thing abolished. The object of our meeting is to end as fast as possible without making a fool of the Chairman."[6] Corporations rarely, if ever, responded to shareholder initiatives. Today, however, all that has changed. Shareholder initiatives hold considerable power within the boardroom and at the annual meeting. The resources controlled by the shareholder have been institutionally redefined.

Acknowledging the open system is not inconsistent with economic theory. Group interests and group behavior are often primary forces in economic as well as political behavior.[7] For example, few modern writers on economics would discuss their subject matter without reference to aggregations, clusters, blocs, and combinations of people and things. Using terms such as *oligopoly, imperfect competition,* and *monopolistic behavior,* economists often refer to a firm's competitive field in defining its type of behavior.[8] However, it would be simplistic to restrict the view of the field to simply the individual firm and its direct competitors. Identifying the presence of the organizational field acknowledges the influence of actors outside the firm's direct value chain. The government, interest groups, insurance companies, investors, the community, the press, and capital markets also play a significant role in defining the form and function of corporate practices.

Rather than juxtaposing these two components of the open system, think of the technical and institutional environments as being always present. Technical environments channel organizational behavior through physical, product, and resource constraints. They have known goals and known means. Institutional environments channel organizational behavior through protocols, processes, and procedural arrangements. They are more ambiguous and less certain. While both are always present, it is their level of primacy that varies. Figure 2.4 depicts how varying levels of primacy might play out.

Figure 2.4.   The Institutional and Technical Components of
the Open System.

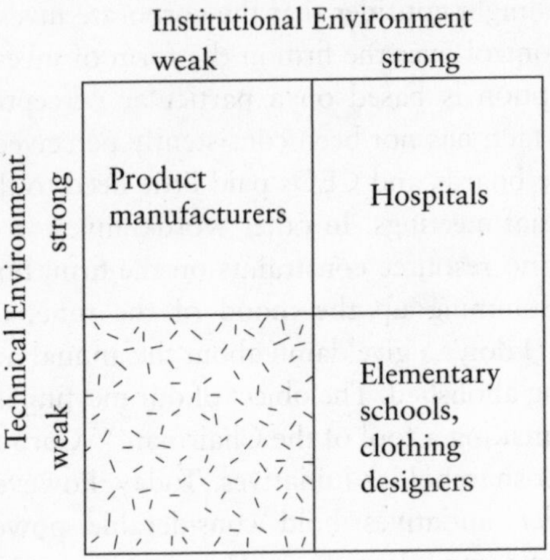

Institutional Environment
weak   strong

		weak ·········· strong
Technical Environment — strong	Product manufacturers	Hospitals
Technical Environment — weak		Elementary schools, clothing designers

Some organizations face environments that have high technical constraints and low institutional constraints (the northwest quadrant). These
might include commodity product manufacturers, whose technical constraints on resource flows far outweigh the institutional challenges of their
purpose and place within the market. Other firms face both high technical
and high institutional constraints (the northeast quadrant). These might
include hospitals, whose operations are constrained by strong demands
for high technical proficiency as well as strong demands from society
regarding their purpose, meaning, and goals. Firms facing high institutional and low technical constraints (southeast quadrant) might include
elementary schools or clothing designers, whose products are based more
on ideological and perceptual grounds than on technical considerations.
Finally, there are few firms that might be described as facing low institutional and technical constraints (southwest quadrant). This would constitute a loose variant of a closed system, where the firm is free of the
constraints of the external environment. Not even a monastery exists
within a closed environment, as it must rely on the outside world for
food, building materials, and so on. So this quadrant remains blank.

Over the past quarter century, corporate environmentalism has placed
strong institutional and technical constraints on the firm. But while laws
have placed technical restrictions on corporate activities, the great institutional uncertainty of the issue has created more severe constraints.

Demands for environmental responsibility have been in a constant state of rapid evolution, and the source of this evolution has been outside the corporation. Although it is beginning to change as of late, the firm itself has traditionally been led along, historically lacking significant credibility to influence the development of such expectations. Furthermore, the channels through which these expectations have been communicated have traditionally been channels outside standard market mechanisms. For this reason, economic literature has long treated environmental protection in the context of "externalities." Pollution, it is argued, is the consequence of an absence of prices for certain scarce environmental resources, such as clean air and water. To trigger action, economists prescribe the introduction of surrogate prices in the form of unit taxes, effluent fees, or, more recently, market incentives to provide the needed inducement to economize on the use of these resources.[9]

But acknowledging the presence of the institutional environment expands the bounds of the concept of market supply and demand. Direct costs are not the only triggers through which the external environment can apply pressures on the firm. External stakeholders also make institutional demands on the firm through the establishment of rules, norms, and common conceptions of behavior. In the case of corporate environmentalism, these types of institutional demands have been extremely influential.

For example, take the most basic question of environmental protection—what is a waste? Seemingly simple, it has been anything but clear or consistent. Firms are not free to decide what is a waste and how and where it is to be disposed. They are bound by the definitions prescribed by the institutional environment. Consider a specific example—at what point is a waste solvent considered a waste? Presumably after it is used and discarded. But what if that discarded waste is collected and recycled? It then becomes the feedstock for the recycler. Should it be regulated as a hazardous waste in the interim? The Safety-Kleen Corporation (a recycler) won a decision in court that ruled that it was not. This institutionally defined answer saved them a considerable sum of money in permitting fees, allowed them a strong position in the competitive market, and set an important precedent—but not without controversy. In making its decision, the court considered opinions from industry, government, and environmental activists. Thus what was to be considered a wasted resource versus a feedstock resource was institutionally debated and defined.

Institutional constraints on corporations' environmental activity do not issue solely from the courts. Firms are not free to define environmental risk management practices alone; they are bound by the norms and values of the insurance industry. Firms are not free to develop their own property in a fashion they deem consistent with their own economic objectives; the community determines the validity of development projects through zoning requirements and political protests.[10] Firms are not free to obtain capital based on their own interpretation of the validity of a proposed project. Instead, financial institutions establish the standard evaluation procedures and norms. Each of these examples emphasizes the institutional aspects of the open system in defining individual corporate action. In explaining the history of corporate environmentalism, this book directs its attention to a model of corporate change based on that aspect of the open system—*institutional theory.*[11]

THE INSTITUTIONAL MODEL OF CORPORATE CHANGE

The institutional model supports an underlying skepticism toward "atomistic" accounts of organizational processes. Firms are not autonomous units, able to develop and implement strategy in isolation from the influence of the external environment. Indeed, institutional arrangements and social processes are central to the formulation of both individual and organizational action. In other words, while the technical environment is one aspect of the corporate environment, its impact is mediated by the institutional environment—the socially constructed, normative world, in which organizations focus on conformity with social rules and rituals rather than on the technically efficient processing of inputs and outputs. In such circumstances, organizational action is a response to external pressures for legitimacy rather than internal demands for efficiency.[12]

For example, a corporation forms a highly visible, specialized department but denies it the power and resources necessary to accomplish its tasks; administrators and politicians champion programs that are established but never implemented; managers gather information assiduously but fail to analyze it; expert consultants are hired not for independent advice but to validate a program already conceived.[13] Why would such actions, appearing on the surface to be irrational, be undertaken? The answer is, to conform to the expectations of the institutional environment. Whether that is to appease specific external constituents, to signal legitimacy to the external environment at large, or to follow the current conventions of best business practices, the motivations are external, not internal, and based on legitimacy, not efficiency. Or, rather, the notions of what is external and what defines efficiency become redefined along the lines of dominant institutional perspectives.

To put this into proper perspective, however, it must be noted that not all institutions are inefficient. Often they provide certainty by triggering commonly understood or socially acceptable scripts of action in response to commonly encountered situations. Such organizational conformity creates efficiencies in external interactions and internal operations. For example, the organizational structure of the American corporation has become largely institutionalized. Ask MBA students to design an organization, and they unfailingly return a hierarchical diagram of boxes, each filled with the titles found in any annual report: chief executive officer, president, chief financial officer, general counsel, treasurer, controller, as well as a series of vice presidents for auditing, public affairs, government relations, environmental affairs, and so on. This structure has become implicitly understood. Within each corporation, these jobs have been, to a large degree, standardized. This facilitates efficiencies in task distribution and the accumulation of corporate competencies. And this also simplifies the search for new recruits by standardizing the training necessary to fill these slots. If a company decided to structure itself differently, it would suffer inefficiencies, finding that its control of the movement of information and personnel was hindered. So, without considering the distinct needs of the individual firm, this structure has become universally accepted.

In understanding and explaining corporate behavior, institutional theory looks to exogenous sources of organizational action, those that are beyond the firm's boundaries but within the broader group of organizations of which the firm is a part. It looks for more than mere organizational reactions to the direct pressures of external stakeholders, however; it asks questions about how the organization's social choices are shaped, mediated, and channeled. This is not to say that action is entirely determined by the institutional environment. As stated in Chapter One, this is not an argument for total external determinism. Rather, through cultural influences, organizational action becomes a choice from among a narrowly defined set of legitimately available options—not a choice from among an unlimited array of possibilities.

Think of an organized sporting event. It is bound by a specific set of rules that define what is considered legitimate and illegitimate actions. These rules do not force conformity but rather define the game. They tell you what you can and cannot do. Or, more accurately, they compose what the game is. Rules define baseball. If you don't conform, it is not baseball. You could pitch with a football or run counterclockwise around the bases, but then you would not be playing baseball. You have free will, but only within the parameters of the game. However, if these rules completely determined the players' actions, there would be no reason to be a spectator. All games would be the same. Clearly this is not the case. But, conversely, does this mean that the games will differ only where the official rules do not apply? Are the games only the same in respect to the mandated definitions of the game? In fact, they are not.

The means by which the objectives of the game are best achieved evolve over time in response to forces that are more implicit than direct technical constraints (rules). For example, if you have been a longtime fan of NCAA football, you might expect each game to be completely different from the next. Yet in the 1970s you would have seen repeated use of the wishbone formation, and in the 1980s you would have seen that formation replaced by the "I" formation as the dominant offense. These types of shifts are not necessarily "improvements" or attempts at greater "efficiency"; rather, they represent conformity to institutional norms. In basketball, the most efficient way to score a layup is to drop the ball into the basket. But since the 1970s, the slam dunk has become the prominent layup technique in professional basketball. This is hardly the most energy-efficient, least injurious, or most certain way to score a basket. It became the norm when style became as important as substance. In professional baseball, shifting norms have even led to arguably less efficient modes of play. Prior to the 1970s, the dominant catcher stance was with one hand behind the other. This was considered more efficient, because the throwing hand was close to the ball for a throw-out to second base. But in the 1970s, Johnny Bench perfected the stance of putting one hand behind his back. Since he had an unusually fast motion, he was able to perfect this unorthodox position. Given his popularity, other catchers soon copied the stance, and today it is the universally accepted catcher position, regardless of the fact that it is not necessarily the most efficient position for catchers. These cases are meant to illustrate that although all sporting events are different, the established practices for accomplishing the goal of winning the game have changed through forces other than efficiency and compliance with the rules. Although sports is an arena with considerable freedom for individual and group innovation, institutional pressures can still be observed.

To observe these pressures within the corporate realm and to explain how institutional dynamics direct organizational action, a structure is necessary. Based on the open-system model depicted in Figure 2.3, three central constructs will be used throughout the next four chapters. Ranging from the macro to the micro level in scope, they are the organizational field, the dominant institutions, and the organizational structure and culture of the firm. Connections and relationships between the three illustrate the dynamics of institutional processes. More important, they allow distinctions between institutional components, so that a collection of data can highlight the whole of the institutional model. In the remaining space of this chapter, each theoretical construct and its empirical representation are discussed in turn.

The Organizational Field

Where are the boundaries of the firm? Clearly, certain external actors have the power and capability to establish or influence certain types of corporate behavior. Governments are the most prominent (and the most studied in institutional analyses), able to establish laws that bind organizations to certain practices and procedures. But more subtle institutional pressures also exist. Academic institutions, professional and trade associations, and other certifying boards can establish normative standards by which organizations abide. Religious organizations and the press can influence cognitive perceptions of reality.

As an example of the latter, consider the following question: Which of the following causes more deaths in the United States, stomach cancer or motor vehicles? Most people surveyed believe that the answer is motor vehicles, but in reality stomach cancer causes more than twice as many deaths. This perception is caused, in part, by the media. A research study in 1989 by Russo and Shoemaker found that during a one-year period, two typical newspapers reported 137 stories that involved motor vehicle fatalities and only one story about a death from stomach cancer.[14] It has been shown that through the frequency or vividness of an experience (for example, through repeated news reports), cognitive perceptions of reality become biased toward more commonly recalled events.[15]

Even regulation can alter perceptions in a fashion more subtly than was originally intended. For example, in a 1983 study of the secondary effects of government policy, DiMaggio found that public policy toward the arts from 1920 to 1940, although designed to foster creativity and diversity, instead created organizational homogeneity. Orchestras and theaters began to present common programs, adopt common structures, and set common goals in the interest of appeasing government funders.[16] These are just two examples of how institutional pressures mediate organizational action. This occurs in virtually all organizational interactions.

But what is the scope of these interactions? How is the organizational field to be defined and bound? In theory, it is defined and bounded by a set of complex social structures and linked relationships. The organizational field contains concrete social relationships between and among organizational actors and comprises resource, historical, and network elements. It embodies materials, resources and meanings. In practice, however, its membership could include critical exchange partners, sources of funding, regulatory groups, professional and trade associations, special interest groups, the general public, and basically any source of normative or cognitive influence that effects individual or organizational action.[17] In this way, the organizational field differs significantly from strategic sectors defined along product lines and market segments.

As a hypothetical example, Chemical Company A produces an organic plastic such as polyvinyl chloride. An equal-sized company, Chemical Company B, produces an organic solvent such as trichloroethylene. In terms of market competition, these two firms are technologically differentiated along product lines and are therefore technologically segregated. However, in terms of the organizational field encompassing environmental protection, these two companies may be institutionally linked. Regulatory or activist pressure may similarly categorize them for institutional pressure, thereby creating the link exogenously. Or they may perceive commonly shared technical or political solutions to environmental problems and form the link endogenously. In the end, what results is a common identity, a common language, common stories, and common interactions and contacts in connection with a single topic.

This example illustrates that the organizational field is not monolithic and that all external actors are not part of the same field. Organizations can exist within multiple fields. As depicted in Figure 2.5, each field is overlaid on the organization, and each has its own cultural rules. These are sometimes at odds with one another or with the firm's existing culture. These fields distinguish themselves by the phenomenon of empirical interest. Each is "topic"-specific,[18] and each has its own particular combination of institutional or technical constraints. For example, in terms of human resources, the firm may face one institutional reality, but in terms of environmental management it may face another and in terms of manufacturing protocols, yet another. To deal with this complexity, firms interact with each field through separate functional departments, employing differentiated attention. This may cause inconsistency in organizational action, with the "right hand" interacting with one field in one fashion and the "left hand" acting to appease another field in a completely contrary fashion. Different fields employ different routes of influence into the organization, triggering different organizational routines and responses. It falls to the corporate executive to mediate among field interests and coordinate a consistent organizational response. This is a daunting challenge and one that is never fully controlled. Organizational consistency can most reliably come through institutional consistency.

Figure 2.5.   The Firm Exists Within Multiple Organizational Fields.[19]

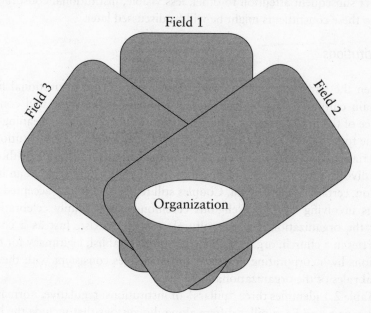

Field 1

Field 3

Field 2

Organization

Moving from this theoretical discussion to the practical presentation in the next four chapters, the next question is, How can the organizational field be measured and presented? What we wish to focus on is not just the specific network ties of a particular organization. The organizational field is more subtle than that. We need to identify who is influential in deciding the institutional norms by which all firms must abide. To identify this group of organizational actors, this history turns to legal data. Data on federal environmental law cases between 1960 and 1993 were collected and sorted according to participating constituents. (See Appendix A for more detail on data sources and collection techniques.) The entrance and exit of individual types of actors involved in lawsuits can serve to illustrate the evolving nature of the organizational field. Law is the visible manifestation of who is authorized to participate in the legal process; it reflects who possesses a voice in determining environmental norms. Law has a direct impact on corporate action, and it casts a revealing light over the external corporate environment, showing who is relevant in determining such action by providing a formal system for actors to act on and influence one another. It is, admittedly, an incomplete inventory, limiting consideration to those actors who utilize legal channels to influence corporate behavior and thus leaving out constituents such as the press, the community, customers, and financial markets. However, it can reveal significant changes in the major constituents of the field, highlighting institutional shifts that may direct subsequent attention to other, less visible, institutional constituents. Who these constituents might be will be discussed later.

Institutions

Given the particular makeup and membership of the institutional field, certain cultural rules, or institutions, emerge as the negotiated convergence of the field's interests. These institutions give collective meaning and value to particular events and activities.[20] For example, "the institution of marriage" connotes a cultural rule, a practice of enduring value. Although the divorce rate suggests that this is becoming more a cliché than an institution, certain rituals remain. Couples still repeat commonly accepted customs involving clothing, religious ceremonies, and family celebrations. For the organization, similar cultural rules also exist. Just as a couple marries in a church, organizations attempt to establish legitimacy for their actions by incorporating practices and principles consistent with the cultural rules of the organizational field.[21]

Table 2.1 identifies three "pillars" of institutions: regulative, normative, and cognitive.[22] Each pillar differs along dimensions that include the basis of legitimacy, the basis of compliance, cultural carriers, social structures, and routines.[23] These levels provide a hierarchy, moving from the conscious to the unconscious, from the legally enforced to the taken for granted. For example, regulative institutions are based on legal sanction. Organizations accede to them for reasons of expedience. Normative institutions are morally or ethically grounded. Organizations comply with them as a matter of social obligation. And finally, cognitive institutions are built on a culturally supported and conceptually correct basis of legitimacy. Organizations follow them without conscious foresight.

But, using Scott's pillars as a jumping-off point, political dynamics can better illustrate how they work. The three pillars are important in that they represent varying degrees to which corporations conform as well as the varying dynamics by which this conformity occurs. The regulative and normative levels of institutions are the product of political dynamics. Cognitive institutions are less defined. The former two are the products of direct human design. The latter is the product of "natural" development. They form through the persistent presence of regulative and normative institutions and are validated by their conformance with other cognitive beliefs. Cognitive institutions could be called taken-for-granted beliefs, myths, prejudices, or clichés. They are powerfully pervasive and can both guide and misguide organizational action. Although he did not use this

Table 2.1.   Institutional Pillars.[24]

	Regulative	Normative	Cognitive
Basis of compliance	Expedience	Social obligation	Taken for granted
Mechanisms	Coercive	Normative	Mimetic
Logic	Instrumentality	Appropriateness	Orthodoxy
Indicators	Rules, laws, sanctions	Certification, accreditation	Prevalence, isomorphism
Basis of legitimacy	Legally sanctioned	Morally governed	Culturally supported, conceptually correct
Cultural carriers	Rules, laws	Values, expectations	Categories, typifications
Social structures	Governance systems, power systems	Regimes, authority systems	Structural isomorphism, identities
Routines	Protocols, standard procedures	Conformity, performance of duty	Performance programs, scripts

terminology, John F. Kennedy spoke eloquently of the influence of cognitive institutions:

> As every past generation has had to disenthrall itself from an inheritance of truisms and stereotypes, so in our own time we must move on from the reassuring repetition of stale phrases to a new, difficult, but essential confrontation with reality. For the great enemy of the truth is very often not the lie—deliberate, contrived, and dishonest—but the myth—persistent, persuasive, and unrealistic. Too often we hold fast to the clichés of our forebears. We subject all facts to a prefabricated set of interpretations. We enjoy the comfort of opinion without the discomfort of thought. Mythology distracts us everywhere—in government as in business, in politics as in economics, in foreign affairs as in domestic affairs.[25]

Given the persistence of cognitive institutions, it stands to reason that they can be either consistent or inconsistent with the more politically volatile regulative or normative institutions. When they are consistent with them, cultural stability exists. When they are inconsistent, cultural tension is the result. For example, a regulation may be either culturally supported or in conflict with societal values. The ratification of the Eighteenth Amendment in 1919 established Prohibition in the United States, contrary to the cognitive institutions of a large percentage of the population. Given the strength of this contradiction, it failed to result in an alteration of those taken-for-granted beliefs, and the law was eventually reversed in 1933, thereby bringing the regulative and the cognitive back in line.

As a further illustration, when you drive your car, you automatically drive on the right side of the road. And when you get on the highway, you may impose a degree of self-control to obey the speed limit. Both actions are enforced by legal sanction. However, the first is an example of a cognitively supported regulative institution; the second is not (depending on the driver). The first represents unconscious conformity to institutional rules; the second represents conscious conformity. Each allows for the efficient use of the road system by standardizing the driving habits of its users. Yet the former represents cultural stability, while the latter creates tension (for the driver, in keeping his or her speed below the limit and when receiving a speeding ticket).

In one final example, the annual report has become the normatively accepted format for reporting corporate economic information. There is no law requiring it; it is an industry standard, consistent with corporate values that stress providing specific information to stockholders. Recently, organizations have attempted to create similar normative standards for environmental annual reports. Not all companies believe in the need for this reporting format. It is not supported by cognitive institutions; yet many believe that it would accomplish the same goal as annual reports, allowing an efficient distribution of important stockholder information. If accepted into the norms of industry practice, firms will be obliged to conform as an ethical and social obligation.

The challenge of reporting the evolution of such a wide-ranging and deeply cultural idea as institutions is in capturing their full range empirically. In depicting the history of environmental institutions, it is critical to indicate how industry viewed their external environment and certain issues within it. Institutions represent a common identity, language, or "story set" within a particular field.[26] In other words, they can be reflected subtlety in the wording, phrasing, and framing used to describe a particular issue, event, or belief. Capturing this subtly is central to capturing cultural institutions over time. At issue here is the question of how the world was viewed from within the chemical and petroleum industries in 1960, 1970, 1980, and 1990.

To answer this question, this history turns to trade journals. They provide both quantitative and qualitative data for characterizing the evolution of dominant corporate conceptions of environmental management. They provide an extemporaneous log of internal industry views, not only on the actions undertaken but also on the motivations behind them and on who was influential in directing them. The particular journals used were *Chemical Week* and *Oil & Gas Journal,* both for their industry specificity and for their comparability in size and scope. Each issue of both journals was reviewed over the time frame 1960 to 1993. Articles were categorized according to who was written about, what subject was covered, and what language and terminology were used. (See Appendix A.) From this, a vivid history of industry environmental perceptions emerges.

Organizational Structure and Culture

Finally, there is the organization to be considered. How are the institutions of the organizational field reflected in an organization's structure and culture? In interacting with their external environment and negotiating among their internal power bases, organizations must allocate scarce resources, and it is not always apparent what might be the optimal mechanism for such allocation. Hence, political power enters into all important organizational decisions, resting on some structural claim over resources.[27] This claim is based both on internal interests and on external institutional demands. For example, the emergence of a strong environmental law may empower the environmental management department to counter traditional power bases within the firm (such as engineering). Or other types of institutional pressures (such as an investor proxy resolution) may activate organizational departments not typically involved in environmental affairs (such as the executive board), thus creating pressures from nontraditional sources within the organization.

The shifting of internal and external power relationships will be accompanied by a shift in the organizational structure. To the firm, environmentalism has represented a steady reassignment of responsibilities and functions. New job tasks are created while old job tasks are altered to incorporate new perspectives and responsibilities that reflect broader societal demands. This can have tremendous implications for organizational and technological change.[28] In essence, what evolves is a new firm, with a form and function determined both by the internal interests of the firm and by the institutional interests pressuring for action. The resulting transformation is both structural and cultural and is based on the institutional norms of the organizational field. In the aggregate, firms, yielding to common pressures for change, adopt similar structures and strategies.

As a result, a convergence in strategies and perspectives occurs, driving the field's membership toward organizational homogeneity, or what is referred to as *isomorphism*. For example, Perrow argued that in the 1970s, sales and marketing personnel attained dominance over manufacturing personnel in the American firm because as manufacturing became routinized, the sales position occupied a more strategic position with respect to the external environment.[29] Fligstein took this one step further by observing that sales and marketing was then replaced by finance due to power shifts created inadvertently by government regulation.[30] In particular, he argued, it was the antitrust environment established in Washington that drove this shift. This environment made mergers between relatively small firms with moderate market shares illegal. Large firms adapted by dropping mergers for market share and turning instead to mergers related to diversified products as a strategy for growth.[31] Thus vertical integration was replaced by financially based diversification, and this became the new dominant concept of the corporation.

In their classic 1983 paper, DiMaggio and Powell specify three mechanisms by which isomorphism occurs: coercive, normative, and mimetic mechanisms, corresponding to the three levels of institutions defined by Scott.[32] Again, this three-pronged distinction is a powerful illustration of the diversity of pressures that influence corporate behavior. Regulation is but one type of external control. Coercive mechanisms, of which costs may be one, include regulation, protests, lawsuits, political lobbying, and direct negotiation. Normative mechanisms include the establishment of occupational standards, rules of thumb, practices, and procedures through governing boards, trade associations, academic institutions, and the like. And finally, through mimetic mechanisms, organizations attempt to model themselves after others whom they perceive to be successful.

Often, mimetic mechanisms are more implicit than the agents know or wish to acknowledge. They can occur with more subtlety through the development of common language, an appreciation for mutual interests, and the establishment of credibility among the field's members. At this level, institutions are developed in the cognitive realm, at which reside the taken-for-granted scripts, rules, and classifications to which the organization abides without conscious thought.[33] Each organization unconsciously adopts common conceptions of reality and behavior, thereby yielding common structures and strategies. Their formation is beyond the direct individual control of the organization, and their influence is not always readily perceptible. As Leibniz states, "Following only [one's] own laws," each "nonetheless agrees with the other."[34]

Looking at the specific manifestation of this institutional pressure on the corporate organization directs us to the area of corporate culture. While institutions guide the actions of firms within the organizational field, culture guides the actions of individuals within the organization. In fact, the two notions are so closely related that Thomas, Meyer, Ramirez, and Boli lament that "we have come to label the present perspective, for better or worse, as an institutionalist model, although we hope that 'culture' eventually can be reclaimed by macro-sociology."[35] The two are interconnected by their origins and development. Edgar Schein defines three levels of culture, corresponding to Scott's three levels of institutions.[36] The importance of these levels is that, like the institutional levels, the first two are the product of political processes and can be forced upon the corporation. The latter represents the extent to which culture is internalized.

Comparable to the regulative level of institutions, the most easily observed level of culture is that of *artifacts:* "the observable organizational structures and processes such as products, procedures, and company records." Artifacts of corporate environmentalism are highly visible and easily constructed. Over the past thirty years, these changes have fallen into three broad categories: the evolution of the environmental management function, the expansion of the boundaries of the firm, and an alteration of the overall structure of the firm.[37]

THE EVOLUTION OF THE ENVIRONMENTAL MANAGEMENT FUNCTION
EH&S, once designed as a buffer for the organizational core against the threat of intrusive regulation, is now becoming a source of innovative ideas and process changes.[38] In 1970, the Conference Board found that "96 percent of companies surveyed handled environmental policy decisions in company headquarters while only 3 percent made such decisions at individual plants."[39] Removed from the core functions of the organization, the purpose of EH&S was to screen this core from the impact of regulation. Today, environmental managers are finding themselves acting more as internal consultants, helping to set goals and provide direction for operating managers to direct proactive environmental efforts.

THE EXPANSION OF THE BOUNDARIES OF THE FIRM The firm's organizational boundaries are becoming increasingly permeable, to receive the input of external stakeholders. For example, McDonald's entered into an alliance with the Environmental Defense Fund (EDF) to target waste reduction opportunities across the business. The alliance produced a forty-two-part comprehensive action plan (the most visible component being the shift from polystyrene clamshell containers to paper wraps). And Dow is organizing community advisory panels, inviting community representatives into its plants for direction and input.[40]

THE ALTERATION OF THE OVERALL STRUCTURE OF THE ORGANI-ZATION Finally, the overall structure of the organization is being altered as environmental responsibilities shift from the periphery into core functions of the firm. Once an isolated responsibility of one department, environmental management is now affecting the departments of marketing, law, human resources, product development, and process design, to name just a few.

Whether any of these artifacts represent true cultural change depends on the level of infusion into the two deeper levels of culture. The second level, similar to the normative dimensions of institutions, is that of *espoused values*: "the professed strategies, goals, and philosophies of the corporation."[41] These are equally as prominent as artifacts. Statements of environmental values have been published both internally as corporate policy and externally as external relations. Even the names of corporate pollution prevention programs attempt to proclaim the values of the company: 3M's 3P program ("Pollution Prevention Pays"), Allied Signal's AS:AP program ("Allied Signal, Against Pollution"), Westinghouse's "Achievements in Clean Technology" program, and Dow's WRAP program ("Waste Reduction Always Pays").

The third and deepest level of culture, comparable to cognitive institutions, is that of *underlying assumptions*: "the unconscious, taken-for-granted beliefs, perceptions, thoughts and values that motivate behavior."[42] This is the level at which the defining factors of a company's environmental commitment are found. Yet it is also the most difficult level to uncover. Although artifacts and espoused values give clues to the existence of this much deeper and all-pervasive system of meaning,[43] to take their connection at face value might result in incorrect inferences about the underlying assumptions of the firm.[44] The challenge in understanding culture is in understanding how these artifacts are created and sustained.[45]

Capturing culture accurately for an empirical history such as this one is a difficult and time-consuming challenge. The history chapters that follow present organizational structure and culture by first presenting whatever broad industry-level data on structure are available. But to fully uncover the culture of an organization, one must enter and become a part of it. One must observe how the members of the firm perceive their environment, the role of the corporation in dealing with it, and their role within that organization. For this reason, a case study of the Amoco Corporation (Chicago) is also presented.

Amoco is the eleventh-largest U.S. corporation (based on 1990 assets), the parent of three wholly owned subsidiaries—Amoco Production Company (APC), Amoco Oil Company (AOC), and Amoco Chemical Company (ACC)—and an ideal candidate for this study. Amoco is both a chemical and a petroleum company, existing in both institutional fields simultaneously. To reveal the structural and cultural evolution of the firm, I worked within the Amoco organization in the summer of 1993 and the months of March and April 1994, collecting data through archival review, participant observation, and personnel interviews (see Appendix A).

It is important to point out, however, that this is not intended to be a book about the evolution of Amoco, per se. Amoco is not the subject but rather a model that represents the changes going on in companies throughout the industry. (At the request of the company, all quotes remain anonymous, and no employees are mentioned by name.)

To sum up, each of these theoretical constructs is represented by a separate data source. By utilizing these isolated and separate data sources—federal environmental case law, trade journals, and a corporate case study—the history in the following pages constructs a story that might otherwise remain obscured. It reports public data, but it utilizes disparate sources that triangulate into a singularly coherent historical record. Taken as a whole, it accurately depicts the very basic shift in thinking that has taken place over the past thirty-five years in corporate environmentalism.

AN INSTITUTIONAL HISTORY OF CORPORATE ENVIRONMENTALISM

PART TWO

AN INSTITUTIONAL HISTORY OF CORPORATE ENVIRONMENTALISM

3

INDUSTRIAL ENVIRONMENTALISM
(1960–1970)

THE STORY BEGINS in 1960. John F. Kennedy was just elected the thirty-fifth president of the United States. Burt Lancaster was packing in the movie theaters with his Academy Award–winning performance in *Elmer Gantry,* and *Leave It to Beaver, Father Knows Best,* and *Ozzie and Harriet* were captivating television audiences. In sports, golf newcomer Arnold Palmer won both the U.S. Open and the Master's tournaments. Floyd Patterson knocked out Ingemar Johansson to become the world heavyweight champion. And Red Auerbach's Boston Celtics dominated the NBA under the skilled hands of Bill Russell and Tommy Heinsohn.

Against this backdrop, two social issues were beginning to ferment. First, in Greensboro, North Carolina, four black men ordered coffee at the white's-only lunch counter of the local F. W. Woolworth's, only to be denied service. The incident helped ignite the civil rights movement. Second, U.S. Army officers were beginning to school South Vietnamese troops in fending off attacks from Vietcong guerrillas, setting American foreign policy on a collision course with the nation's moral conscience. The topic of environmental protection was barely a whisper on the lips of the American public. That, too, would shortly change.

The technological age was at hand. The economy was healthy, consumer income and expenditures were at record levels and rising, and enthusiasm for the future, bolstered by advances in science and engineering, knew few bounds. In a 1957 poll by the National Association of Science Writers, nearly 90 percent of the U.S. public agreed that the world was "better off because of science," and an equal proportion could not cite a single negative consequence of science.[1] In his 1961 inaugural address, Kennedy's words optimistically challenged the nation: "Together, let us explore the stars, conquer the deserts, eradicate disease, tap the ocean depths, and encourage the arts and commerce."[2] As its 1961 "Man of the Year," *Time* magazine picked fifteen scientists for their contributions to "remaking man's world" and "transform[ing] the earth and its future."[3]

The heart of this optimism about technological advancement lay within industry. Although several dramatic environmental incidents had cast a suspicious shadow over the by-products of industrial processes, the "golden age of engineering" had not yet come to a close.[4] (In 1952, a deadly smog settled over the city of London, England, killing four thousand people. And between 1953 and 1960, hundreds of residents of the Japanese village of Minamata were killed and thousands more suffered crippling nerve disorders from eating seafood tainted with mercury dumped into the bay by a Tokyo chemical company.)

Particularly within the U.S. petroleum and chemical industries, the perception was that engineers and scientists were improving the quality of life for individual Americans and the strength of the nation as a whole. The petroleum industry was proudly mobilizing America by fueling the record number of automobiles being produced and the economy's expanding industrial base. And the chemical industry was providing miraculous new materials that were revolutionizing fields such as medicine, food production, and fashion. Despite growing concerns over pesticide hazards, particularly with respect to DDT, and the gradual disappearance of U.S. cities behind veils of smog, few questioned the wisdom of industrial development.

The 1960s, however, would bring the beginning of such critical analyses, marking the dawn of the "modern" environmental movement. Although in 1960 industry attention to environmental issues was low and external pressure was virtually nonexistent, the environmental movement would begin for the chemical industry in 1962, centered around the issue of chemical pesticides, and for the oil industry in 1963, centered around the issues of urban smog and gasoline reformulations.

With these issues as touchstones, these two industries (and the society of which they were a part) would begin a journey toward awareness and change that continues today. The progression of each industry has been similar, moving from reactively challenging to actively managing environmentalism. This evolution has been reflected in the broad institutional norms governing corporate responsibility and within the culture of the individual corporation. The structures for dealing with environmental affairs have been transformed from an adjunct responsibility of engineering departments to the dedicated responsibility of large EH&S departments. And all this has been motivated by an evolution in the environmental constituency, which has called for new rules, norms, and values regarding corporations' responsibility toward the environment.

Corporate environmental management was no longer simply a venue of government intervention; activists, investors, insurance companies, and competitors all served to redefine our conceptions of it. As noted in Chapter One, the history of this progression follows four stages: industrial environmentalism (1960-1970); regulatory environmentalism (1970-1982); environmentalism as social responsibility (1982-1988), and strategic environmentalism (1988-1993). Each of these stages represents the development of each of the three variables of the institutional model: the organizational field, the dominant institutions, and the corporate culture and structure.

These stages are presented as an analytical device for descriptive purposes. They should not be viewed as strictly homogenous, but rather as depicting dominant trends between shifting points. It is the shifting points that are of the most importance, as they mark the entrance (or exit) of institutional actors and changes within the dominant institutions of that field. The dates, likewise, are not intended to be precise. The data depict institutional shifts that vary from the first, rather definitive shift in 1970 to more diffuse shifts from 1981 to 1983 and 1987 to 1989. The first aligns with a discrete and formative event, the creation of the EPA. The subsequent stages align with less prominent events, which will be discussed later. However, to delineate the stages, the mean date of each shift will be used as the shifting points: 1970, 1982, and 1988.

THE ORGANIZATIONAL FIELD: INDUSTRY-FOCUSED

From 1960 until 1970, the chemical and petroleum industries existed virtually alone in the organizational field. The persistent norms and beliefs of the period were focused on technological solutions and the denial of environmental problems. These were indicative of industries that were defining the environmental issue on their own terms. There existed little significant pressure from external interests to redefine their perspectives or behavior. Although government influence was increasing through the Departments of Agriculture, Interior, and Health, Education and Welfare, the rules they enacted were of little consequence for industrial change. Other constituents were virtually nonexistent in terms of directly affecting industry affairs.

An average of only 0.54 federal environmental lawsuits were filed per year over the period. And in coverage of environmental issues, industry-related articles accounted for the majority in both journals: 56 percent in *Chemical Week* and 66 percent in *Oil & Gas Journal*. Environmental activists, first noted in *Chemical Week* in 1967 and in *Oil & Gas Journal* in 1970, were given little significant attention.

While the organizational field might be viewed as nonexistent at this time, given environmental concerns and growing interindustry debate, it is more accurately described as coalescing. Yet through this period the field was singular in its membership. Industry was essentially left to its own devices in protecting the environment; it was the only significant constituent defining corporate environmentalism.

THE DOMINANT INSTITUTIONS

As the decade unfolded, the chemical and the oil industries sought the solutions to environmental problems through their own technological capabilities. Interference from both government and environmentalists was considered unnecessary or intrusive.

Industry as the Solution: The Chemical Industry

In 1960 and 1961, the overall tone in *Chemical Week* articles reflected a mild interest in environmental matters and the sense that both resentment toward controls on technological development and antagonism toward government intervention were growing. The editorial direction was blunt: articles called antitrust laws "archaic,"[5] complained that "antivivisection harasses research,"[6] and labeled people who complained about food additives "cranks."[7] Subscribing to the philosophy of "nothing ventured, nothing gained," the general view was that the chemical industry "should not be concerned solely with the elimination of risk but rather with a judgment of risk versus gain." If government controls allowed too little risk, "progress will be slowed."[8] Challenging this view on risks, the environment became a critical issue in July 1962, when the industry's self-image of promoting a better quality of life through technological advancement (by increasing food production) was dealt its first serious blow by the publication of Rachel Carson's *Silent Spring*[9] (see inset page 56).

As shown in Figure 3.1, chemical industry attention to environmentalism grew slowly following the publication of *Silent Spring*. Although the

Figure 3.1.   Chemical Industry Attention to Environmentalism, 1960-1970.

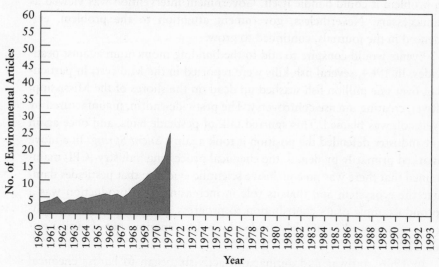

Year

Note: All data reported by quarter; five-quarter rolling averages.
This graphical format will be revisited continually through the text as subsequent
portions of the graph are filled in.

most significant growth in attention to the issue occurred after 1967, this was the first environmental issue to warrant significant editorial interest—which was scathing, continuing well into 1963. For example, "Those opposed to chemical pesticides ... are a motley lot, ranging from superstitious illiterates and cultists to educated scientists."[10] And "industry must again take up the Sisyphean task of repeating that its research is aimed at profits through knowledge, not a public be damned approach."[11] In a more mocking tone, the Monsanto chemical company produced a parody of *Silent Spring,* called *The Desolate Year.* In prose and format similar to Carson's, it described a small town beset by cholera and malaria and unable to produce adequate crops because it lacked the chemical pesticides necessary to ward off harmful pests. Taking the challenge to debate Carson in a public forum, Robert White-Stevens, assistant director of research and development for American Cyanamid Company's agricultural division, became the spokesman for the Manufacturing Chemist's Association, or what *Chemical Week* referred to as "defender of an entire industry in the face of serious attack."[12]

As a result of the uproar over *Silent Spring* and the subsequent debate over possible government intervention, pollution was mentioned for the first time in *Chemical Week*'s 1963 year-end list of important issues facing the chemical industry. The industry, however, stuck to the view that it was a problem it could handle itself. Government intervention was viewed as unnecessary. Nevertheless, government attention to the problem, evidenced in the journals, continued to grow.

Events would conspire to add to the building momentum against pesticides. In 1964, several fish kills were reported in the Midwest. In particular, over one million fish washed up dead on the shores of the Mississippi River, creating intense controversy. The pesticide endrin, manufactured by Velsicol, was blamed. This spurred talk of pesticide bans, and once again the industry defended the position it took against *Silent Spring*. In a move marked primarily by denial, the chemical processing industry (CPI) maintained that there was no conclusive scientific evidence that pesticides damage the ecosystem and that its role in increasing food production was a proud example of its contribution to progress. Talk of government controls was viewed as unfairly guided by public opinion, not scientific evidence.

In 1966, antiwar and antinapalm activists began to harass chemical firms. Editorials recommended that CPI firms conduct their interviews off campus to avoid protests and to facilitate assistance from local police. Of those companies targeted by public and campus protests, Dow Chemical was the object of the most intense scorn. These events coincided with an increase in the level of attention paid to the environmental issue within the industry and a shift in the tone of journal articles and editorials toward greater acceptance of some environmental responsibility: "We have reached a point in our economic development where we are concerned not only with dollars but also [with the] social and aesthetic implications of our work."[13] Believing that a solution could be reached amicably, one editorial recommended that the "process industry should face up to the pollution problem. Granted, we are more often blamed for others' sins. But if we act voluntarily, we will avoid community ill will."[14] And rather than scorning it as in the past, signs were emerging of an acceptance of (cooperative) government intervention: "Government-industry partnership, as in atomic energy and space programs, is the best approach to achieve clean water."[15]

In 1968, the need became evident for a common set of national rules to establish regulatory consistency. Legislation was being developed at the local, regional, and state levels, as well as within the Departments of Agriculture, Interior, and Health, Education and Welfare. One editorial argued, "Anti-pollution agencies must settle jurisdictional disputes soon. Federal vs. state vs. city vs. county jurisdictions are overlapping and contradictory."[16] Calling for a set of national standards, the journal predicted that "anti-pollution performance may fall short of [its] promise because of local official wariness or plant manager lack of authority. We need alignment of plant managers' incentives and enforcement from a higher authority."[17]

In 1969, as the level of attention to environmentalism within the industry rose to unprecedented proportions, optimism concerning the industry's technological capabilities reached equally new heights: "We predict that by the end of the century, we will have prevented further environmental degradation and will have begun to reverse the process towards melioration."[18] Industry began the process of calling attention to the legitimacy of its efforts. In January 1969, a story announced that Standard Oil of New Jersey had spent $1.4 million in 1968 for environmental advertising and would spend another $1.4 million in 1969, focusing on their advances in pollution control and the need for industry flexibility.[19] A June 1968 cover story titled "Meet the Pollution Managers" introduced business managers at Allied, Stauffer, and Union Carbide whose sole responsibility was pollution control.[20] In 1970, optimistic predictions again reached bold proportions: a nonpolluting auto by 1975, economically competitive extraction of oil from shale by 1980, and an inexpensive method for removing sulfur from coal before burning by 1983.[21] At this time, companies were also beginning to acknowledge some joint ownership of the environmental problem. In June 1970, American Cyanamid's CEO, Clifford Siverd, discussed the environment as part of a broader interview: "Our plants have done more than required, but we could do more. There are some companies, unfortunately—usually smaller ones with cost problems—that skimp a little. This gives us all a black eye."[22]

In April 1970, the country reveled in the first celebration of Earth Day (see inset page 58). Industry was shunned from the festivities, as executives attempted to participate but were jeered by students. Again, Dow was the primary target of activists, due to its production of napalm and agent orange. This prompted Dow's president, H. D. Doan, to announce publicly that increased regulation was necessary. In late 1970, President Nixon's decision to establish the EPA was viewed within the industry as a positive step to "help to bring order out of confusion."[23] One editorial optimistically looked for "pollution policy that is both sane and enforceable."[24] Few anticipated that the agency would soon become the bane of corporate existence.

Industry as the Solution: The Oil Industry

The environmental movement started later and with less of a sudden jolt in the oil industry than it had in the chemical industry. Pesticides were not an issue that concerned oil operations. However, urban smog and oil spills were, and these were the touchstones that set environmentalism in motion for this industry.

From 1961 through 1963, little attention was paid to urban smog and the health effects of lead. In both cases, articles denied the existence of a problem. In June 1960, one *Oil & Gas Journal* editorial read, "Now oil must concern itself with pure air. Unfair blame is being put on refiners for evaporative losses from storage tanks in major cities."[25] It went on to argue that blame should be put on automobiles manufacturers and dry cleaners. In December 1961, an article presented its evidence that "leaded gasoline poses no threat to public health."[26]

In 1963, articles started to acknowledge that federal pollution laws were likely to be enacted. Although occasional articles argued a preference for state rule over federal rule, this was not accompanied by the same kind of concern over the federal bureaucracy as was apparent in the chemical industry. The tone of oil industry journal articles was more conciliatory toward government efforts. This may have been due to the extent to which the industry had already been regulated from Washington through energy and conservation policies from the Departments of Energy and Interior. Regardless of whether or not the oil industry's tone was more relaxed, as Figure 3.2 shows, attention to the environment within the industry started a rocky but most definitely upward trend in 1963.[27]

From 1965 through 1967, the first major environmental debate emerged around gasoline reformulation for reduced volatility, sulfur, and, most important, lead concentrations. The industry continued to argue that such emissions were not harmful and regulation was unnecessary. The debate began to pit oil producers both against automakers and against one another. In April 1969, one *Oil & Gas Journal* article asked, "Oilmen oppose lead rush but does Washington know it? Someone certainly needs to blow the whistle on the gamesmanship of auto-makers, some refineries, and federal authorities. Auto-makers want to push onus of air pollution control from their hardware to fuels. Some refineries took heat to gain advantage but others reacted violently."[28] And in January 1970, "Automotive pollution: time for a decision. Government must settle the debate between oil and autos. How far should Detroit reduce compression rates and how far should petroleum go in matching required octanes? The stakes are too high for an individual industry to take off on its own."[29]

Showing an enlightened attitude more reflective of what would come in the 1990s, an August 1964 article touted, "Vapor control at refinery improved refinery efficiency and paid financial dividends. But refiners are

Figure 3.2. Petroleum Industry Attention to Environmentalism, 1960–1970.

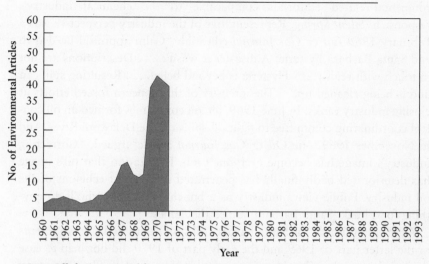

Note: All data reported by quarter; five-quarter rolling averages.

As with Figure 3.1, this graphical format will be revisited continually throughout the text as subsequent portions of the graph are filled in.

now willing to go further and assume considerable burdens to end the cause. This will pay dividends through improving industry's public image."[30] This reference to public opinion was also reflected in a growing acknowledgment of the industry's responsibilities to society. In November 1967, the journal said, "Like it or not, the inescapable fact is that government and business are so inextricably mixed up in each other's affairs that they cannot be put in separate compartments. The public demands from government broad social programs which will not be denied no matter how much they impinge on industry. Industry has the responsibility to adjust, adapt, and respond to these social charges."[31] And in March 1968, "Oil's new look in public relations. The old idea of a publicity campaign to make the public like what it gets from oil is shifted to give the public what it wants. There is a new social and economic environment in this country. People are no longer content that an industry give good products and service. They demand that business become an active force in the country to improve living conditions in all respects."[32]

This optimistic social activism came to an abrupt end in 1969 when Union Oil's Platform A began spilling crude oil into the Santa Barbara shipping channel and onto local beaches (see inset page 57). Public anger over the incident spurred editorial activity within industry journals that, coupled with the lead debate already under way, created a peak in environmental-related editorials comparable to the chemical industry's response to *Silent Spring*. Representative of the industry perspective was a February 1969 *Oil & Gas Journal* editorial: "Calm appraisal needed to end Santa Barbara hysteria. A disaster it wasn't. . . . Descriptions are not in touch with reality. . . . Hysteria is beyond belief. . . . Resulting spill can and is being cleaned up."[33] The intensity of this concern forced efforts at closing industry ranks. In June 1969, ten oil companies formed an oil control coordinating committee to fight oil spills on the Delaware River. And in November 1969, one *Oil & Gas Journal* article argued, "Correcting industry's image has become everyone's job. Realization that oil's image has deteriorated badly finally has penetrated the highest echelons of the oil industry. Public views industry as a bunch of fat cats who'll do anything for a buck. Santa Barbara fanned the flames."[34]

As the attention to the Santa Barbara oil spill began to die down, events of the latter part of 1969 and the early part of 1970 did not help to ease the scrutiny on the oil industry over its shipping practices. In a matter of just five months, four prominent oil spills pushed the industry further into a defensive posture. These included the *Marpessa*, off West Africa; the *Arrow*, off Nova Scotia; the *Delian Apollo*, off Florida; and Chevron's Platform C, off Louisiana. In response, industry articles continued to argue that oil spills caused no damage to the ecosystem. And, in even greater defiance, industry arguments began to pit the objective of energy security against that of pollution control, to counteract conservationists who used the spills to argue for controls over oil-drilling leases on public lands.

•

Publication of *Silent Spring* (1962)

The publication of Rachel Carson's *Silent Spring* was a turning point in how society viewed the world and the role of technology in altering it. Carson did not discover the dangers of DDT, nor was she the first to write about them. But writing as a scientist and with eloquent style—and at a time when people were open to hearing her message—her book had an unusual power to convince and persuade. Also unusual was that the book was written by a woman, one of the few female marine biologists of her day, and that it was researched and prepared without any institutional or academic backing.

Carson's specific target was DDT. She argued that by barraging the environment with this synthetic pesticide, we were also poisoning the entire food chain and, ultimately, ourselves. But her more general target was what she referred to as the "arrogance of man." Introducing the concept of the "web of life," through which all parts of the ecosystem are interconnected, she raged against the idea that, with our technology, we could possibly subdue nature without causing irreparable harm to the overall ecosystem of which we are a part. She therefore argued that nature should be protected, not for its future exploitation, but for its own innate value.

When it was published, the book gained widespread publicity. Although many journals turned it down for fear of losing advertising revenue,[35] it was serialized in the *New Yorker* and became a selection of the Book-of-the-Month Club. Carson was interviewed on national TV by CBS and went on the lecture circuit to profess her arguments and her warning. As a direct result of the book, President Kennedy convened a special panel of his Science Advisory Committee to study the problem of pesticides. The panel's report supported her thesis. In the end, *Silent Spring* forever changed how industrial activity and technology were viewed in the context of balancing improvements in our standard of living against degradation of our natural environment. It challenged the "golden age of engineering" and helped bring about the demise of the technological optimism that was so much a part of the previous decades.

The Santa Barbara Oil Spill (1969)

On January 28, 1969, a highly visible oil spill occurred from Union Oil Company's Platform A in the Santa Barbara Channel. Drilling operations had encountered an unexpected geological anomaly in the form of an uncharted fissure in the ocean floor. As a result, once punctured, oil immediately began to seep out in large quantities. Although it took ten days for the leak to be capped, given the irregularity of the fissure, oil continued to seep for long afterward. By mid May, an estimated 3.25 million (U.S.) gallons of thick crude oil had formed a slick that covered the entire city coastline as well as most of the coastline of Ventura and Santa Barbara Counties.[36]

This was by no means the first nor even the worst oil spill the industry had seen. Just two years earlier, the *Torrey Canyon* spilled more than ten times that amount (34.9 million gallons) on the shores of Land's End, England. What was critical about the Santa Barbara spill, however, was its location and the affected constituency. Santa Barbara was home to a disproportionate number of upper-class and upper-middle-class citizens. They chose Santa Barbara because of its ideal climate and gentle beauty. It was for this beauty that tourism had become the economic base of the region. Given the status of its citizenry, the Santa Barbara oil spill reached national attention with unusual speed.[37] Fueled by prominent media coverage, the public outcry became national in scope, reaching across the political spectrum. A local group calling itself Get Oil Out (GOO) collected 110,000 signatures on a petition to the government to stop further offshore drilling. In response, the Nixon administration imposed a moratorium on California offshore development, temporarily shutting it down. Of more far-reaching implications, the leak increased societal awareness of the effects of drilling on environmentally sensitive areas. In particular, it helped fuel opposition to proposed drilling in the highly sought after and potentially lucrative reserves of the Alaskan tundra.[38]

Earth Day (1970)

In the closing years of the 1960s, an emerging environmental movement was beginning to take shape. It lacked a clear center or unifying purpose, however. Drawing from one of the early tactics of the anti–Vietnam War movement, Wisconsin senator Gaylord Nelson proposed the idea of a "National Teach-In on the Crisis of the Environment" in September 1969. He hoped that a teach-in would help crystallize the new environmental constituency while also distancing it from the more radical New Left and counterculture activists. The idea caught on quickly, and to handle the growing interest in it, a new organization called the Environmental Teach-In, Inc., was formed (later to become Environmental Action). Nelson also brought in twenty-five-year-old Harvard Law School student Denis Hayes to help organize the event. The event was intended to project a less confrontational style than much of the antiwar protests and to involve all of society, in particular the silent majority of the middle class.

The event took place on April 22, 1970, with nearly twenty million Americans taking part on campuses all over the country. It successfully captured the growing awareness of environmental issues apparent in the country's politics and the press. For example, two months prior to Earth Day, President Nixon devoted a major portion of his State of the Union address to the environment. This was largely a response to concern over the inroads being made by Maine senator Edmund Muskie, who was first to use the environment in his political platform. Simultaneously, the press embraced environmentalism as the all-inclusive cause of the day, introducing the American public to issues such as population growth, air and water pollution, the loss of wilderness, and pesticide use.

For its part, industry also tried to participate in the festivities. Companies like Dow and Ford contributed financial support. Others took out advertisements, set up displays at corporate headquarters, and made speakers available at teach-ins. For the most part, however, they were not greeted warmly on the day of the event. At the University of Illinois, students disrupted a Commonwealth Edison speaker by coming on stage, throwing soot on one another, and coughing loudly. In Florida, activists presented a dead octopus to representatives of Florida Power and Light, a major contributor to thermal pollution in Biscayne Bay. At the University of Alaska, Secretary of Interior Hickel was booed off the stage when he outlined administration support for the Alaska pipeline.[39]

Conversely, critics also challenged the validity of the event. Some charged that its motives were suspect since it took place on the hundredth anniversary of Lenin's birth. Others were critical of the movement's challenge to the preeminence of the existing social movements surrounding the Vietnam War, civil rights, and poverty. And even some within the traditional environmental movement (such as the older conservation groups like the Sierra Club and the Audubon Society) chose to abstain from the festivities.[40]

Regardless, the event galvanized environmentalism into the national consciousness. While many factions still existed and the movement was still somewhat splintered, its presence had become established within the American culture. Following Earth Day, an avalanche of environmental developments would ensue, causing some to label it the dawn of American environmentalism.[41] Attempts were made to repeat Earth Day and Earth Week celebrations on a yearly basis. However, interest and visibility for the event gradually waned.

•

ORGANIZATIONAL STRUCTURE AND CULTURE: PROBLEM SOLVING

Within the corporate organization, technological optimism toward environmental management matched the technological optimism industry maintained toward all of its efforts. In other words, it gained little preferential treatment. Chemical and oil firms treated environmental management merely as an ancillary technological problem to be handled on a part-time basis by operations engineers. What was often called "pollution-control management" followed an often fairly relaxed course. At Diamond Shamrock, for example, the plant engineering manager looked after pollution control in his spare time, not because it was part of his specific responsibilities but because "it was kind of a hobby."[42] External pressures were not evident, as the organization approached the problem as internally defined. Management efforts focused primarily on wastewater control, and in particular on only visible forms of pollution. For example, Mobil Oil's first environmental department was an ad-hoc group, set up in 1964, called the "air and water conservation task force."[43] Often, expenditures for such departments were so minor that firms did not even break them out as separate items in cost statements.[44]

Organizational Structure at Amoco

Corporate environmental management at Amoco saw its beginnings in 1966 with the creation of the Air and Water Conservation Department, a one-man department within the Manufacturing Department of what was then the American Oil Company. In related functions, the Product Safety Department had been in existence since 1948, and industrial hygiene was handled by the Employee and Public Relations Department.

Organizational Function at Amoco

Records from this period in regard to the corporation's environmental management practices are scanty. However, interviews both with senior members of the EH&S staff and with retirees help provide an understanding of how it was handled. One environmental engineer formerly assigned to the Whiting refinery in the 1960s described a staffing situation where environmental concerns were handled as a secondary responsibility to other more central issues: "At that time, most engineers in Sanitary were working on water issues. There was some concern over air issues, but the Clean Air Act was not passed until 1970. The plant had two to three people in Environment in the sixties and into the seventies, but their responsibility was usually shared between that and other more operations-oriented responsibilities. The engineering department would supply people on a short-term basis as needed." Another engineer formerly at the company's Wood River refinery concurred: "At that time [prior to 1970], the larger refineries had maybe one part-timer who did Environment. It was maybe in the mid fifties when people were first marked down as 'environmental' types. That original work was in removing phenolics from wastewater. The focus was not on health hazards, though. It just smelled and looked bad when it got into drinking water." Furthermore, he pointed out that environmental concerns garnered little interest from line personnel: "In the 1960s and 1970s there was no buy-in on environmental issues . . . from operations. Even between divisions there was a lack of coordination and communication. Everyone ran their own business and did their own thing."

THE INSTITUTIONAL DEFINITION OF CORPORATE ENVIRONMENTALISM, 1960–1970

Through the 1960s, chemical and oil industry attention to environmental issues grew steadily. By the end of 1970, attention had reached unprecedented levels, far above those at the beginning of the decade. The modern environmental movement had begun. Although direct pressure from an organizational field of external constituents had not yet formed, attention levels peaked for the oil industry in 1970, a full year before the chemical industry. This corresponds to the enactment of the Clean Air Act in 1970 versus the Federal Water Pollution Control Act of 1972 (later to become the Clean Water Act in 1977), which impacted each industry disproportionately. The former had major implications for the oil industry, while the latter strongly impacted the chemical industry.

This can be seen in how the issue of the environment was conceptualized. Simply put, aside from the industry-specific issues of pesticides and oil spills, both industries perceived it as primarily an air and water issue. Yet, as shown in Figure 3.3, the precise proportion of this perception dif-

Figure 3.3. Media Perception of the Environmental Issue, 1960–1970.

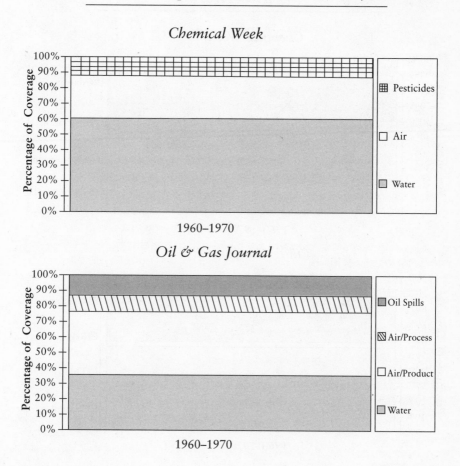

Chemical Week

Oil & Gas Journal

fered. *Chemical Week* coverage focused 43 percent of its attention on water issues, while *Oil & Gas Journal* devoted only 28 percent of its coverage to water. The oil industry defined the issue more in terms of air pollution, and unlike the chemical industry, the air aspect dealt with the formulation of their product—gasoline—not with emissions from their plants. As will be seen, in successive years this focus on the various media—air, water, soil, and so forth—would expand significantly.

Interestingly, it may be more accurate to state that until the celebration of Earth Day and the formation of the EPA in 1970, there was no "environmental issue" per se. There were separate medium-specific issues of air and water that lacked an overarching umbrella. This explains why the

Figure 3.4. Organizational Perception of the Environmental Issue, 1960–1970.

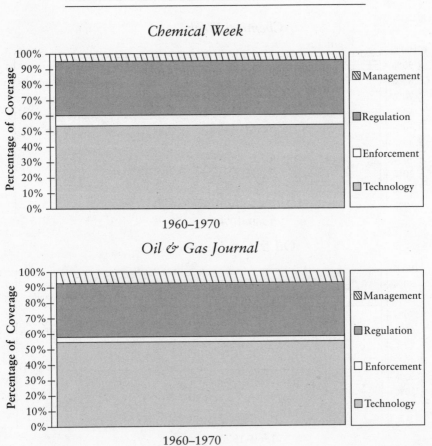

organizational structure established to deal with environmentalism involved merely the part-time efforts of a manufacturing engineer. The environmental issue, as we know it today, was not a discrete issue for the firm. Air and water issues were separate and relatively unimportant issues to be handled on an ad-hoc basis.

Moving beyond media conceptualizations of the environmental issue, how was it conceptualized in terms of corporate concerns? In both cases, as shown in Figure 3.4, it was regarded as technological in nature. Regulatory and enforcement were of secondary prominence, and management aspects were barely covered. Overall, both industries remained firm in their position that pollution was a problem they could solve through their own technological prowess. This corresponded to the dominant coverage focusing on industry as the primarily important member of the organizational field.

One central aspect of this technological optimism, and an issue that would form a major portion of the environmental debate to follow, was the issue of risk. As stated in a 1962 *Chemical Week* article, "In pest control—as in medicine, law, or international diplomacy—we must weigh risks against benefits. Is the chance of restored health worth a dangerous operation? Is the survival of civilization worth a few pounds of fallout?"[45] The industry's chief spokesman on the issue, Dr. White-Stevens, added: "Man is constantly learning to control nature to his own ends and will occasionally make blunders. But it is better to make mistakes than to give up the struggle."[46] In the ensuing decade, it was not just the issue of whether risks should be taken that was significant but, more important, who should be able to decide what those risks will be. In effect, the preeminence of technology and scientific knowledge would come under criticism, while the autonomy of the firm in deciding its environmental impact would be curtailed. Such changes would serve to elevate the prominence of environmentalism within the corporate organization from what it was in the early 1960s, an ancillary aspect of operations, to an issue of significant importance to the corporate decision maker by the close of the decade. Two critical events driving this transformation were the publication of *Silent Spring* and the Santa Barbara oil spill. As will be shown, these were but the first of a series of events that played a central role in driving the history that has since unfolded.

4

REGULATORY ENVIRONMENTALISM (1970–1982)

THE INDEPENDENT response to environmental concerns that was predominant within industry in the 1960s quickly came to an end in 1970, not by force but with industry support. By the end of the sixties, federal, state, and county environmental regulations had grown to significant and divergent levels, such that both the chemical and petroleum industries began to look for a common and converging set of standards. That convergence came on December 4, 1970, when President Nixon signed Reauthorization Plan No. 3, which created the Environmental Protection Agency (EPA). The new agency legitimized the need for corporate environmental management as a matter of regulatory responsibility, while establishing the dominant conceptions of what form it would take.

First, although many at the time recommended a complete restructuring of the nation's existing environmental programs—away from a medium-segmented focus and toward a holistic, "intermedium" approach to protecting the environment—political realities forced the creation of the new agency through the consolidation of existing compartmentalized programs scattered among various departments in Washington (see Figure 4.1). An intermedium approach would regulate a plant as a whole, considering the impact of its operations on the environment as a whole; a medium-segmented approach would consider the plant's operations in terms of their impact on air, water, and solid waste individually. In the end, the new organization plan integrated nearly six thousand existing employees into offices for air, water, pesticides, radiation, and solid waste.

Second, the regulatory format created by the agency's first administrator, William Ruckelshaus, was adversarial in nature. Ruckelshaus was a rising political star whose appointment added clout to the new agency.

Figure 4.1.   Functions Transferred to the EPA by Reauthorization Plan
No. 3 of 1970.[1]

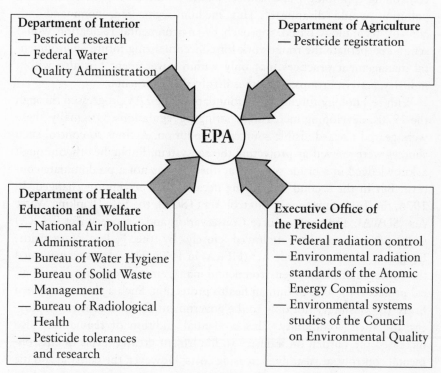

Department of Interior
— Pesticide research
— Federal Water
   Quality Administration

Department of Agriculture
— Pesticide registration

EPA

**Department of Health
Education and Welfare**
— National Air Pollution
   Administration
— Bureau of Water Hygiene
— Bureau of Solid Waste
   Management
— Bureau of Radiological
   Health
— Pesticide tolerances
   and research

**Executive Office of
the President**
— Federal radiation control
— Environmental radiation
   standards of the Atomic
   Energy Commission
— Environmental systems
   studies of the Council
   on Environmental Quality

However, his penchant for strong enforcement, acquired in his previous position as assistant attorney general for the Department of Justice, would determine the agency's primary focus. Ruckelshaus felt that once government set standards and began to enforce them, industry would fall in line, and the problem would eventually disappear.[2] During the first sixty days, the EPA brought five times as many enforcement actions as the agencies it inherited had brought during any similar period.[3] This focus on punishing polluters was justified on political grounds to establish agency credibility, but it also established an adversarial, "command-and-control" type of relationship between government and industry.

Third, this coercive conception of environmental regulation led to a prescripted, technological-fix approach. With air and water pollution the primary focus, the Clean Air Act (1970) and the Federal Water Pollution Control Act (1972) mandated the installation of pollution-abatement equipment that was deemed to be the "best available technology" (BAT). These technologies were fairly well known and required merely a financial investment, with little organizational restructuring for regulatory compliance. The catchword for the early 1970s was "technology forc-ing"—new federal rules would force industry to use new pollution-controlling technology, and as new plants replaced old, the problem of pollution would disappear.[4] This medium-segmented, command-and-control, technology-based approach to environmental regulation would set and perpetuate the framework for conceptualizing future environmen-tal management practices, not only within government but also within industry, activist groups, and other involved constituents.

With technology forcing as its foundation, the EPA progressed through the 1970s, developing increasingly stringent regulations. Originally, these were geared toward visible sources of pollution. Actions to control such sources were viewed as protecting the ecosystem. Public health, although acknowledged in a crude sense of aesthetics, was not a predominate con-cern. But in the second half of the decade, that perception changed. In 1976, the Toxic Substances Control Act (TSCA), the Safe Drinking Water Act (SDWA), and the Resource Conservation and Recovery Act (RCRA) were passed into law, followed closely by the Federal Insecticide, Fungicide, and Rodenticide Act (FIFRA) in 1978. These laws transformed the conceptualization of environmental management from one of ecologi-cal protection to one of human health protection. Such a shift established firms' responsibility not only to the government but also to their employ-ees and their community. This sequential addition of regulations also increased the burden on industry to implement greater levels of environ-mental controls, at steadily increasing costs. However, the demands on the organization and the necessity to change core operations remained low. Even though many requirements began to mandate "performance stan-dards," these were often based on BATs and therefore, in effect, remained technological fixes.

But even though these regulations made low demands for significant industrial change, they placed increasing demands on the EPA for enforce-ment. By the end of the 1970s, EPA Administrator Doug Costle quipped, "The laws were written so that we would need a policeman at every cor-ner."[5] The EPA was beginning to feel the weight of unrealistic objectives. No one realized how complex the job of protecting the environment would be. Most thought that the big problems would be taken care of eas-ily and that the remainder of the effort would be a matter of maintenance. That was not the case. Lawsuits, with environmentalists on the one side and industry on the other, became a fact of agency life. Adversarial rela-tions became the order of the day. It quickly became clear that what industry first saw as a welcome sign of regulatory convergence and com-mon-sense legislation had turned very sour. Although industry continued to look to the government to define society's expectations for its environmental management practices, it grew increasingly hostile and frustrated at the direction regulation was taking. By the end of the decade, tensions were ready to explode. All that was needed was the spark.

THE ORGANIZATIONAL FIELD: GOVERNMENT-FOCUSED

With the formation of the EPA, industry lost its dominant control of the organizational field. Corporate environmental responsibility shifted from an industry-defined to a government-defined concept. In other words, environmental responsibility meant regulatory compliance, and this compliance would be achieved through the rapid domination of industry by the new agency. As shown in Figure 4.2, EPA administrative actions increased dramatically in 1972, with civil actions following closely in 1975. This legal focus established the form of debate over how environmental management practices would be defined. Industry replied to EPA actions with legal actions of its own. As shown in Figure 4.3, firms filed an average of 28.92 lawsuits per year, with 98 percent of them directed at the EPA (the remaining 2 percent were directed at other firms).[6]

Riding a growing wave of enthusiasm following the Earth Day celebra-

Figure 4.2.   EPA Enforcement Actions, 1960-1982.[7]

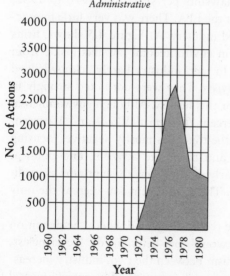

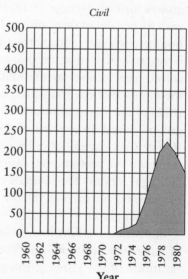

Note: *Three-year rolling averages.*

Figure 4.3.   Federal Environment-Related Lawsuits (Industry as
Plaintiff), 1960–1982.

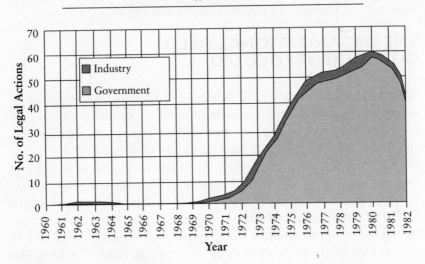

Note: *Three-year rolling averages.*

tions and the creation of the EPA, environmental activists also became
prominent in the organizational field. Their sphere of influence did not
include industry directly, but they did influence industry indirectly,
through the government. As can be seen from Figure 4.4, environmental
groups filed an average of 16.49 lawsuits per year from 1970 to 1982,
with 91 percent of those directed at the EPA. There was very little interaction between environmentalists and industry. As Figure 4.5 shows, firms
were rarely named as defendants in environmental lawsuits (aside from
enforcement actions by the EPA). In fact, industry barely acknowledged
the presence of environmental activists. They were not noted strongly in
either of the journals considered for this history. Although environmental
groups gained an average of 5 percent *(Chemical Week)* and 1 percent
(Oil & Gas Journal) of coverage, the tone was mostly negative, focusing
primarily on protests, regulatory and corporate activism, and political
and legal actions. The journals clearly did not view these groups as credible partners for rational discourse. The government was seen as the only
significant player.

In essence, the EPA had become the battleground where the definition
of corporate environmentalism would be determined. Nevertheless,
regardless of any growing antagonism between the two, industry increasingly looked to the EPA for guidance and definition of its environmental

Figure 4.4. Federal Environment-Related Lawsuits (Environmental Groups as Plaintiff), 1960–1982.

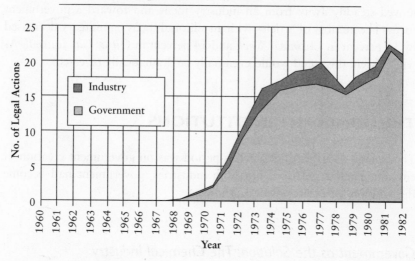

Note: Three-year rolling averages.

Figure 4.5. Federal Environment-Related Lawsuits (Industry as Defendant), 1960–1982.

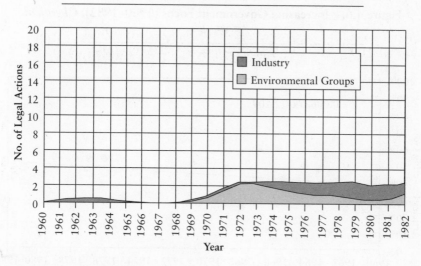

Note: Three-year rolling averages.

responsibilities. This can be seen in the coverage within both journals. As can be seen from Figures 4.6 and 4.7, as the decade progressed, attention moved steadily away from an industry focus and toward a government focus. The number of articles with an editorial focus on industry decreased by 18 percent in *Chemical Week* and 14 percent in *Oil & Gas Journal*. As will be seen, this trend would eventually be dramatically reversed.

THE DOMINANT INSTITUTIONS

The general focus throughout this period was on government creation of environmental regulation. For both industries, government had become the solution for environmental problems.

Government as the Solution: The Chemical Industry

With the formation of the EPA in 1970, the chemical industry viewed the growing controversy over the issue of environmentalism as resolved. As can be seen from Figure 4.8, attention to the issue in *Chemical Week* peaked in 1972 with the Federal Water Pollution Control Act but declined dramatically over the next two years. This decline was facilitated by the

Figure 4.6.   Increasing Government Focus (1960–1982), *Chemical Week*.

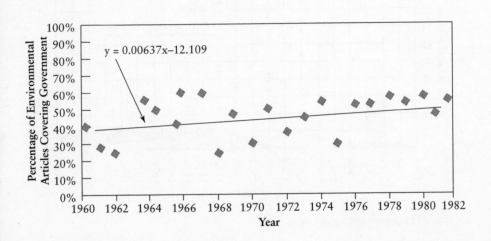

Figure 4.7.   Increasing Government Focus (1960–1982), *Oil & Gas Journal.*

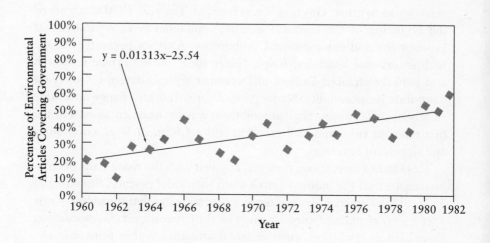

Figure 4.8.   Chemical Industry Attention to Environmentalism, 1970–1982.

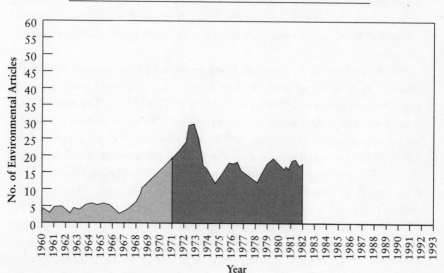

Note: Five-quarter rolling averages.

energy crisis of 1973, which displaced environmental concerns from industry's radar screen.

Although attention to environmentalism was declining and government was seen as a solution to the external controversy over it, another controversy began to grow. This time it was internal. The year 1970 also marked the beginning of the chemical industry's antagonism to environmental expectations and environmental proponents. Activists began the decade with sensational headlines; Ralph Nader sued Union Carbide in March and publicly attacked DuPont in December. Establishing the Project on Corporate Responsibility, Nader pressed for corporate change on a wide variety of social issues. High among them was environmentalism. For the first time, an environmental group gained a *Chemical Week* cover story and significant coverage.

This kind of threatening pressure, coupled with the rising costs of compliance, pushed the industry into a confrontational posture. Beginning in 1971, articles emerged several times a year stressing that the industry was "yet again" spending record amounts on the environment. Accompanying these high expenditures, environmental attention within firms was elevated: "Pollution problems may no longer be addressed by the assistant plant manager but may require board approval."[8] And in September, the industry felt its privacy was being violated as these expenditures were set to become public information, whether companies liked it or not: "the SEC [Securities and Exchange Commission] wants companies to disclose pollution expenditures to stockholders."[9] Reflecting the growing prominence of environmental issues, in November 1971, Monsanto's managing director of industrial chemicals, C. Preston Cunningham, offered *Chemical Week* an interview dealing strictly with corporate environmental concerns.

All this attention to growing costs and rising expectations within the industry was soon eclipsed as the energy crisis displaced environmental protection as the central social issue from 1973 to 1975. The energy crisis was more than a distraction, however; many within the industry viewed it as an opportunity. In August 1973, one *Chemical Week* article asked, "Will pollution standards ease in the face of the energy crisis? Congress waives EIS [environmental impact statement] for Alaska pipeline. This may signal a softening stance."[10] In 1974, it declared, "Energy crisis makes pollution control job tougher."[11] And in February 1975, it noted, "The Ford Administration is urging relaxation of some environmental standards to improve the nation's energy supply and to lift the sagging economy."[12] Reflecting an about-face in just four years, industry conferences repeatedly cited energy conservation as the predominant issue. This was not to last, however.

By the end of 1975, the energy crisis had subsided and the environment had returned as the chief industrial social issue. *Chemical Week* coverage of government enforcement again began to rise, from an energy-crisis low in 1974 to an all-time high in 1978. This reignited the defensive posture initiated before the energy crisis. However, this time the industry stance had extremely frustrated undertones: "EPA writes the rules, plays against you, keeps score, and makes arbitrary decisions."[13] "After four years of debate, Congress seems determined to add one more regulation (TSCA) to the already 27 H&S regulations we must answer to. This will make EPA a chemical czar. No agency in a democracy should have that authority."[14]

In July 1976, sparks really started to fly when Dow Chemical was denied a permit by the California Bay Area Air Pollution Control District to build the first stage of a $500 million petrochemical plant along the Sacramento River in Solano County. This added to industry's perception of a lack of rationality in the expectations of environmentalists and the government. Although the plant would have operated within legal emissions levels, it would have "significantly impacted" the region's air quality, which was struggling to meet the EPA's ambient air standards. The district's board felt that, regardless of the economic benefits of such a plant, environmental concerns should take precedence. This decision made Dow's estimated $10 million investment in planning worthless and raised questions about the competing goals of creating jobs and protecting the environment. Also called into question was the role of government in making trade-offs in this area in order to lure corporations into their districts.

This incident also helped introduce a new concept into the national debate. The "not in my backyard" (NIMBY) syndrome became a significant part of the legal aspects of activist and community efforts to control polluting activities. Adding fuel to the NIMBY fire, in August 1976, a toxic cloud of the chemical dioxin was accidentally released over the town of Seveso, Italy (see inset page 78). The confusion and panic that ensued created repercussions for relations between communities and chemical plants throughout the United States. For many in the United States, the incident at Seveso cast a sinister light on their local chemical plant. Communities became fearful of the unknown, not knowing what was occurring behind chemical plant walls and wondering whether they *should* know.

Community and activist antagonism toward chemical companies grew, and confrontational lawsuits seemed the most visible manifestation. The industry responded angrily. *Chemical Week* editorials in 1977 started to complain of the increasing litigation brought on by external interests: "Environmentalists have decided that law is the only way to settle, and they've set up NRDC [Natural Resources Defense Council], EDF [Environmental Defense Fund] and the Center for Law in the Public Interest. This could tie us up in court for decades."[15] And later, an article reported that "the NAS [National Academy of Science] says EPA should have fewer lawyers, more scientists."[16]

By 1978, the industry appeared to shift from a defensive to an embattled posture. An expanding field of activists was pressuring corporations on environmental as well as safety and consumer issues. In February, one editorial asked, "Who's David and who's Goliath? Hardy activist groups with Ralph Nader as their prophet have forced a series of government actions that add up to a Consumer's Bill of Rights. The Goliaths of modern industry are armed with slingshots while the consumerist Davids carry the heavy artillery."[17] *Chemical Week* editorials began to see anti-industry and anti-technology biases everywhere: on TV, in Hollywood *(The China Syndrome)*, and in the newspapers. One editorial attacked "the hidden agenda of the 'coercive utopians'—not to stop or slow the wealth-generating machine of society, but to control it."[18]

In 1978, yet another environmental calamity would cast an even more sinister shadow over corporate activities and motives. The Love Canal disaster hit the news (see inset page 78). This was covered in *Chemical Week* not with a story about the first notice of chemical hazards at the site, which occurred in 1976 when chemicals began to leak into the sump pits of houses in the area, but about state actions to buy out the first group of contaminated homes. The articles focused on Hooker Chemical, with a tone that was supportive of the company's plight. Finding a silver lining to this dark cloud, the industry perceived an opportunity in hazardous waste remediation as a way to take the initiative on an emerging environmental issue. Articles continued to present the growing federal bureaucracy as a menace and argued that site cleanups were an industry problem that industry could tackle on its own. However, as legislation made its way to the president's desk, the industry saw this potential slip through their fingers. In December, *Chemical Week* said, "The passage of Superfund may be the first skirmish in the battle on personal liability."[19] Superfund held companies responsible for the cleanup of sites long since closed. Furthermore, under a "strict joint and several liability clause," companies could be held liable for all of the cleanup costs even if their proportional liability was small. In short, the enactment of Superfund was viewed by the industry as patently unfair.

With the introduction of retroactive liability into the lexicon of environmental management, insurance coverage became an issue for environmental articles. This created a new level of internal concern for corporate managers. This internal component was further inflamed by the passage of the Resource Conservation and Recovery Act (RCRA) and new workplace air standards under the Occupational Safety and Health Administration (OSHA). To respond, innovative organizational responses became necessary. In July 1978, Allied Chemical was reported as "one of the few, if not the only one to make environmental affairs the sole responsibility of a Vice President."[20] This growing importance was not entirely welcome. It was accompanied by growing frustration.

By 1980, the posture of the industry shifted from embattled to defeated. The growing federal bureaucracy was now viewed as out of control and virtually running the chemical industry. The first *Chemical Week* editorial in January, headed "David, You've Knocked Off Goliath. Now What?" asked, "Have the Davids we used to cheer assumed some of the trappings of a Goliath? In little more than a decade, the U.S. Chemical Industry has been smothered with upwards of 30 health and safety enactments. It is an industry virtually run, not just regulated, from State and Federal Agencies. Have the Davids upset the political 'ecology' to such an extent that the field is left to the biggest predator of them all, big government?"[21] A few weeks later, in an editorial titled, "In Terms of Regulation, You Ain't Seen Nuttin Yet,"[22] the journal lashed out with criticism of OSHA, TSCA, and the myriad other health and safety laws, explicitly comparing the situation to that in the George Orwell book *Nineteen Eighty-Four.*

In an attempt to counter this growing threat, the Chemical Manufacturers Association (CMA) emerged as a new industry spokesman in 1980. A February editorial proclaimed that "industry must enter the debate" and called the CMA's newly adopted role of advocacy "an interesting test of industry's commitment to joining the public debate on chemical industry issues."[23] In June, the journal stated, "CMA hopes to save industry $4 billion in the battle over hazardous waste control rules."[24] In January 1981, it reported that "the CMA learned that it does pay to advertise" and noted, "Its efforts at lobbying suffered a setback with Superfund. Justifiably or not, the chemical industry did not emerge as the one wearing the white hat. But the bill did not turn out as bad as it might have."[25] So, while the industry bore the mantle of the unfairly persecuted, the CMA adopted the role of proactive champion. Within two short years, this latter role would replace the former.

Government as the Solution: The Oil Industry

As with the chemical industry, the decade began with a decline in attention to the environmental issue (see Figure 4.9). Also consistent with the chemical industry, the rhetoric quickly shifted to a confrontational tone: "Environmentalists Forcing Energy Crisis on Nation" blared one headline. This March 1971 editorial in the *Oil & Gas Journal* went on to argue that "environmentalists don't care a snap about the economic impact from the instant changes in American life they demand. The approaching energy crunch has all the markings of a national tragedy."[26] In June, the journal said, "It's time to blow the whistle on run-away environmentalists. The reckless tendency of environmentalists to whip up emotions for instant zero pollution has gone too far. They exaggerate the perils and totally disregard the consequences."[27]

Attention to the issue dropped dramatically from 1972 until 1974 and stayed low for the rest of the decade. But even though the level of attention may have been subdued, the level of rhetoric was anything but. Articles in the *Oil & Gas Journal* responded to the exaggerated claims of

Figure 4.9.   Petroleum Industry Attention to Environmentalism, 1970–1982.

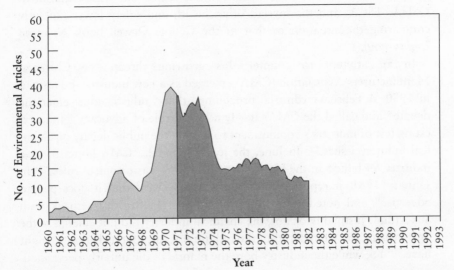

Note: *Five-quarter rolling averages.*

environmentalists with some exaggerated declarations of their own. In September 1972, the journal reported, "Bad Auto-Emission Controls Being Forced on Motorists. There is a distinct possibility that the personal auto will be put out of financial reach of many Americans by politically inspired auto standards,"[28] and in November, "Environmental Deeds, Oil Supply on Collision Course. Demand for additional petroleum supplies created by new environmental regulation (lead standards) cannot be met."[29]

By the end of 1972, the impending energy crisis displaced environmental concerns in the industry's attention as quickly as they had emerged just three years before. But this also created new competitor relationships, where before there were none. In particular, oil companies began to find themselves in opposition to automakers. In January 1972, friction between the two industries erupted when a General Motors executive argued publicly that unleaded gasoline should be priced two to four cents lower than regular. Concurrently, a broader debate flourished over the merits of catalytic converters and their associated need for low lead and sulfur fuel content.

Confrontational strategies with the EPA also flourished. In December 1973, the Ethyl Chemical Corporation sued the EPA to prove that lead was a health hazard. In May 1978, Exxon challenged the EPA's authority to regulate drilling in the outer continental shelf. In February 1979, the American Petroleum Institute (API) filed suit to overturn the new ozone standards. By October 1979, Getty Chairman Harold E. Berg called the EPA "the worst enemy the U.S. oil industry has."[30]

These deeds were matched with rhetoric, as the oil industry mirrored the chemical industry's frustration with perceived persecution at the hands of the EPA and its expanding regulatory base. In particular, the oil industry grew angry over governmental delays in energy development projects. In December 1979, an article challenged that "basic environmental law[s] must be revamped in the U.S." Railing against delays over drilling on George's Bank, the article continued, "How much longer will the administration permit the delay of energy development projects?"[31] In August 1980, an article titled "Congress Near Choice for Nature and Against Man" complained that "the Alaskan lands bill is another example of high sounding but mindless environmental action." Yielding to such arguments, the article contended, amounted to "selling future generations down the river."[32]

As this internal frustration grew, external scrutiny and pressure would not let up. The decade ended with two major oil spills that refocused public attention on crude oil transport and public ire at oil company operations. In 1978, the *Amoco Cadiz* ran aground off Brittany, France, spilling 65.6 million gallons of crude oil over prime fishing grounds. And in 1979, a blowout in the Bay of Campeche off Mexico by Petróleos Mexicanos (Pemex) began what would be a steady eight months of flowing crude oil into the Gulf of Mexico. Although industry frustration over access to drilling sites would not diminish, the rationality of the antagonism toward the EPA was soon to be challenged.

•

Seveso (1976)

On July 10, 1976, an explosion occurred at Hoffmann-LaRoche's ICMESA chemical plant just outside the Italian town of Meda. As a result, a toxic cloud of TCDD (2,3,7,8–tetrachlordibenzo-*p*-dioxin) was accidentally released into the atmosphere. A specific component of the cloud, dioxin, was widely feared at that time to be the most toxic chemical known to man. Although this disaster was named after the town most seriously affected, Seveso, the cloud contaminated a densely populated area about six kilometers long and one kilometer wide that included the municipalities of Seveso (population 17,000), Meda (19,000), Desio (33,000), and Cesano (34,000).[33] As with the Santa Barbara oil spill, demographics played a critical role in the prominence of the incident. The entire affected area was part of the Brianza district of Lombardy, one of the wealthiest and most industrialized regions of Italy. This guaranteed rapid publicity throughout the world.

Also critical in shaping public perception of the event were both the slow response of the company and the uncertainty of the release's effects. Although the explosion was met with alarm by the community, the company waited for ten days before confirming that dioxin had been released. With this admission came a sense of dread. For what distinguished this accident from other accidents such as the Santa Barbara oil spill was the factor of the unknown. Fears ranged from malformed babies to widespread and lingering illness and death. No one knew the real dangers of a dioxin release, and few trusted the assessments of "experts" from government or industry. In the end, victims were compensated, workers were redeployed, a substantial program of long-term health monitoring was established, and the site of the accident was made into a park. In the accident's wake, the United States acted to ban the production of dioxin. In Europe, the European Community established the Seveso Directive, a new system for regulating industrial safety, emergency preparedness, and the public disclosure of safety information.[34]

Love Canal (1978)

In the 1890s, entrepreneur William T. Love began digging a canal to connect the upper and lower Niagara River and capture cheap hydroelectric power for his industrial "city of the future." His project was eventually abandoned, and residents of the city of Niagara Falls used the unfinished canal as a swimming hole. In 1942, Hooker Electro-Chemical Company (which was acquired by Occidental Chemical Corporation in 1968) bought the property and dumped 21,800 tons of toxic chemicals into the clay-lined pit over the period from 1942 until 1953. In 1953, under pressure from the City of Niagara Falls, the company covered the landfill with a protective clay cap and sold the sixteen-acre parcel to the city for one dollar, with a warning in the deed that chemical wastes were buried there. Anxious to accommodate an expanding population, the city built an elementary school on top of the landfill, homes around it, and roads and sewer lines through it. By the mid 1970s, the chemicals that Hooker had buried twenty years earlier literally rose to the surface, pouring into the basements of local homes and erupting into noxious lagoons.

What followed was a nightmare for local residents and an education for the country. After several weak-willed government responses and sensational community protests (at one point, five EPA officials were taken hostage), the New York Commissioner of Health declared the area a health hazard on August 2, 1978. President Jimmy Carter declared the nation's first federal emergency for a nonnatural disaster on August 9, 1978, and authorized the purchase of the first ring of homes closest to the canal. Over the next two years, 803 homes were bought by the government, 239 of which were destroyed. Today, with years of remediation efforts complete, the 21,800 tons of waste remain under a multilayered plastic and clay cap, and the surrounding neighborhood has been tested and cleaned where necessary. In 1988, the New York Department of Health deemed the area safe for habitation, and 234 of the remaining 492 homes went up for sale. Today, all of the homes have been sold, and the remaining areas are slated to be turned into an industrial park.[35]

The legacy that Love Canal left behind is multiple. For one, the disaster created a whole new dimension to the environmental issue. No longer were environmental problems foreseeable, originating from an expected source. Now they could emerge from a place as seemingly safe as your own backyard. Second, as a direct result of Love Canal, President Carter signed into law on December 12, 1980, the Comprehensive Environmental Response, Compensation and Liability Act (CERCLA), or Superfund. Under this act, chemical and oil companies (among others) would be charged a feedstock tax to cover its funding. More important, companies would be charged for the cleanup of any waste sites that they had had even minor involvement with. In essence, companies would be penalized, retroactively, for actions that had been legal when they were undertaken.

At the time, few knew the scale of this undertaking. A 1979 EPA study concluded that there were between 1,200 and 2,000 sites that could potentially cause serious problems to human health and the environment and that the total costs would range between $3.6 and $44 billion.[36] Today, the Superfund program has 1,246 hazardous sites on its National Priority List[37] and another 26,000 potentially hazardous sites in its Hazard Ranking System.[38] Further, the General Accounting Office estimates that the list of hazardous and potentially hazardous sites could grow to 368,000 if a more comprehensive inventory were taken.[39] Estimates to clean up the all of these sites reach as high as $750 billion.[40] Today, Superfund remains one of the most controversial of all environmental legislation.

•

ORGANIZATIONAL STRUCTURE AND CULTURE: TECHNICAL COMPLIANCE

The regulatory focus of environmental management established with the formation of the EPA was immediately reflected within the corporate organization. In 1970, environmental management was elevated to a corporate-level function. Yet it continued to receive only ancillary attention and was regarded as a "necessary evil" and a "cost of doing business." Attention was generally directed strictly at regulatory compliance. All efforts to control pollution were externally empowered by regulatory mandates. Thus it appeared that internal motivations, at this time, were being directed by the government. As such, there was little need for an advanced staff to manage environmental affairs. The environmental management department remained low in terms of organizational power; line operations paid it scant attention, preferring to keep attention on the primary issue, producing and refining the company's products. Few appeared aware of the potential levels to which environmentalism would rise in altering operations.

Most companies set up EH&S departments separate from the operating core of the company. According to a 1974 survey by the Conference Board,[41] 96 percent of companies made environmental policy decisions at headquarters, not at the plant. More than half set up a special pollution-control unit, identifying it by such titles as "environmental quality," "air and water pollution control," or "air and water conservation."[42] In most cases, a new staff function was created, but titles varied. At DuPont and Union Carbide, it was "director of environmental affairs"; at Dow, "manager of environmental affairs"; at Hercules, "environmental health coordinator"; at Allied, "director of pollution control." But the job in each case was basically the same. This manager worked with specialists in public and legal affairs and with plant management, but he had no direct authority over these personnel. In general, with the exception of adding these small

specialized staffs of control specialists, companies made no major organizational changes in their efforts to manage environmental problems.[43]

Therefore, the level of organizational power these departments received
remained low. Most companies viewed uniform federal standards as
unnecessarily stringent,[44] and fewer than 7 percent of companies viewed
pollution control as profitable.[45] No companies surveyed by the
Conference Board viewed pollution control as an opportunity to improve
production procedures. According to the board's report, "these factors
reflect[ed] the widespread tendency in most of industry to treat pollution
control expenditures as non-recoverable investments."[46]

Despite such similarities in response, companies saw little common purpose or objective in their environmental actions. Fewer than 5 percent of
companies surveyed reported receiving policy or program guidance from
their trade associations or some vehicle of industrywide consensus.[47] This
would change dramatically in the late 1980s. Also, emerging as an early
trendsetter in the field, Dow began to develop its "product stewardship"
program in 1970, which would form the foundation for what would later
become a major trade association initiative.[48]

Organizational Structure at Amoco

In 1970, to respond to the growing national focus on environmentalism
exemplified by the creation of the EPA, environmental affairs at Amoco
was elevated to a corporate-level function under the Research and
Development Department. As shown in Figure 4.10, the staff grew to six
in 1974, at which point the group was renamed the Environmental

Figure 4.10.   Amoco Environmental Department Staffing, 1966–1978.

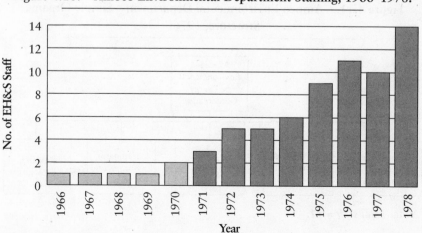

Conservation Department. By 1976, the staff had grown to eleven, and the groups was again renamed as the Environmental and Energy Conservation Department. The group also moved out of Research and Development to become, for the first time, an autonomous corporate function. The organization was loosely structured, subdivided by individual specialties rather than individual responsibilities or functions (see Figure 4.11).

Organizational Function at Amoco

Throughout this period, the function of the group was a technical one. Their objective was to ensure that Amoco's operating companies had the necessary support to understand and respond to the newly emerging environmental regulations. Since these regulations prescribed specific technology or performance standards, there was little need for a large staff to analyze corporate response. Gaining buy-in from line operations proved a challenge. According to one former environmental coordinator at the Cooper River plant, "In 1978, environment was not considered any big deal. They weren't cavalier in meeting compliance. That was simply always the stated objective, 'Amoco will be in compliance.' It was easily met. Regulations at that time were straightforward and concerned with only a couple of media." A former manager of the Yorktown refinery recalls, "In the 1970s, no one thought that environment would be a full-time job. It wasn't a nonissue; it just wasn't the driving force it is today. It was a compliance kind of thing. A refinery usually had a half-time person focused on rules and regulations. . . . It started like an adjunct to doing business. It was a necessary evil, viewed as an element of doing business,

Figure 4.11. Amoco Environmental Department—Simple Organic Structure, 1976.

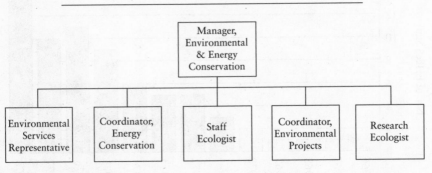

Note: Total staff = 11.

an administrative function just like legal or accounting. It wasn't our main function. It was just something that had to be done. It was viewed as innocuous, not offensive."

What empowered the environmental staff to gain line-level cooperation? One manager sums it up simply: "It was the law that really empowered these people to come in and do what they did. The corporate mission played into it, but the law was really the empowering force." A former refinery manager adds, "The environmental folks were more looked at as the equivalent of accounting. We didn't like to see them come around, since they always had bad news, but we knew it wasn't their fault. We used to joke about shooting the messenger, but we knew that they had a job to do. They weren't really viewed as an imposition; we just accepted their role as a cost of doing business."

Regardless, managers and line operators were concerned over the career implications of requesting expensive undertakings that the law required. One manager (now retired) whose job it was to obtain funding from senior management for refinery wastewater treatment units recalls that his was not an enviable task:

> People at that time were reluctant to initiate investments that would raise costs without a payback. It seemed that at that time management was always looking for another plant to close. That made the managers very uneasy about keeping profits up.... The first few times going before the board were hard. They would have lots of questions. Our regular planning coordinator wouldn't do it, because they weren't money-making projects. He didn't want to get that mark on his soul. But the minute you told them that the law requires it, they'd do it. I don't know anyone in Amoco that would deliberately break the law. The oil company vice president would simply say, "Well, I guess it's just a part of doing business," and it was approved. I thought that they would sit and discuss it and then vote, but he just said that and decided and moved on to the next item. These were one- to three-million-dollar plants. Later, in the late seventies, the next plant upgrade would be more in the twenty- to thirty-million-dollar range.

These increased expenditures would cause the company and the industry considerable consternation.

Beyond the difficulty in gaining cooperation, environmental management lacked the political power to attract the company's upwardly mobile executives. Promotion-track careers—individuals slated for refinery manager or executive management—never included EH&S. One former refinery manager explains:

Early on, through the seventies, you needed technical know-how to comply with the regulations, but it was really just an adjunct function. If you were a true line operator, it wasn't your cup of tea. It wasn't that they [the environmental staff] were necessarily looked down upon as an EPA pawn. It's just that our business was to make gasoline or lube oil. That's where we put our best people. EH&S just wasn't an important place to go to move ahead. It wasn't a career move. We didn't need to dilute our technical efforts by sending talent over to EH&S. It just doesn't make sense to send the best and the brightest to just figure out how to deal with compliance. It wasn't quite a dumping ground; our best-quality people just weren't put there.

THE INSTITUTIONAL DEFINITION OF CORPORATE ENVIRONMENTALISM, 1970–1982

The formation of the EPA legitimated environmentalism as a corporate responsibility and established a significant external source of pressure for taking that responsibility seriously. With this source of pressure came an illusion of certainty. Responsible environmental management meant regulatory compliance. Attention to the issue, therefore, declined through the decade to reach a low in 1980. But while attention diminished, rhetoric heated up. While environmental activists blended into the institutional background, their role was seen as anything but secondary. Industry saw a biased posture within the new agency and railed against its growing power and political slant.

Through the decade, the newly emerging legislation and the expanding awareness of the scope of the environmental issue manifested itself in a wide range of media perceptions of the issue. By 1980, the regulatory framework of corporate environmental management had been almost entirely institutionalized. It had evolved beyond a strictly ecological concern to include human health and economic liability concerns. And as Figure 4.12 shows, the previous air and water focus had been displaced by concerns for toxics, waste site remediation, and hazardous waste. Of particular note, hazardous waste management became a significant component for both industries, while for the oil industry, Superfund cleanups were not yet a major concern.[49]

This expansion of the issue bred resentment at environmental expectations. By 1982, environmental attention had decreased from an early-in-the-decade peak to a level that had remained relatively flat since 1974, and both industries had reached a critical point of frustration in dealing with the environmental issue. By the end of the decade, they appeared beleaguered at rising compliance costs and increasingly onerous legislation. Not surprisingly, then, the managerial perception of the issue, as depicted in Figure 4.13, had shifted from one of technological optimism to one of regulatory and enforcement pessimism. Within the corporation, this managerial shift could be seen as new departments were established to handle not *environmental* affairs but *regulatory* affairs.

The tension at the close of the 1980s was extreme. A powder keg was about to explode; all that was needed was a match. That match came in the form of regulatory reform under the newly elected president, Ronald Reagan. But as will be seen, Reagan's efforts became a test of the depth and institutional power of the environmental issue. By providing that test, Reagan exposed the core strength of the environmental movement's sup-

Figure 4.12.   Media Perception of the Environmental Issue, 1970–1982.

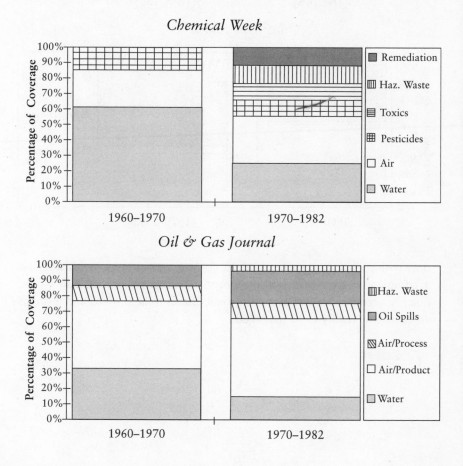

Figure 4.13.   Organizational Perception of the Environmental Issue,
1970–1982.

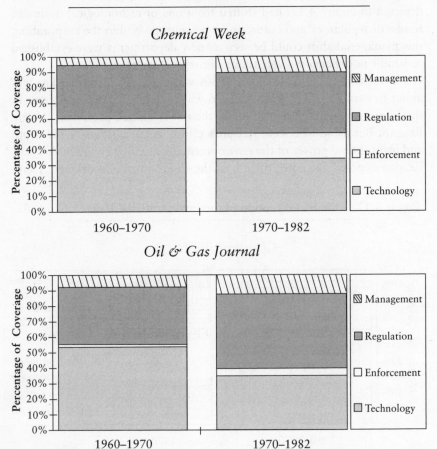

Chemical Week

Oil & Gas Journal

port within American society and set corporate environmental history on
a completely new path. For the corporation, environmentalism would
quickly become seen less as an economic threat to be resisted and more as
an economic reality to be managed.

5

ENVIRONMENTALISM AS SOCIAL RESPONSIBILITY (1982–1988)

THE ECONOMIC AND SOCIAL ENVIRONMENT of 1981 created a perfect context for the defederalization agenda of incoming president Ronald Reagan. An ongoing worldwide recession continued to diminish the national mood, already darkened by a failed attempt to rescue the fifty-two hostages seized at the U.S. embassy in Teheran two years earlier. The U.S. economy was faltering. Inflation rose to an annual rate of 14 percent, while unemployment grew to 7.4 percent. Automobile production was at its lowest point in twenty years, and the cost of medical care climbed 12.5 percent to the highest level since records were first kept in 1935. Reagan's agenda was clear and simple—government controls were the source of the problem.

His solution was marked by severe budget cutbacks and regulatory reform of programs that restricted corporate activity. Environmentalism could not be missed by such an agenda, and with public attention to environmental issues at a ten-year low,[1] his initiatives gained early momentum. Reagan appointed James Watt to head the Department of the Interior and Ann Burford Gorsuch as EPA administrator, while Rita Lavelle took control of Superfund. Later, this group would become known as the "gang of three," and those within the EPA would refer to Gorsuch's term as the "acid reign." For it was the EPA that was the prime target of Reagan's defederalization. In the words of Gorsuch, "There is no riper pasture for regulatory reform than EPA."[2] After her appointment, she immediately announced that she wanted cooperation rather than confrontation with the regulated community. Even though both EPA enforcement and industry lawsuits had been on the decline under the Carter administration, Gorsuch slowed agency activity down even further. In particular, Lavelle was charged with the task of slowing Superfund activity. This was at first a welcome sign to industry, which sensed an optimistic future based on a partnership with the EPA.

However, closed meetings soon created an air of favoritism and secret deals. And Gorsuch's slashing of the EPA's budget and staff created a critical backlash within the public and subsequently within the government. In 1983, the gang of three were hastily removed from office, and in 1984 voters elected a Democratic Congress that stopped antienvironmental initiatives. (Lavelle was fired in February, Gorsuch resigned in March, and Watt resigned in October; in December, Lavelle was sentenced to serve six months in jail and pay a $10,000 fine for perjury committed in hearings on Superfund enforcement.) Congress went on to renew and strengthen RCRA (1984), Superfund (1986), the Safe Drinking Water Act (1986), and the Clean Water Act (1987). This turn of events set industry on a new tack. With this clear demonstration of the strength of the environmental movement in the country, both the chemical and oil industries began to adopt a more cooperative posture. Recognizing that this was an issue that would proceed either with or without industry involvement, they had no choice but to accept it. The dominant theme was now that it was a corporation's social responsibility to protect the environment. This justified the idea of going beyond regulation and adopting internally defined environmental goals.

THE ORGANIZATIONAL FIELD: SOCIALLY FOCUSED

The cooperative tone of corporate environmentalism in the mid 1980s emerged from the confusing state of affairs that followed Ann Burford Gorsuch's efforts to dismantle the EPA's infrastructure. Even before her removal from office, what began to settle out was a different form of organizational environment. While new members did not emerge, the relationships among existing members (government, activists, and industry) were altered. Environmentalists, in particular, entered the field as influential players, and the government's credibility was tarnished. Bypassing the previously intermediary EPA, environmental activists began to take direct aim at industry through expanded legal actions supported by an increased power base gained through increased membership and budgets.[3] From 1982 through 1988, environmental activists more than doubled their legal activities of the 1970–1982 period, and instead of directing all of their attention at the government, they now directed a full third of their efforts at industry itself (see Figure 5.1).

Similarly, the EPA underwent a shift following Gorsuch's ouster. In an attempt to regain its lost legitimacy, the agency increased civil and

Figure 5.1. Federal Environment-Related Lawsuits (Environmental
Groups as Plaintiff), 1982–1993.

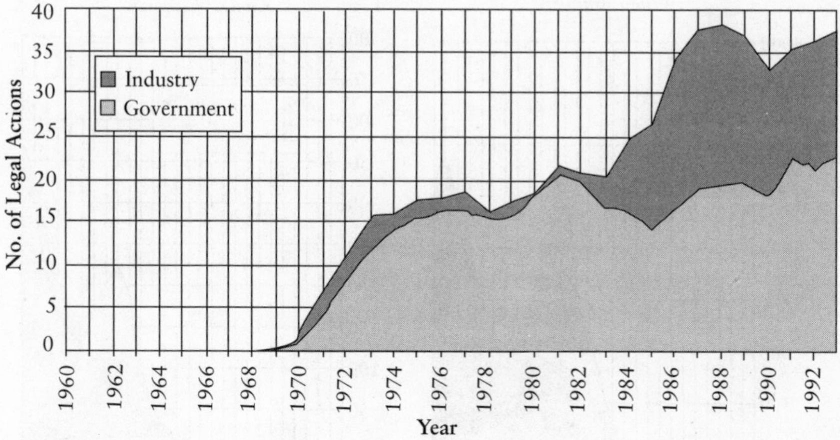

Note: Three-year rolling averages.

administrative actions and introduced, for the first time, criminal actions
against industry (see Figure 5.2). Reagan's efforts to soften regulatory
restraints on industry had yielded the exact opposite effect.

These shifts in the roles of activists and the government were accompanied by a shift in industry perspectives on who should define what constituted responsible environmental management. Government was no longer
a completely reliable source, as regulatory compliance was no longer considered a legitimate signal to society of corporate responsibility. In defining its new role and responsibility, industry would have to look more
toward itself for solutions to environmental problems. This change in
mindset can be seen in the journal coverage. Shown in Figures 5.3 and
5.4, the trends in coverage of both *Chemical Week* and *Oil & Gas
Journal* reversed in 1982 (see Appendix B for statistical analyses).
Switching from an increasing focus on government prior to 1982, the
post–1982 focus was now increasingly directed at industry.

DOMINANT INSTITUTIONS

Following Reagan's failed attempt to disable the EPA and the associated
restructuring of the organizational field, environmentalism for the chemical and oil industries became redefined as an issue of social responsibility.
With this shift in perspective came a more cooperative posture toward
goverment regulation.

Figure 5.2.   EPA Enforcement Actions, 1960–1988.[4]

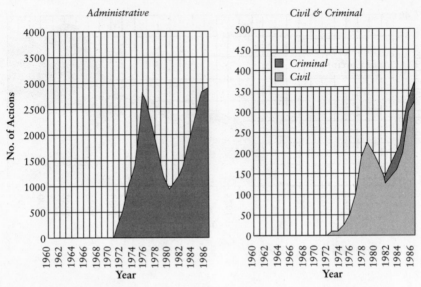

Note: Three-year rolling averages.

Figure 5.3.   Linear Regression: Industry Focus, *Chemical Week*.

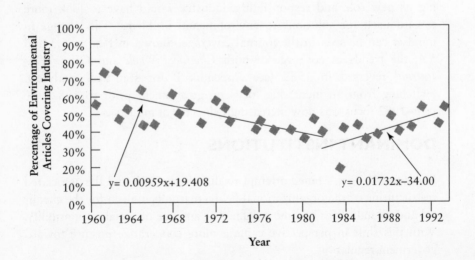

Industry and Government as the Solution: The Chemical Industry

In May 1981, the appointment of Ann Burford Gorsuch offered relief to a much beleaguered chemical industry. She was seen as someone who would bring rationality to the environmental issue by working cooperatively with industry. However, concerns soon arose in October about whether the "knife has cut too deep."[5] *Chemical Week* editorials stressed that an EPA in disarray could mean problems for the industry. This was the most active editorial stage in the thirty-four years covered by this history. In stark contrast to past editorials, many were now supportive of the agency. For example, one *Chemical Week* editorial said, "EPA has been criticized for going too slow on RCRA. Still, we think that it is doing a good job. Give and take is part of the process."[6] Later, the journal wrote, "Many are complaining that the administration is dragging its feet on acid rain. We believe that the argument against power plants is a strong one, but alternative solutions should be considered."[7] And again, "Criticism [of EPA] is unnecessary. Critics expect an overnight fix. EPA deserves credit for its pace and accomplishments."[8] Editorials were also supportive of Gorsuch. In February, *Chemical Week* noted "A bright, tough-minded Gorsuch set out to change the direction and style of EPA. But she has alienated environmentalists and Congress. We sympathize with her effort."[9] With Gorsuch's removal from office in March 1983, and once the effects of the decimation of the EPA had been seen, the chemical industry feared a backlash. Figure 5.5 shows that attention to the issue began a slow increase.

Figure 5.4.   Linear Regression: Industry Focus, *Oil & Gas Journal.*

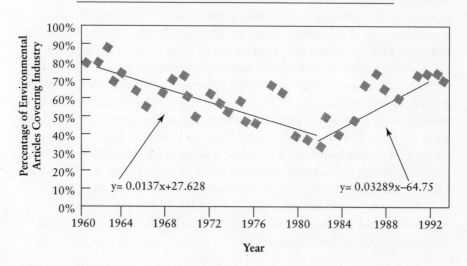

$y= 0.0137x+27.628$

$y= 0.03289x-64.75$

Figure 5.5. Chemical Industry Attention to Environmentalism, 1982–1988.

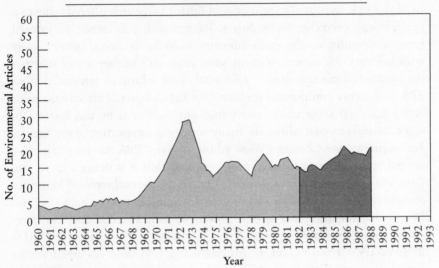

Note: Five-quarter rolling averages.

This increased attention was matched by a shifting mindset as rhetoric began to acknowledge the importance of stern but fair legislation. Industry once again began to see itself (in cooperation with the government) as a part of the solution to environmental problems.

Activists were also now seen in a more constructive light. Displacing their previous focus on protests, articles in *Chemical Week* now highlighted the results of policy and of scientific research they performed. Gaining uncharacteristic recognition, activists were the subject of a positive *Chemical Week* cover story in October 1983: "Environmental Activists: They've Grown in Competence and They're Working Together." However, the industry was not yet prepared to fully trust them. The article went on to warn, "They have more influence in Washington and they are talking more with industry. How far will it go?"[10] Less confrontational industry stances were repeatedly advocated, and cooperation was encouraged. As part of the industry's strong focus on voluntary efforts to clean up waste dumps, Clean Sites, Inc. (CSI), was formed in May 1984 to help negotiate better remediation solutions. And in July 1984, an editorial titled "Nice Guys May Be Back in Style" stated that "the 60s and 70s saw too much confrontation with NRDC and EDF versus the Pacific Legal Foundation and National Legal Center for the Public Interest. But new alliances like Clean Sites, Inc., and the National Coal Policy Project may begin an 80s era of cooperation."[11] A June editorial revived its former technological optimism: "With Superfund, CSI, and other efforts, we see waste dumps resolved by the end of this decade."[12]

In December 1984, this optimism came to a sudden halt as the Bhopal disaster put the industry back into a confrontational posture (see inset page 96). Unlike previous disasters, this was viewed as an industrywide issue rather than a specific company's problem. Articles presented a defensive style reminiscent of earlier years. In April 1985, *Chemical Week* proclaimed, "No, you're not paranoid. A report by the Media Institute substantiates that the mass media accentuate the negative when it comes to chemical risks."[13] A week later, the journal warned of "killing the golden geese": "Litigation by environmental witchhunters kills off one useful product after another."[14]

This defensive posture lingered for two years, but by the end of 1985, the aftershocks of the Bhopal disaster had blown over, and the industry returned to its previously cooperative posture. In November 1995, the CMA established the Community Awareness and Emergency Response (CAER) Program, an associationwide initiative for more interaction between plant personnel and the local community. This program would become the predecessor of another CMA industrywide initiative that would set the tone for the 1990s as a decade of environmental action. Bhopal, in its aftermath, expanded the focus of environmental management beyond ecological and human health concerns to include even greater concern over liability issues and new demands for more open plant operations. The community's "right to know" (RTK) became the new watchword within community, regulatory, and industry circles. The Toxics Release Inventory under the SARA Title III requirements made RTK into law, requiring that firms publicly report all forms of pollution created at their plants.

Not running from the trend set by the new disclosure requirement, the industry made arguments for more proactive management as well. In April 1987, *Chemical Week* proclaimed: "Environmental Law: More Than Compliance. Companies obeying the letter of the law are heading for trouble. Congress is trying to legislate an ethic: Thou shalt not pollute."[15] More cooperation was also advocated. In August, the journal asserted that "the root of the environmental problem is the lack of consensus in a public policy making approach to science, technology, industry, and environment. Industry must build partnerships with academic institutions, policy makers, and the public."[16] And the CMA continued to win praise for its efforts in the environmental arena, being applauded for "more lobbying, public awareness, and pro-active action."[17]

Industry and Government as the Solution: The Oil Industry

President Reagan's 1981 appointment of Ann Burford Gorsuch was met in the oil industry, as in the chemical industry, with initial optimism. The industry perceived an opportunity for gain in Gorsuch's term as administrator. In March 1981, *Oil & Gas Journal* reported, "Better Balance Seems Assured Between Energy and Environment. Reagan administration seems about to relax environmental standards."[18] In June, it declared, "Clean Air Act and Regulations Need Big Revamp to Reflect Reality."[19] And in July, "Clean Air Rules Need Overhaul for Environmental and Economic Program."[20] An August headline proclaimed, "Lead Phasedown Should Be Among First Targets in Regulatory Reform."[21]

And as with the chemical industry, Gorsuch's removal from office induced fears of a backlash. In April 1983, *Oil & Gas Journal* proclaimed, "U.S. environment [and] economy will lose if the EPA issue is used for political gain. With Burford out and Ruckelshaus in, the U.S. is at a critical crossroads in policy. Will we put this risky episode behind us and clean the environment? Or will we continue the scandal for the Democrats? This would produce a reckless pursuit of a pristine environment."[22] As Figure 5.6 makes clear, Gorsuch's ouster stimulated a change

Figure 5.6.   Petroleum Industry Attention to Environmentalism, 1982–1988.

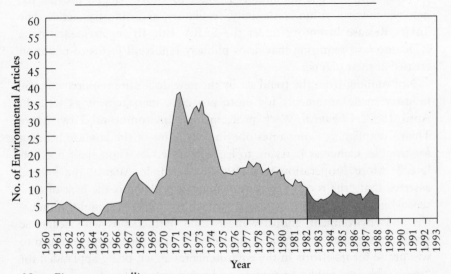

Year

Note: Five-quarter rolling averages.

in attention to the issue. Halting the previously declining trend, attention to environmental issues stabilized and slightly increased through 1988.

Reflecting a cooperative tone similar to that of the chemical industry, industry rhetoric also made a turnaround. Even before Gorsuch's term was over, and marking what may be the beginnings of a cooperative posture, a December 1981 editorial read, "Environmental Self-Policing Serves Industry's Best Interests. Oilmen have learned the importance of protecting the environment. Unfortunately, a few bad actors threaten to spoil things in the traditional oil patch. If self-policing doesn't work, the entire industry will be made to pay for the mistakes of a careless few."[23] In July 1983, the American Petroleum Institute sent out placards to member organizations for display at gas stations about the risks from breathing gasoline vapors, citing scientific studies that showed an increased cancer risk from prolonged exposure. In June 1985, Chevron and Unocal developed a research group to study waste treatment technologies and began soliciting partners.

In addition, coverage became supportive of the EPA. In one case it even went so far as to suggest a public relations partnership. In August 1984, *Oil & Gas Journal* admonished that the industry "shouldn't rush reauthorization [of Superfund] for political reasons. Give EPA time to analyze options."[24] When the bill was finally passed in October, the industry saw a partial victory: "New bill is hard for industry. Raises taxes on petroleum; it's too big. But Reagan should sign it because it could have been much worse."[25] In October 1987, the journal lauded the agency: "EPA jumps on the right track with draft oil waste report."[26] And a month later, it proclaimed, "Clean Air Act deadline delay the right move for clean air." This article went on to argue that "industry should not only welcome EPA's decision to extend the CAA deadline . . . but it should help the agency defend its actions in controversies certain to follow."[27]

But concern over the availability of federal land for oil drilling remained an ever-present concern. In February 1984, an article titled "Concern over Environment or Economic Obstructionism?" argued that environmentalists trying to stop leasing on federal lands had seized a higher priority on the national agenda than they deserved. In many cases, it argued, it was a disguise for efforts to "stop all development at any cost."[28] And in November 1985, the journal asserted, "Balance Needed in Environmental Values, National Energy Interests." That article went on to argue that "new ideas of protecting 'integral vistas' and 'greater ecosystems' are just another way for an extreme group to shut oil and gas drilling out of more federal land. Restricting access of oil firms will increase exports and raise costs so that people won't be able to drive to the parks."[29]

On the whole, the strategic posture by the end of 1988 appeared to be cooperation, or perhaps more accurately, resigned acceptance. In a June 1987 article titled "Environmentalism Should Acknowledge Successes, Failures," the journal argued that "the principal triumph of environmentalism is that business has learned to behave with greater environmental responsibility." But before closing, it added the caveat that environmentalism had "also restricted economic development."[30]

•

Bhopal (1984)

Between 10:00 P.M. on December 2 and 1:30 A.M. on December 3, 1984, approximately forty-five tons of methyl isocyanate (MIC) gas escaped from an underground storage tank at a Union Carbide pesticide plant in Bhopal, India. Although this release did not affect a wealthy population like the Santa Barbara and Seveso incidents, it gained worldwide notoriety for its horrific consequences. By the next morning, two thousand people in the neighboring slums were dead, and another three hundred thousand had been injured. Fifteen hundred more people died in the ensuing months, and at least seven thousand animals perished. Damage to the environment remains largely unassessed to this day.[31]

The local authorities were completely unprepared to handle the incident. Police instructed people to run away from the area, causing a flight of nearly four hundred thousand people, many of whom inhaled yet more gas and succumbed to the poison. Authorities unfortunately did not know that lying down with a wet towel over your face could deflect the toxic effects. For those that remained, immediate efforts were directed at medical recovery. However, local doctors had no information on the toxicity and epidemiology of MIC poisoning, and even publicly available data did not reach them until several days after the accident.[32]

The plant was shut down immediately, and a few months later another Union Carbide plant, in Bombay, was also closed. In March 1985 the government of India took Union Carbide to court, and on a petition by Union Carbide, the case was moved from New York to India. The case moved from an Indian district court to a state high court and then the Indian supreme court, where in January 1989 a mediated settlement of $470 million was reached.[33]

Aside from the financial ramifications, the Bhopal disaster initiated a significant restructuring in personnel and business activities at Union Carbide. Given the company's stock drop from a predisaster price of between $50 and $58 to between $32 and $40 per share following the incident, Union Carbide found itself a vulnerable candidate for a hostile takeover bid from GAF Corporation. To put the event and the unsuccessful takeover behind them and to make preparations for a stronger future, key top managers at the time of the accident were transferred, retired, or left the company. And the company cut back its operations and emerged a smaller, yet profitable, firm.

For Union Carbide, this incident created a shadow and a drop in morale unparalleled in its history. With trials lasting for more than ten years, the company found itself saddled with the difficult challenge of shedding the Bhopal stigma. For the rest of industry, the incident was a stimulus for major changes the world over. For one thing, it altered the structure of overseas insurance liability. For another, companies were sufficiently shaken to initiate voluntary environmental and safety investments to avoid future Bhopal-type disasters. Finally, communities and society changed their perceptions of technological and industrial risk.[34]

•

ORGANIZATIONAL STRUCTURE AND CULTURE: MANAGERIAL COMPLIANCE

In 1982, petrochemical companies were prepared for an increase in spending for pollution control. Some industry estimates set spending as high as 46 percent over the previous year.[35] As a result of this and a changing mood regarding corporate environmental management, structural changes were afoot. As one article in *Chemical Week* noted, "The industry-wide move indicates the effect of environmental regulation and underscores a growing sense of responsibility for the environment. It is no wonder, then, that the director of a chemical company's environmental affairs department has one of the toughest jobs in industry today."[36] Environmental management was being elevated within the organization as a vital corporate function, and its head carried significant clout. For example, Velsicol (of endrin fame in the 1960s) hired a former regional director of the EPA to head its corporate environmental unit. And Monsanto's director of environmental management noted receiving "more than full support of management."[37]

Centralized environmental affairs departments were the norm for maximizing organizational power. In 1982, the director of environmental affairs for Hoescht Celanese stated, "the problem was bigger than the individual plant. . . . It was a corporate problem."[38] Union Carbide's director of EH&S added that the tidal wave of environmental laws in the 1970s created the need for "stronger central direction."[39] Throughout the industry, these centralized departments merged divisions for environmental protection, toxicology, safety and loss prevention, and industrial hygiene, often with an information services group responsible for tying the parts together through a shared computerized database.

The organizational goal of these departments was now more than strict compliance. Environmental management was now a matter of internal cultural change. According to Monsanto's environmental director, "making a profit is like breathing at the operating level. We want our people to treat environmental issues the same way."[40] To facilitate changes in internal perceptions, companies began to direct attention toward also reducing external confrontation. Stated the vice president for government and public affairs at Dow Chemical, "One way to lose a reputation for combativeness is to stop being combative, and that's what we've done. Another thing we're doing is to spend more time finding out what people are thinking."[41]

In terms of direct pollution control, the mid 1980s also marked a process shift from regulatory compliance at the end of the pipe to waste minimization in the process. The institutional tie between environmental protection and economic efficiency was beginning to be forged. A survey of chemical plant operators by the nonprofit group Inform found that 41 percent of the plants reported a total of forty-four waste reduction practices in place.[42] And of these, 41 percent involved basic changes to the manufacturing process. Ciba-Geigy used new processes to eliminate the use of mercury at its Tom's River plant. Monsanto's plant in Addyston, Ohio, gradually changed its polystyrene process from batch reactions to closed-system continuous reactions, which achieved a 99 percent reduction in air emissions.[43]

In a departure from previous motivations, the dominant factors driving these initiatives were not just regulation but also "cost factors, liability concerns, public scrutiny and the indirect impact of regulations."[44] A new optimism about the potential for opportunities in corporate environmental management was spreading. The Office of Technology Assessment surveyed industry executives and found that "increasing numbers of successful examples of waste reduction yielding net cost savings and more competitive operations support the argument that waste reduction promotes industrial revitalization and economic growth."[45] Momentum was building for the notion that "substantially more waste reduction was possible."[46] According to one DuPont executive, "We will see considerable reductions in the percentage of waste generated per pound of product produced, just as we have seen reductions in the consumption of energy over the last ten years."[47]

Organizational Change at Amoco

Within Amoco, the organizational changes seen in the industry as a whole were reflected in new corporate goals and structures. Slightly preceding the shift in the organizational field, Amoco began to undertake a two-stage consolidation of its environmental functions in 1979. The medical department was integrated with Industrial Hygiene and Toxicology in 1979 and dubbed Environmental Conservation and Toxicology; three years later, the safety department was also merged in, and the resulting department was renamed Environmental Affairs and Safety (EA&S). At this point, the department began to take on a significantly expanded role beyond that of the previous twelve years, one based more on internally directed goals with social legitimacy as their objective. Three events helped spur this shift ahead of the rest of the field.

The first wake-up call was what was then a surprising forecast of where environmental laws were going. Two representatives, one each from the chemical and oil companies, were charged by executive management with the task of determining how much environmental regulations would cost the company in the coming decade. One of the representatives recalled, "I think we gave an estimate of about $500 million over five to ten years. They almost laughed us out of the room." Another environmental director explained the basis for their disbelief: "They said that the U.S. government would never let things get that bad. In actuality, those guys hit the target."

These estimates prompted Amoco's president to commission a task force in July 1980 to study the impact of future environmental and health standards on company operations. A report was completed in April 1982 that recommended a closer examination of corporate environmental policies and the potential environmental impacts of the company's products and processes. However, by the time the report was released, many of these recommendations had already been initiated, as the department was undergoing significant changes. But more important, the report showed that senior management was now becoming aware of the full potential scope of environmental regulations.

A second wake-up call occurred in 1978 when the *Amoco Cadiz* ran aground off the coast of Brittany, France, spilling 120,000 tons of crude oil. This proved to be the worst environmental disaster the company had ever experienced. Although there appeared to be little direct effect on corporate staffing (beyond the creation of a small spill response group staffed with marine biologists), Amoco executives feel that it called attention to the potential costs of environmental mishaps or accidents, both in terms of economics and corporate reputation. According to the EH&S vice president, "The *Amoco Cadiz* was coincidental in its timing with the growth in EH&S in the early 1980s. It did have its effect, though. It forced people to reconsider the implications of environmental [mishaps]. It taught us that if you [have an accident], it can cause much pain. The consequences can be expensive, both financially and in terms of the company reputation." And according to the corporate counsel, "The *Cadiz* affected the reputation of the EH&S people. This was the first time that the EH&S department came into the forefront. They provided advice and technical support to the French government." This elevated the importance of the department in the eyes of the rest of the company.

But if the *Cadiz* incident taught by the stick, a third wake-up call used the carrot. The vice president explained, "The other wake-up call was the construction of the Cooper River [chemical] plant. It started in 1978 and won a national award for best environmental development. This was around the same time that Dow was having its troubles siting a plant in California. This taught us that if you do the right thing, there can be great benefits."

Facilitating this environmental awakening was also a shift in demographics. A new generation of executives was beginning to see the subtleties and full impact of corporate environmentalism. One senior executive remembers, "people started popping up like Lawrence Fuller [the present chairman and CEO] and Lawrie Thomas [the present vice chairman], and they did more listening. They were the next generation of executives, who ushered in a new era. They understood the new things. They weren't the dinosaur types who couldn't understand that anything other than pure profit would guide company activity." However, one EH&S executive is cautious about crediting internal management alone with this transition: "I don't think the executive transition was the cause for the shift in internal attitudes. It was more driven by external events. Both legislation and public-political pressure. However, it's a kind of chicken-and-egg thing. It's not necessarily the accidents that have caused it. I don't think that they've really grown in frequency. We have always had the Love Canals and the Times Beaches. But people's responses to them have changed. This is the real shift taking place here." What, in effect, he was referring to is the shift in the dominant institutions that guide both societal interpretations and corporate responses to environmental concerns.

Organizational Structure at Amoco

Beginning in 1982, attempts were made to centralize the three company EH&S departments. According to a former Amoco Chemical Company (ACC) environmental manager, the reasons for this consolidation were that "We wanted to develop uniformity in the environmental programs within the various operating companies. We were concerned that the three companies were interpreting the regulations differently. For example, chemical would build a new plant based on the proposed regulations. Oil would wait until the law came out before they would initiate anything. There was too great a difference in philosophies."

With the consolidation, the staff grew dramatically, from a size of fourteen to a size of sixty-three, in only four years (see Figure 5.7). Although this growth involved the transfer of thirteen industrial hygienists and toxicologists and seven safety specialists from the medical department, it also included the addition of twenty-four professionals. Also with the consolidation, the corporate environmental department adopted a discipline-based structure, less focused on specific media and more focused on internal functions (see Figure 5.8). The group now had six major disci-

Figure 5.7. Amoco Environmental Department Staffing, 1966–1987.

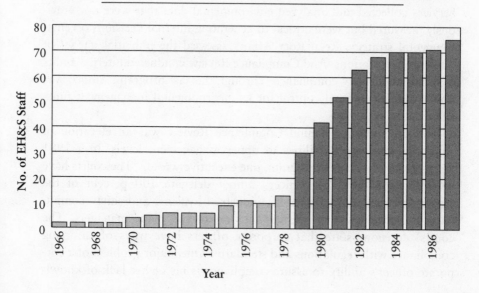

Figure 5.8.   Amoco Environmental Department, Discipline-Based Structure (1982).

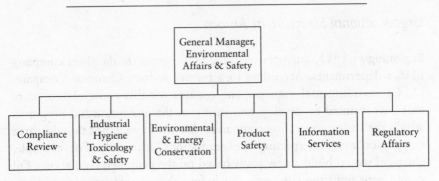

Note: Total staff = 64.

plines, which included not only the original three departments of Industrial Hygiene, Safety, and Environmental and Energy Conservation but also the three new functions of Information Services, Regulatory Affairs, and, most important, Compliance Review.

Organizational Function at Amoco

These last three departments represented the expansion in the corporation's environmental goals toward internally directed change. Information Services collected and analyzed environmental data that were not previously measured but were critical to generating internal decisions on environmental strategy. Regulatory Affairs assessed the potential impact of upcoming regulations. And Compliance Review conducted internal audits to ensure regulatory compliance. Through this last program, Amoco was now assuming internal control for its environmental management function.

One driving force behind Compliance Review was an elevation of environmental responsibilities to upper management levels. In a 1981 discussion over the new program, one executive wrote, "The courts have held that top corporate officers cannot delegate 100 percent of the responsibility for environmental, industrial hygiene, and safety compliance to subsidiary management and on to the plant managers. The courts' decisions state that corporate officers have ways of enforcing compliance with regulations and standards. One major problem of a corporate officer's ability to assure compliance is his or her lack of knowledge of actual environmental, industrial hygiene, and safety practices and problems at various locations. However, the courts have also held that 'deliberate ignorance is no excuse.'" Another senior environmental manager wrote, "Environmental and industrial hygiene compliance reviews are now being widely discussed in both industry and government. The purpose of these reviews is to assure upper management of compliance with policies and numerous environmental and industrial hygiene laws and regulations. It is a method for management to obtain a baseline indication of operational practices."

Aside from the direct changes in organizational function, 1982 marked the beginnings of new types of coordinating structures designed to define internal environmental activities and coordinate those activities throughout the company. In 1982, the Health, Safety, and Environment Coordinating Committee was formed "to respond to the expanding volume of new regulations and enforcement activities by state and federal agencies." For the first time, a central environmental group brought together representatives from Law, EH&S, Medicine, and the three operating companies. Underscoring this growth in corporate environmental concern was the concurrent creation of Amoco's first environmental, occupational health, and safety policy in 1982. Signifying the new level of executive endorsement, it was signed by company president Richard M. Morrow (president of what then had become the Standard Oil Company of Indiana).

Just as the EH&S Department had grown in size and influence within the company, environmental responsibilities started to diffuse in the early 1980s to other support and line functions within the organization. At the plant level, environmental affairs was growing from simply "a cost of doing business" requiring little organizational attention to a significant part of the daily responsibilities of support and line functions in the 1980s. Waste minimization efforts in the chemical and oil companies began in 1983 and 1984, respectively, requiring engineering-EH&S collaboration in determining how best to initiate process adjustments and additions. And, reflecting greater environmental responsibility at the plant level, the EH&S function was cleaved off from the operations department to become a stand-alone department in the refineries in 1982 and in the chemical plants in 1987.

One former refinery EH&S manager recalls that environmental managers were gaining in credibility: "Starting in the early eighties, people started to see EH&S as being more useful to operations. There was a little more buy-in. EH&S had to show that there was an important benefit to the company by adopting environmental principles. The role of operations managers was also starting to change at the refinery due to environmentalism. Managers started to have goals such as energy efficiency and NPDES [National Pollution Discharge Elimination System, under the Clean Water Act] discharge violations added to their traditional results management [performance review] goals of output and yield."

THE INSTITUTIONAL DEFINITION OF CORPORATE ENVIRONMENTALISM, 1982–1988

President Reagan's efforts to reduce the impact of environmental regulation on industry served instead to increase the institutional pressures on firms to adopt environmental controls. Only now the government was no longer the primary arbiter of corporate environmental responsibility. With environmental activists taking a more prominent role and industry itself adopting responsibility for self-control, Reagan's efforts catalyzed a shift from a focus on regulatory compliance to a focus on social responsibility. The shift may have likely happened regardless, but Reagan's efforts made it happen quicker by bringing the underlying tensions of the late 1970s to the surface.

In the process, attention to environmental issues began a rebound, slowly increasing through the middle 1980s while industry's posture became more cooperative. The media perception of the issue, shown in Figure 5.9, was now completely formed. It shifted in its relative proportions: air and water concerns had decreased, while toxics and hazardous waste gained greater attention, and remediation was added as the final piece of the institutionalized legislative framework. More to the point, however, a new pattern was beginning to emerge: what was originally a two-dimensional issue (air and water) was steadily becoming a multidimensional issue.

A dramatic shift was also under way in who would be perceived as the source of solutions to environmental problems. Regulatory compliance was no longer considered a legitimate signal to society of corporate responsibility. In defining its new role and responsibility, industry began to look more toward itself for solutions to environmental problems. The trends in coverage in both journals reversed in 1982, switching from an increasing focus on government prior to 1982 to an increasing focus on industry after 1982. In short, industry was becoming more open, adopting a cooperative strategy, seeking input from a wider range of sources, and proactively undertaking environmental initiatives.

Despite the EPA's reduced credibility, a pattern was also emerging in how the environmental issue was perceived in terms of the organization.

Figure 5.9. Media Perception of the Environmental Issue, 1982–1988.

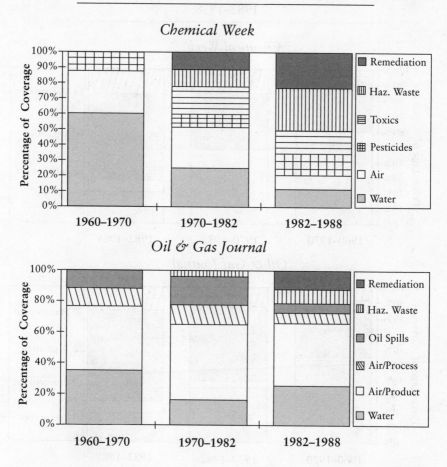

Chemical Week

Oil & Gas Journal

As shown in Figure 5.10, the early technological bias was steadily eroding in favor of regulatory and enforcement considerations. As will be seen, however, this would soon change as organizational perceptions of the environmental issue became managerial in nature.

Within the corporation, these changes could also be seen. In a small way, environmentalism was becoming an integral part of the objectives of the corporation. The firm was instituting programs to achieve regulatory compliance based on internal, rather then external, procedures. In the process, the company was laying the groundwork to develop internal objectives as well as internal procedures for achieving them.

Beginning in 1988, the pace of both this specific organizational change and the broad institutional change surrounding it would increase dramat-

Figure 5.10.   Organizational Perceptions of the Environmental Issue,
1982–1988.

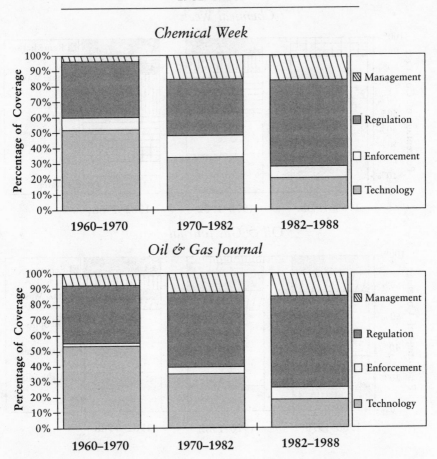

Chemical Week

Oil & Gas Journal

ically. So far we have seen how the field evolved to include first the government and then environmental groups. As we shall see, in 1988 the field would change once more, to include constituents who would drive institutional arrangements to a more fundamental level. This level was based on structures reflecting the vested interests of a new set of actors more centrally linked to corporate objectives. And, as this history has repeatedly demonstrated, it would be the confluence of many high-profile events that would create an avalanche of pressure for the next institutional shift.

6

STRATEGIC ENVIRONMENTALISM
(1988–1993)

THE FOCUS OF ANN BURFORD GORSUCH'S TERM at the EPA was to reduce the growth in regulatory constraints upon industry. Although her objectives and methods were suspect, she did focus attention on the increasingly complex structure of environmental regulations, the unnecessarily antagonistic government-industry relationship those regulations were producing, the growing economic burden they were placing on industry, and the need to reconsider the system as it had become institutionalized. In 1983, Reagan reinstated William Ruckelshaus as EPA administrator, and his efforts focused on ways to integrate the agency's regulatory structure to make it more cooperative, more holistic, less segmented by medium, more efficient, and less onerous on industry. He was followed by administrators Lee Thomas, William Reilly, and Carol Browner, who continued pursuing this objective, prioritizing regulation to direct attention where it was most needed (for example, away from abandoned hazardous waste sites and toward acid rain and ozone depletion). Their efforts came to the fore in the late 1980s, as budget deficits increased and environmental regulation was becoming increasingly stringent. The combination of these two factors yielded a drive toward more cost-effective policies that could simultaneously build international competitive strength and a safer environment.[1]

Successive administrations continued searching for new mechanisms to bring about corporate change. As a result, regulation in the late 1980s began to move away from the incremental, command-and-control approach adopted at the EPA's formation and toward voluntary and market-incentive schemes that attempted to cooperatively initiate corporate change.[2]

This shift coincided with a shift in industry's posture and rhetoric on environmental issues from cooperative to proactive. Pollution prevention became the increasing focus of environmental management, and the issue, on the whole, took on a more international scope and scale. Alliances between environmental groups and industry began to emerge as industry's perception of environmentalists as a group shifted from a previously negative focus on protests and legal actions to a more positive focus on the research work they performed. In what appeared a somewhat cyclical pattern, industry returned to self-directed strategies much like those of the first stage of modern environmentalism, in the 1960s. However, that self-direction had taken on a completely new flavor. The definition of *self* had evolved. It now included the perspectives, opinions, input, and institutions of an organizational field that was vastly different from what it was in the 1960s.

There are many events that took place at this time to facilitate such a dramatic shift. There were so many, in fact, that it is difficult to identify any specific one as predominant. It may be more accurate to state that the timing of so many events occurring almost simultaneously built an avalanche of momentum for dramatic institutional change on environmental matters. Dunlap identifies the causes for the concurrent shift in public opinion as "an endless array of newsworthy events—Bhopal, Chernobyl, frequent chemical spills, hazardous ocean beaches, oil spills, rainforest destruction, and filled-up waste sites—that receive tremendous media attention."[3] Buttel, Hawkins, and Power cite the global warming debate for providing a shot in the arm to "an environmental movement that had enjoyed few victories during the decade."[4] Each of these emerging issues and events (see insets pages 119 to 122) added to the collective growth in public awareness and concern for environmental problems. Indicative of this heightened concern, in lieu of its usual man or woman of the year, *Time* magazine in 1989 picked the endangered earth as "planet of the year"—a far cry from its 1961 choice of fifteen scientists for their contributions to "remaking man's world." *Time*'s editors supported their unorthodox choice by arguing that the "new journalistic challenge . . . is to help find solutions" to the kind of environmental disasters that had been so prominent in the preceding year.[5]

For industry, these disasters added to the collective growth in the organizational field. Once the domain of actors traditionally outside firms' strategic interests (such as activists and the government), the field was now under pressure for increased corporate environmentalism emerging from within core business networks. These new sources of pressure would raise corporate environmentalism from a social responsibility to a strategic concern. The final result was that the introduction of economic and strategic interests into the organizational field triggered economic and strategic responses from within the organization. Thus the institutional perspective on environmental management in this stage shifts from one of responding to external social demands to one of focusing on internal strategic and management issues.

THE ORGANIZATIONAL FIELD: STRATEGICALLY FOCUSED

Looking over the past thirty years, the dominant conception of environmental management has been embodied in the shape of the field: industrial environmentalism emerged from a field dominated by industry, regulatory environmentalism was driven by a government-controlled field, and social environmentalism was directed by social activism. Likewise, strategic environmentalism was embodied in a field constituted of strategic interests. Insurance companies, competitors, and investors joined the field of actors pushing for corporate environmental change. Simultaneously, the institutional roles of government and activists evolved to become more cooperative in the search for new environmental solutions.

As Figures 6.1 and 6.2 show, insurance companies began suing industry in 1986, and industry began to retaliate in 1987. Suits involving insurance companies grew quickly to an average of 16.75 suits per year with insurance companies as plaintiffs and 30.65 per year with insurance companies as defendants. In both cases, the opponent was industry. According to industry analysts, this was due in part to a broad change in insurance policy coverage as well as to a change in the form of environmental incidents. First, policies generally stipulated that pollution must be "sudden and accidental" to be covered under most general liability contracts. This condition excluded the newly emerging and slowly developing problems of waste site remediation and leaking underground storage tanks. Second, after 1986, general insurance coverage became more strict with the creation of pollution exclusion clauses. Pollution protection become more difficult and expensive to acquire as separate coverage. A 1988 General Accounting Office report found that "the number of insurers writing pollution insurance, the number of policies written, and the total pollution liability coverage decreased dramatically from a 1984 peak. Simultaneously, the average premium increased as much as 11 times [beyond] its 1982 level."[6] As a result, lawsuits were filed to contest the norms regarding the definition of environmental incidents and environmental liability. The outcome of these contests had significant implications for corporate competitiveness.

Figure 6.1.   Federal Environment-Related Lawsuits (Industry as Defendant), 1960–1993.

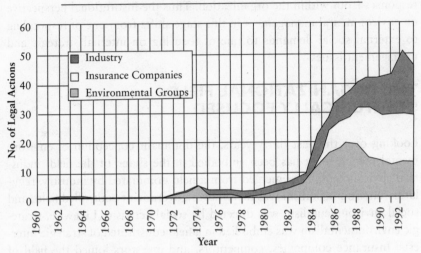

Note: *Three-year rolling averages.*

Figures 6.1 and 6.2 also show that in 1988 industries increasingly sued one another in an attempt to define the proper allocation and limits of environmental liability, particularly as it pertained to Superfund responsibility. Owing to Superfund's strict joint and several liability clause, companies hotly contested who would pay what share of a waste site's cleanup costs. In fact, the EPA would often sue one major contributor to a given waste site for the entire cleanup and leave it to that corporation to recoup those costs from the other contributors independently. Up from only two in 1987, lawsuits between firms jumped to eight in 1988, ten in 1989, and an average of 14.3 from 1988 through 1993.

Finally, investors joined the field in 1989, filing environmental proxy resolutions in suddenly large numbers, as shown in Figure 6.3. Filed at annual stockholder meetings, proxy resolutions would put to an open vote a set of concerns of a particular investor group. Up from only three in 1989, forty-three environmental resolutions were filed in 1990, and an average of 59.6 were filed from 1990 through 1993. Of these resolutions, roughly 37 percent were directed at virtually every major chemical and oil company. Target companies included Allied Signal, Bristol-Myers Squibb, DuPont, Dow, Eastman Kodak, W. R. Grace, Great Lakes Chemical, Procter & Gamble, Union Carbide, American Cyanamid, Ethyl, Amoco, ARCO, Chevron, Coastal, Exxon, Phillips, Unocal, Occidental, and Mobil.

Figure 6.2.   Federal Environment-Related Lawsuits (Industry as Plaintiff), 1960–1993.

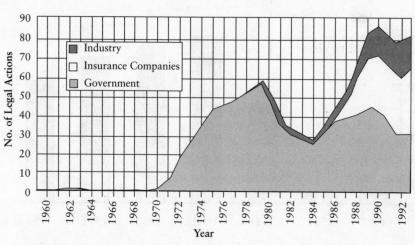

Note: *Three-year rolling averages.*

Roughly 68 percent of these were resolutions to sign the Valdez Principles, a set of ten guiding environmental principles sponsored by the Coalition for Environmentally Responsible Economies (CERES) in 1989 (see inset page 122). Other resolutions dealt with such issues as the establishment of an environmental policy committee, revised health and safety policy, toxic wastes in ethnic and minority communities, controlling carbon dioxide emissions, and eliminating the use of specific compounds. The addition of this new mechanism for institutional pressure triggered a new form of organizational response to environmentalism, introducing external environmental concerns directly to the board of directors through the annual shareholder meeting.

Aside from the addition of these new institutional influences, activists and government also evolved in their institutional roles. First, as a result of the growing public awareness of environmental issues, membership in environmental groups grew from 1988 to 1990 in numbers equal to those of the entire 1980s to that point. Figure 6.4 shows this growth for the sixteen largest environmental groups. In terms of legal activity, environmental activists increased lawsuits against the government by 21 percent and against industry by 28 percent (up 53 and 79 percent against the chemical and petroleum industries, respectively.) Also, alliances between industry and activists were on the rise (for example, McDonald's and EDF) as each party recognized common objectives in environmental protection.

Figure 6.3.   Investor-Initiated Environmental Resolutions.[7]

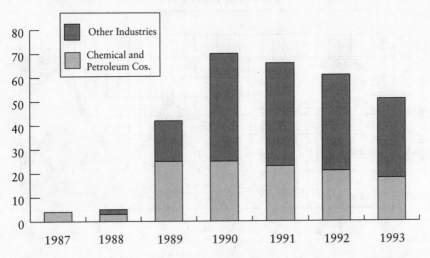

Figure 6.4.   Membership of the Largest Sixteen Environmental Groups, 1982–1993.[8]

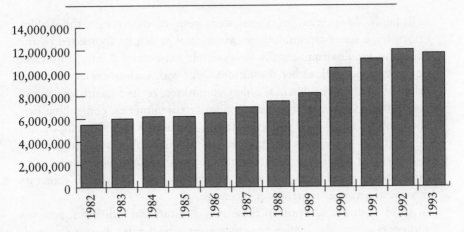

The EPA also began to shift toward more cooperative programs between the agency and the regulated community. Although criminal actions continued to increase, they formed a small percentage of the agency's administrative and civil actions, which were in decline following a 1990 peak (see Figure 6.5). Moving away from the strict command-and-control mindset of the 1970s, EPA administrators Bill Reilly and Carol Browner pushed voluntary programs (for example, the 33/50, Green Lights, and Environmental Leadership programs) and market-incentive programs (for example, the tradable permit program under the Clean Air Act amendments of 1990; see inset page 122) to augment the established

Figure 6.5.   EPA Enforcement Actions, 1960–1993.[9]

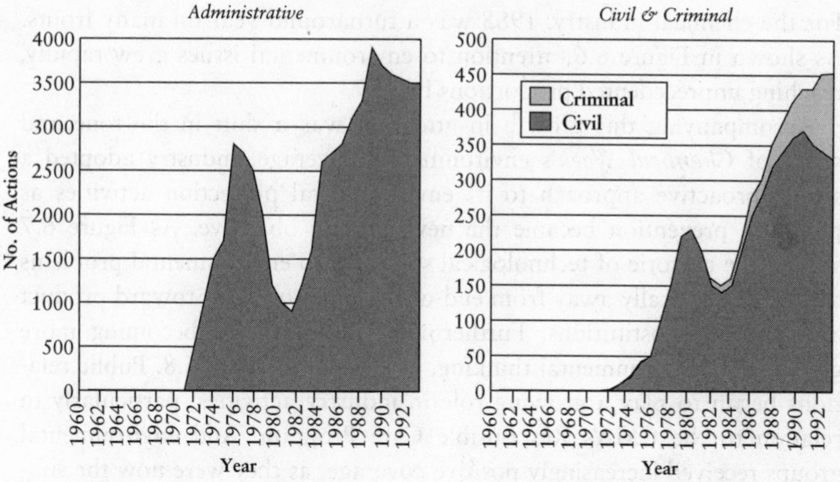

Note: Three-year rolling averages.

regulatory structure. Also significant was the development of the 1986 Toxics Release Inventory (SARA Title III), whose first reports were due in 1987. This required that companies reveal the extent of their polluting emissions, thus empowering environmental activists and local communities with valuable data on the environmental record of individual firms. This combination of changes left the agency with a slightly schizophrenic posture, dictating command-and-control enforcement on the one hand and seeking cooperative partnerships on the other.

In response to these institutional shifts, industry continued to be more cooperative and less confrontational. As shown in Figure 6.2, lawsuits against government decreased nearly 40 percent from a 1988 peak. And as Figures 5.3 and 5.4 showed, journal coverage continued to be geared increasingly toward industry news and decreasingly toward government action.

THE DOMINANT INSTITUTIONS

With the organizational field restructured with a strategic orientation, proactive environmental management became the dominant conception. Attention to environmentalism reached new heights by the early 1990s. That increasing attention and proaction was continued through 1993 for the chemical industry but was unsustained by the oil industry, which faced new challenges from the Clean Air Act amendments, the lurking threat of global control on greenhouse gas emissions, and public resentment following the *Exxon Valdez* spill.

The Organizational Field as the Solution: The Chemical Industry

For the chemical industry, 1988 was a turnaround year on many fronts. As shown in Figure 6.6, attention to environmental issues grew rapidly, reaching unprecedented proportions by 1993.

Accompanying this growth in attention was a shift in the tone and scope of *Chemical Week*'s environmental coverage. Industry adopted a strong proactive approach to its environmental protection activities as pollution prevention became the new guiding objective. As Figure 6.7 shows, the rhetoric of technological solutions to environmental problems shifted dramatically away from end-of-the-pipe solutions toward product and process substitutions. Furthermore, industry was becoming more global in its environmental thinking, as shown in Figure 6.8. Public relations began to play a growing role in industry activities, particularly in relation to the CMA's Responsible Care Program. And environmental groups received increasingly positive coverage, as they were now the subject of attention for their alliances in industry and government efforts.

In *Chemical Week*, the *Exxon Valdez* disaster, global warming, the CMA's Responsible Care Program, the Valdez Principles, and several new legislative initiatives—the Clean Air Act amendments, the Pollution Prosecution Act, and the Pollution Prevention Act—were the central

Figure 6.6. Chemical Industry Attention to Environmentalism, 1988–1993.

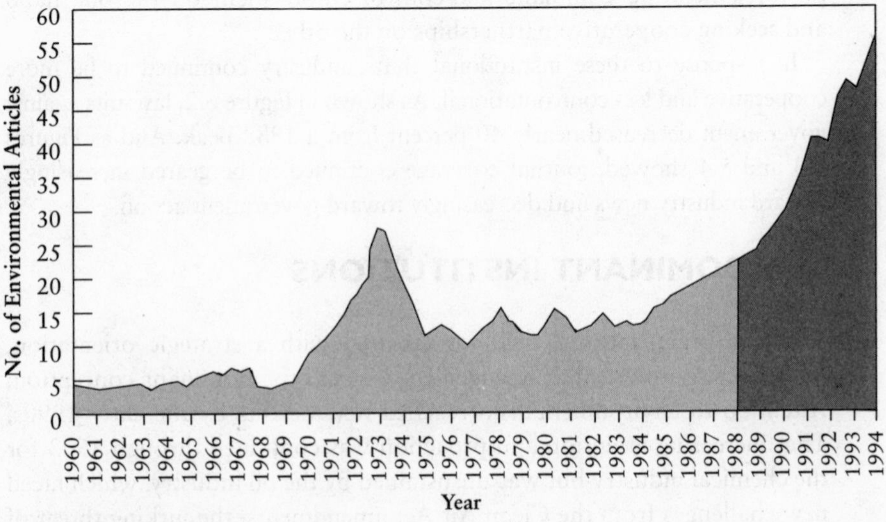

Note: *Five-quarter rolling averages.*

Figure 6.7. Focus of Technology Articles, *Chemical Week.*

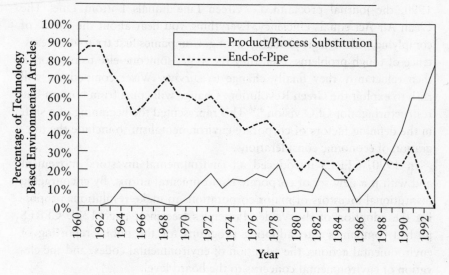

Figure 6.8. International Focus of Environmental Articles, *Chemical Week.*

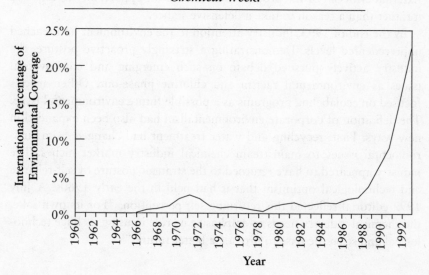

focus. In response to each, cautious optimism was visible. In November 1990, the journal proclaimed, "Green Line Equals Bottom Line. The Clean Air Act equals efficiency. Everything you hear about the 'costs' of complying with CAA is probably wrong. Companies first try to deny existence of tough problems, then they try to get someone else to pay for it, then reluctantly they finally change to survive. Wiser competitors will rush to exploit the Green Revolution. Change will come from bottom-line restructuring, not CEO vision."[10] This represented the beginning of a shift in the defining factors of corporate environmentalism to include the integration of economic considerations.

In 1990, CERES introduced an environmental investors' movement and with it a new set of corporate environmental norms. By encouraging institutional investors of major corporations to make resolutions proposing the adoption of the Valdez Principles (see inset page 122), CERES pushed companies into adopting programs for the public reporting of environmental actions, the adoption of environmental codes, and the elevation of environmental concerns to the board level.

And in what represented the industry's most aggressive proactive effort, the CMA's Responsible Care Program exploded as an issue in 1991. Two entire issues of *Chemical Week* were devoted to covering it in each of the years 1991, 1992, and 1993. Interestingly, this burst of attention to Responsible Care came a full year after the program was first unveiled in April 1990. The industry appeared to be tentatively testing the waters with a gradual introduction of the program. However, once it was fully introduced, the industry seemed much more thick-skinned about it. External criticism of the program was seen as an opportunity to improve it rather than a reason to take a defensive stance.

By the end of 1993, industry attention to the environment had reached unprecedented levels. Demonstrating a strikingly proactive posture, the industry actively pursued debate on such emerging and controversial issues as environmental racism and chlorine phase-out. Other articles focused on ecolabeling programs as a possible future environmental issue. The definition of corporate environmentalism had also been expanded in new ways. First, recycling and water treatment had changed from environmental issues to mainstream chemical industry market niches. The industry appeared to have returned to the strategic posture of self-reliance and technological optimism that it had held in the early 1960s. A July 1992 editorial reflected this returning self-perception: "For its own sake, the chemical industry needs to emphasize its role in using its huge technological and scientific base to provide a better future."[11]

The Organizational Field as the Solution: The Oil Industry

As with the chemical industry, attention to environmental issues in *Oil & Gas Journal* grew significantly in 1988 and, as shown in Figure 6.9, reached a peak in 1990. However, the continued optimism present in the chemical industry was not sustained in the oil industry, as attention dropped from this 1990 peak to a 1993 low comparable to that of the early 1980s.

The year 1988 began for the oil industry with a focus on similar events and issues as in the chemical industry. However, the relative weight given each issue and the perspectives from which they were viewed were quite different. The *Exxon Valdez* disaster garnered a tremendous amount of attention (see inset page 121). And in contrast to articles surrounding previous spills, those about the *Valdez* did not question the validity of environmental claims but rather focused on the broad impact the accident would have on the industry as a whole. In April 1989, *Oil & Gas Journal* reported, "*Exxon Valdez* Disaster Leaves Industry with Much to Repair. For Exxon, embarrassment. For industry, the biggest setback since the 1969 Santa Barbara spill. Industry, not just Exxon, will pay for the spill."[12] Some articles were uncharacteristically critical of Exxon for the

Figure 6.9. Petroleum Industry Attention to Environmentalism, 1988–1993.

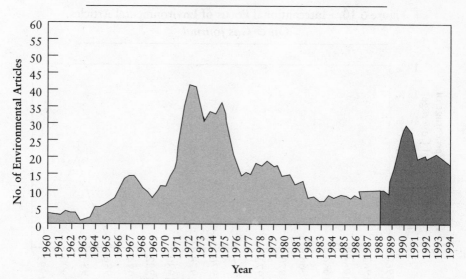

Note: Five-quarter rolling averages.

company's slow response and the ramifications the aftermath of the spill could have on the entire industry.

Proactive environmental management grew as a serious industry movement. In April 1990, an editorial promoted industry efforts at "Winning the environmental lead."[13] In December, an editorial touted the "good lessons from a bad year,"[14] citing the April launch of the American Petroleum Institute (API) Strategies for Today's Environmental Partnership (STEP) program (a counterpart to the CMA's Responsible Care Program), and in a May 1991 article, the API's president called "the environment the top issue for U.S. industry."[15] Environmentalists began to emerge as partners in scientific and policy development, while the Valdez Principles introduced pressure from owners and investors. Although to a lesser extent than the chemical industry, the oil industry showed signs of seeing the environmental issue on more global terms (see Figure 6.10).

But in 1990, the dominant institutions of the oil industry would, for the first time, diverge from those of the chemical industry. Attention would drop and pessimism would return, slowing the proactive developments of the late 1980s. Beginning in 1990, economic, political, and technical realities set in that tainted the drive for environmental leadership. Growing public and political pressure over global warming and the Clean Air Act amendments (see inset page 122) put the oil industry back into a defensive position. Or, more accurately, both the real and the potential economic

Figure 6.10.   International Focus of Environmental Articles,
Oil & Gas Journal

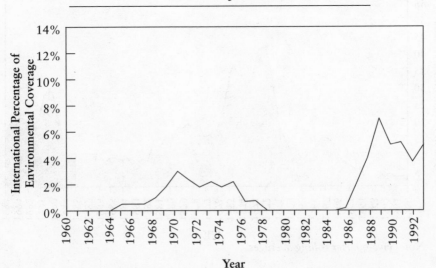

Year

impacts of these issues stalled environmental action. Concern over these issues was reflected in a thirty-year peak in environmental editorials in *Oil & Gas Journal* that attacked global warming as "alarmist,"[16] as the "politics of sacrifice obscuring science,"[17] and as "offering great potential for error"[18] and attacked the CAA's mandate for oxygenated fuels as "a response to an air pollution crisis that exists nowhere outside of L.A. and the collective imagination of an oversold citizenry."[19]

By the end of 1993, the level of industry attention to the environment rapidly approached levels similar to the 1960s. Also similar to the 1960s, almost 70 percent of the articles in *Oil & Gas Journal* focused on industry actions (compared to roughly 50 percent in *Chemical Week*). Rather than being seen as an opportunity, corporate environmentalism had become an area marked by guarded optimism, based on tempering environmental objectives with economic realities. Articles argued for caution, citing the need for a strong economy before the environment could be protected.

•

The Ozone Hole (1985) and the Montreal Protocol (1987)

Until the early 1970s, chlorofluorocarbons (CFCs) were considered one of the great success stories of the chemical industry. They were inert, nontoxic, inexpensive to produce, and useful in a wide variety of applications. But in 1970, scientists began to detect the destructive effects of these chemicals on the stratospheric ozone layer. By the late 1970s, due to a combination of market forces and societal concerns, companies began withdrawing the use CFCs in aerosol cans. However, the issue did not rest there. In May 1985, a paper published in *Nature* by Joe Farman of the British Antarctic Survey presented data showing a 40 percent depletion in stratospheric ozone over Antarctica from 1957 to 1984. Thus the "ozone hole" was born, and the powerful imagery of this metaphor captivated the public's imagination.[20]

In the process, the ozone hole also accelerated the international negotiations over CFC reductions. In September 1987, virtually all of the world's industrial nations met in Montreal under the auspices of the United Nations Environment Programme and pledged to cap production of CFCs in their respective countries at their 1986 levels by 1989. Total use would be phased out by 2000. Hydrochlorofluorocarbons (HCFCs), which were originally touted as CFC replacements, would be banned in developed countries in 2020 and in developing countries in 2040. This agreement, called the Montreal Protocol, had important implications for norms regarding environmental issues. It introduced the need for international control of global environmental problems. As well, it linked these global concerns to the behavior of individual citizens. While many uses of CFCs were in industrial operations, they were also used as refrigerants in home and car air conditioning units, devices near and dear to the consumer.

Chernobyl (1986)

On Saturday, April 26, 1986, a chemical explosion at the nuclear power station at Kiev in the Soviet Ukraine sparked an uncontrollable graphite fire and an accidental release of more than 450 radionuclides (about 3.5 percent of the fuel in the core). Official reports put the immediate death toll at thirty-one and the subsequent death toll among cleanup workers at between seven and eight thousand. A total of 135,000 civilians were evacuated, but total casualties were not known. What is critical about this disaster is the confusion and lack of adequate response procedures that followed. According to eyewitnesses, personnel at the station did not comprehend the significance of the accident when it happened.[21]

What is even more chilling about this incident is that it continues today. A thirty-kilometer evacuation zone is still in effect and will remain so for the foreseeable future. The sarcophagus surrounding the ill-fated reactor is unstable and undergoing constant repair. And the long-term health effects of this level of radiation exposure are far from certain. This emphasized to the world that the ramifications of technological miscalculation or mismanagement can have lasting effects well beyond the present. And more important, it made it clear that these effects are far from understood.

The *Mobro 4000* Garbage Barge (1987)

In the spring of 1987, the eyes of the American public were fixated on the *Mobro 4000,* a garbage barge that sailed from port to port, unable to find a place to dump its cargo. The barge picked up 3,168 tons of municipal garbage from Islip, Long Island, on March 22 and then spent the subsequent fifty-five days traveling up and down the seacoast, unable to find a willing recipient of the waste.[22] Although many argue that the barge's voyage was the result of the miscalculation of an entrepreneur hoping to make a quick buck,[23] what it came to symbolize for the American public was that we were running out of landfill space to dispose of our ever-growing production of solid waste.

Medical Waste on East Coast Beaches (1988)

In the summer of 1988, ocean beaches in New York and New Jersey became a focal point for the nation, as garbage, driftwood, and medical waste began washing up on shore. The debris, which included hypodermic needles, forced the closing of over eight hundred beaches.[24] Bathers fled in fear of becoming infected by the AIDS virus, and the shore counties of Monmouth, Ocean, Atlantic, and Cape May lost an estimated $100 million in tourist revenue. Although the fears of contracting AIDS were unfounded (medical experts stated that after a needle had been in salt water for a prolonged period of time, the risk of contracting HIV from it was reduced significantly if not eliminated),[25] government action followed the public outcry.

Many coastal sewage treatment plants were closed, and many others were upgraded. New Jersey and New York issued new rules for disposal of medical waste, requiring hospitals and other disposing institutions to document that wastes actually reached their final destination. And the federal government issued a ban on ocean dumping of municipal waste, which went into effect in 1992. Added to the *Mobro 4000* incident, this incited public fears that we were losing control of our capacity to manage our waste disposal practices.

Calls to Reduce the Emission of Greenhouse Gases (1988)

In 1970, the Council on Environmental Quality issued the first warning that industrial activity might be changing the weather. Throughout the seventies, climatologists had hypothesized that man was triggering atmospheric changes that were either cooling or warming the surface of the earth. The primary mechanisms by which this was argued to be occurring were as follows: by increasing the carbon dioxide (CO_2) content of the atmosphere through the burning of fossil fuels, we were raising the earth's temperature by creating the "greenhouse effect"; by clouding the atmosphere with dust and soot, we were cooling the earth's temperature by blocking out incoming sunlight. By 1983, the argument for global warming prevailed, and the EPA issued a report warning that it may be too late to avoid the rising atmospheric temperatures expected from increasing levels of carbon dioxide and other "greenhouse gases."

The issue reached the level of global concern in 1988 when the World Conference on the Changing Atmosphere (the first of its kind) convened in Toronto in June. Sponsored by the United Nations and Canada, the conference recommended an initial global reduction of carbon dioxide emissions by 20 percent of 1988 levels by 2005.[26] Although these recommendations were not binding, they brought the concept of global warming to the fore of public debate, again through the use of an evocative metaphor—the "greenhouse effect."

The *Exxon Valdez* (1989)

On March 24, 1989, the Exxon oil supertanker *Valdez* ran aground on Bligh Reef in Prince William Sound off the southern coast of Alaska. In the days immediately following the grounding, Exxon concerned itself with off-loading the ship's cargo, while local fisherman were concerned with the effects of the leaking oil on fish populations. In all, 10.1 million (U.S.) gallons of crude oil coated about 1,200 miles of shoreline. Estimates of wildlife loss include approximately 350,000 seabirds and 5,500 sea otters.[27]

Although the chronology immediately following the spill is a story of hesitation, disagreement, and, ultimately, mismanagement (making Exxon into an ideal villain), it is less the spill's magnitude and more the period in which it occurred that made it so prominent. There were no wealthy constituents as in Santa Barbara and Seveso (most of those affected were local fisherman), and there were no human deaths (as in Bhopal and Chernobyl). It was not the worst oil spill in history; it was, however, an accident that occurred at a time when environmental awareness was at an all-time high and public opinion was quick to respond with condemnation. Legal judgments against Exxon reached over $5 billion, with many cases still pending. As a direct result of the incident, the Oil Pollution Act of 1990 was enacted to mandate safety controls on ocean crude transport.

The CERES Valdez Principles (1989)

On September 7, 1989, CERES publicly announced the Valdez Principles, a set of ten guidelines for environmentally responsible behavior. This type of pressure was used successfully in at least two other occasions. In 1977, the Sullivan Principles used investor resolutions to convince companies to discontinue operations and cut ties (such as licensing and franchise agreements) with South Africa. Similarly, the McBride Principles coerced companies through investor resolutions to endorse a nondiscrimination code aimed at creating equal opportunity for Catholics in Northern Ireland.

Using the same tactics, CERES formed as a collaboration between socially responsible investors and representatives of several prominent environmental organizations. Of the ten guiding principles, the most important outlined requirements for public disclosure of environmental performance, the addition of an environmentalist to company boards of directors, and the creation of an environmental vice president position.

In December 1989, letters went out to potential signatories of three thousand companies, including all of the *Fortune* 500. Aside from the blanket mailing, investor-initiated resolutions were also proposed at a select number of upcoming corporate shareholder meetings. In the ensuing years, CERES has been able to gain approximately eighty signatories, which include five *Fortune* 100 companies: Bank of America, General Motors, Polaroid, Bethlehem Steel, and Sun Oil Corporation.[28]

The Clean Air Act Amendments of 1990

In 1990, the Clean Air Act was amended to meet problems unaddressed or insufficiently addressed by previous amendments to the act (in 1975 and 1977). These included acid rain, ground-level ozone, stratospheric ozone depletion, and air toxics. Given this expanded scope, the amendments have been considered to be the most expensive environmental legislation ever written. Compliance costs for utilities alone are estimated to reach $4 billion per year.

Beyond the scope and cost, the most groundbreaking and innovative aspect of the amendments is the clause allowing the trading of "marketable permits" for sulfur and nitrogen oxide emissions. Plants that can reduce emissions of these precursors of acid rain and ground-level ozone below the levels required by the law receive permits that they can sell to firms that cannot meet the standard. Since it is presumed that a plant will not pay more for such a permit than it would cost to reduce the same amount of pollutants itself, the costs of pollution control (in the aggregate) will be reduced. To facilitate trading, a pollution commodities exchange was established at the Chicago Board of Trade. The upshot of this program is an attempt to integrate economic and environmental concerns as one, thereby enticing companies to protect the environment as a way of increasing profits.

•

ORGANIZATIONAL STRUCTURE AND CULTURE: PROACTIVE MANAGEMENT

In the early 1990s, leading U.S. companies began to pay greater attention to environmental issues through executive-level appointments. In 1991, forty-nine of the *Fortune* 100 companies had environmental vice presidents, and thirty-one of the *Fortune* 50 had them.[29] And, as of the middle of 1992, well over one-third of the *Fortune* 100 companies' boards of directors had either a public policy committee or an EH&S committee.[30] Table 6.1 shows a list of companies that had environmental vice presidents or environmental committees on their boards as of 1992. And Table 6.2 shows how other companies went even further, placing an environmentalist directly on the board of directors.

At the same time, pronouncements of environmental ethics were increasingly espoused by top executives at companies such as Dow, DuPont, Sun, and Monsanto. According to a 1991 survey by the Conference Board, 50 percent of companies viewed the external role of the CEO to be the personification of company environmental philosophy.[33] Seventy-six percent of American companies felt that environmental standards were reasonable or technically feasible and that "there was general agreement that, philosophically, pollution must be controlled."[34] And more than 77 percent of companies had a formal system in place for identifying key environmental issues. Thirty percent used a combination of inside staff and outside expertise for this task. The motivating factors driving environmental policy were listed, from most to least important, as follows: legal requirements, social responsibility, liability pressure, community pressure, and shareholder pressure.[35]

Survey data also show that by 1992, a total of 40 percent of American companies had a formal environmental policy statement in place, and

Table 6.1.   Executive-Level Involvement in Environmental
Decision Making.[31]

Company	Environmental Vice President	Environmental Board Committee
Allied Signal	x	x
American Cyanamid	x	x
Amoco	x	x
ARCO	x	x
Ashland Oil	x	x
Chevron	x	x
Dow Chemical	x	x
DuPont		x
Exxon	x	x
W. R. Grace	x	x
Mobil Oil	x	x
Monsanto	x	x
Occidental Petroleum	x	x
Phillips Petroleum	x	x
Sun Oil	x	x
Texaco	x	x
Union Carbide	x	x
Unocal	x	x

another 11 percent had added environmental responsibility to their existing company ethics statements.[36] The inclusion of the general counsel was
consistent with 84 percent of the policy statements being written, suggesting that these companies believed their environmental codes required the
same careful drafting as legal documents. These statements had an underlying administrative or compliance purpose, or they detailed enforcement
mechanisms.[37]

These changes in internal management seemed to be generating more
commonality among firms, through direct interaction. Individual industries
appeared to be accepting a common obligation toward environmental management. As shown in Table 6.3, industrywide standards initiated at the

Table 6.2.   Environmentalists on the Board.[32]

Company	Environmental Director	Affiliation
Ashland Oil	Patrick Noonan	President, Conservation Fund
ARCO	Frank Boren	Conservation Fellow, World Wildlife/Conservation Fund
Chevron	Bruce Smart	Senior Counselor, World Resources Institute
DuPont	William Reilly	Former Administrator, EPA
Exxon	John Steele	Senior Scientist, Woods Hole Oceanographic Institute
Monsanto	William Ruckelshaus	Former Administrator, EPA
Union Carbide	Russell Train	Chairman, World Wildlife/Conservation Fund; Former Administrator, EPA

trade association level were proliferating rapidly. Also, a survey by the Conference Board found that companies were gaining input and uniformity outside the realm of direct industry partners by "undertaking an increasing number of voluntary alliances with non-profit environmental research and advocacy groups."[38] The most prominent example was the McDonald's-EDF alliance in 1990, but companies such as Ashland, Goodyear, Kodak, AT&T, Monsanto, Dow, Ciba-Geigy, and others were now getting into the game.[39] Overall, by the end of 1993, companies had developed internal structures and external outreach programs that indicated an elevated strategic importance that would have been unthinkable in 1960.

Organizational Change at Amoco

Although attention to environmentalism rose and fell between 1988 and 1993 for the oil industry as a whole, Amoco maintained an increasingly self-directed and proactive trajectory, similar to that seen in the chemical industry. Again, the shift preceded that of the organizational field, in this case by one year. By the end of this stage, the company found itself at a threshold, with environmentalism evolving into a significant position within the organization. First, environmental responsibilities had diffused throughout much of the organization, moving up to the executive level,

Table 6.3.   Industry Environmental Programs.[40]

Industry	Program	Year Formed
Chemicals	Responsible Care	1990
Petroleum	Strategies for Today's Environmental Partnership	1990
Automobiles	Automobile Pollution Prevention Project	1991
Lead	Product Stewardship Program	1991
Paper	Pollution Prevention Program	1991
Textiles	Encouraging Environmental Excellence	1992
Printing	Environmental Management Program	1992
Dry cleaners	IFI Certification Program	1994
Forestry	Sustainable Forestry Initiative	1995

down to the operating level, and across functional boundaries. Second, the function of the EH&S department had evolved and had become driven by internal objectives, with the goal of gaining a competitive advantage. Third, the company actively sought input from and dialogue with external activists, government, and competitors in regard to environmental management. Just as environmentalism had diffused inward, it had likewise projected outward, expanding the boundaries of the firm beyond the corporate structure. And interlaced within all of these changes were signs of a fundamental cultural change: viewing environmentalism as an aspect of the business environment, to be internalized into the objectives of the firm.

Organizational Structure at Amoco

In terms of staffing, 1987 saw the beginnings of the third major growth in the environmental function at Amoco (see Figure 6.11). At the same time, the operating company EH&S departments were decentralized from the corporate level, and reporting responsibilities were reassigned directly to the operating company presidents (see Figure 6.12). This was enacted in concert with the decentralization of other support functions throughout

Figure 6.11.   Amoco Environmental Department Staffing, 1966–1993.

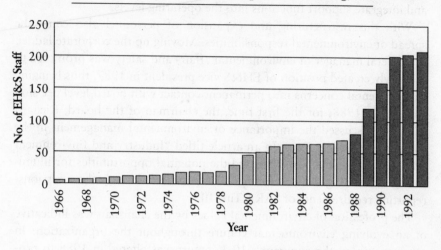

Figure 6.12.   Amoco Environmental Department, Decentralized
Operating Company Structure, 1994.

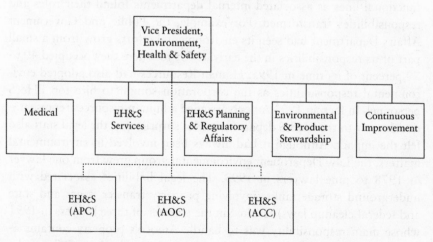

Note: Total staff = 220; AC = 132, APC = 27, AOC = 38, ACC = 23.

the company, in an attempt to both reduce corporate-level operating costs and integrate support functions into the operating levels.

With this restructuring and expansion of personnel also came the spread of environmental responsibilities. Moving up the corporate ladder, the general manager of environmental affairs and safety was promoted to the newly created position of EH&S vice president in 1987, thus bringing environmental concerns into permanent contact with board-level decision making. In 1988, for the first time, the chairman of the board, Richard Morrow, discussed the importance of environmental management in the company magazine, *Span*. In an article titled "Industry and Environment Can Be Compatible," he discussed the potential opportunities for illuminating Amoco's good environmental reputation through the emissions-reporting requirements of SARA Title III.

The profession of environmental values by the chairman was indicative of an evolving environmental culture throughout the organization. In other examples, the company's 10–K report was altered in 1988 to proclaim the company's new "pro-active approach to environmental management, which aggressively addresses increasingly complex and diverse environmental challenges." And on this theme of perceiving environmentalism as an opportunity and not a threat, a senior legal counsel wrote a 1988 memo to the corporate general attorney on the importance of "creating and nurturing an environmental ethic at Amoco" through top-down leadership and financial rewards and recognition. He saw this as an opportunity to reduce compliance costs and operate in a manner consistent with appropriate environmental principles.

This cultural shift was not restricted to EH&S. It was diffusing across functional lines as associated internal departments found their roles and responsibilities transformed. For example, the Public and Government Affairs Department had seen its environmental efforts grow from a small part of its responsibilities in the early 1970s to where they occupied 40 to 50 percent of its time in 1993. Human Resources had also adopted environmental responsibilities as the corporation sought to hire top EH&S personnel. In fact, in 1992 Amoco assigned a human resources representative directly to the EH&S department. Not surprisingly, the legal staff also felt the impact. Although it had always been involved in environmental matters, the Law Department environmental group grew from one lawyer in 1978 to nine lawyers in 1993. The legal liabilities associated with underground storage tanks (involving property transfer issues and state and federal cleanup laws) resulted in the transfer of three lawyers in 1991 whose main responsibility was to handle Amoco's property contamination claims. Environmentalism even plays an integral role in defining the company's product, as it has altered definitions of quality. Amoco's former advertising agency, D'Arcy, Masius, Benton, and Bowles, believes that the public is beginning to perceive environmental benefits as synonymous with quality. Such an association will force the integration of environmental values into standard advertising programs.

Organizational Function at Amoco

In addition to the general diffusion of environmental responsibilities throughout the organizational structure, the specific functions of the EH&S Department also evolved dramatically. The department focused less on functions that respond directly to regulatory mandates and more on internally directed objectives. In 1990, Product Safety was expanded to handle more than the regulatory requirements for safety labels; its new responsibilities included considering more internally driven objectives of product responsibility. (Eventually, the department was renamed Product Stewardship, as it is called in the Responsible Care Program.) Regulatory Affairs was expanded, promoting more lobbying efforts at the federal and state levels. EH&S Training was created to teach environmental procedures and objectives throughout the organization. And in 1993, Continuous Improvement was formed, its sole objective being that of initiating cultural change within the corporation.

In addition, two new programs significantly furthered the organizational shift toward proactive environmental management: Program and Process Review and Crisis Management. The former was a significant departure from its predecessor, the Compliance Review program, which had focused on ensuring regulatory compliance in a randomly selected set of facilities. The newly devised program presented a more sophisticated and internally directed auditing effort. For the first time, sites were assigned a quantitatively weighted risk factor based not only on regulatory and economic factors but also on environmental considerations. Factors included facility size, number of permits, location, presence of sensitive receptors, toxicity of raw materials and products, and past performance. High-risk sites would be more rigorously inspected. Recommendations from these inspections would encompass both performance criteria (regulatory and company technical requirements) and goal criteria (management systems, company, and trade group objectives). Amoco executives felt that this represented a more "systems-oriented" approach to compliance review. According to one senior manager, "The shift from Compliance Review to Program and Process Review represents the evolution we have gone through. The first was focused on making sure we were in compliance. The second is focused on checking to see if we have the systems in place to manage our corporate responsibility. In the seventies, it was compliance with a minimal staff; in the eighties, it was awareness; and in the nineties, it is management of issues."

The second program, Crisis Management, was initiated in 1989 in direct response to the *Exxon Valdez* disaster (March 1989), which caused Amoco, and most other oil companies, to take a careful look at how well prepared they were to handle a major environmental incident. According to one executive, it was a response to "the public's view that environmental and safety issues should be a top priority for government and industry, and that steps should be taken to reduce exposure to such risks." The resulting program called for a "seamless web" of responsibilities for responding to the many facets of an environmental disaster: government relations, major media coverage, shareholder communications, and internal issues such as effects on other operations and allocation of adequate response resources to quickly resolve the incident. Designated Amoco personnel from the board level to the operating line were required to participate in ongoing drill and exercise programs to ensure that the system was intact. As stated in one of the founding documents, this system was "developed from a pro-active point of view (for example, to provide for the anticipation and management of issues), as called for in the policy statement. To support this, we require that plans for at least the initial response, to be an over-response (for example, to be sure we have the capability to back up the 'get ahead and stay ahead' attitude that we want underlying all of our crisis and emergency management efforts)."

In 1990, reflecting the growing international focus of corporate environmentalism, the company also began to expand its international environmental focus. A task force initiated by the board of directors began to define the operating standards the company would use "with respect to health, safety and the environment in those parts of the world where such standards do not exist or where they are so minimal as to be unacceptable." Since that time, fourteen "international standards of care" have been written that establish common environmental practices in every country in which Amoco operates. Amoco executives feel that this gives the corporation advantages not only in marketing its services to foreign governments but also in avoiding potential liabilities should regulations be developed after foreign operations begin. They also believe that it helps improve employee self-esteem and community goodwill in those locations. In a March 3, 1993, letter to one of the board members, the EH&S vice president stressed that "if Amoco's workforce knows that we care about them as individuals, additional benefits will be derived in terms of performance, ownership, and employee pride."

In 1991, Amoco elevated environmental concerns to the director level by establishing a board-level EH&S committee, similar to the actions of others in the industry. Acknowledging the institutional influence on the company, internal Amoco memos cite several external motivating factors for this decision:

> Environmental concerns are gaining increasing support from the public and the political institutions. This support is evidenced in many ways, including several resolutions from Amoco shareholders, recent public opinion polls, and comments by both Republican and Democratic pollsters, and more recently by the efforts of the Coalition for Environmentally Responsible Economies (CERES), to enlist investors who control more than $100 billion to support only those companies that subscribe to a list of principles of environmental protection. Fundamentally, this means that instead of the use of government command-and-control types of influence, we can expect people to act more directly on Amoco by way of shareholders and customers.

Although CERES was downplayed by company executives, one senior EH&S manager admits the external influence of the council in helping to precipitate the formation of a board-level committee: "We were already looking at what other companies were doing. But, we didn't want to be caught by a shareholder proxy forcing us to do it. So, for a lot of industries, Amoco included, it was a defensive maneuver to counteract CERES." Appropriately, the committee's first responsibility was to decide whether or not the corporation would become a signatory to the Valdez Principles. (They decided against signing.)

Concurrent with the formation of the board-level EH&S committee, in 1991 the company's EH&S policy statement underwent a fundamental shift from a compliance-oriented document to a proactive one, pledging the corporation to commit to environmental leadership. Representing a new level of corporate commitment, this policy statement was signed not only by the CEO but also by four members of the board of directors, the presidents of each of the three operating companies, the company's general counsel, and the vice presidents of human resources, government relations, technology, and EH&S.

Although it was again downplayed by executives, CERES appears to have been influential in this organizational change as well. In a May 30, 1991, letter to the CEO, responding to his suggestion that the company develop "some 'Amoco Principles' that we could adopt rather than negotiating on the Valdez Principles," the EH&S vice president pointed out that an internal set of principles would be preferable and that he had "recently undertaken a process to redraft Amoco's Health, Safety, and Environmental Policy."

External Relations at Amoco

Perhaps the most significant change in Amoco's corporate ideology at the time was the acknowledgment that external relations with environmental groups, the government, and other companies were critical in assessing salient issues and devising an appropriate response. In an April 22, 1988, speech at a senior management meeting, the ACC environmental affairs manager acknowledged that "the relative importance of industry's key stakeholders in terms of our response on health, safety, and environmental issues has shifted. Within the traditional group listed, our efforts have primarily focused on employees and compliance with governmental agencies. But now, customers and downstream users are demanding a much greater expenditure on our part. In addition, a relatively new group of stakeholders, primarily from the public sector, are now making demands on industry in a more organized and powerful way than ever before. Effectively addressing these groups is essential to the success of our business." And later, in an October 9, 1990, memo to one of the board members, the EH&S vice president suggested that "there are environmentalists, really conservationists, that we can and must work with in order to obtain the permission of society to do the things we need to do. . . . I would prefer not to brawl at all with the fringe because there is no benefit, but I feel we have no choice but to work closely with those we can." And finally, summing up, a 1991 task force report recommended that "to accommodate societal demands, a significant effort must be made to improve Amoco's relationship with the various publics and the regulators."

This evolving perspective was manifested in a wide-ranging effort at expanding the company's external relations. To initiate dialogue with environmental activists, the company joined the Keystone Center and the Global Tomorrow Coalition in the late 1980s. Later, the company formed direct alliances with the World Resources Institute, the Natural Resources Defense Council, and the Environmental Law Institute. As one EH&S manager put it, "We discovered the potential for such an alliance when we realized that we were seeking some of the same things that traditional environmental groups were also seeking—environmental programs that get the most effective results." The benefits these groups offered Amoco included established relationships within certain key circles in Washington, an associated knowledge of how to influence change in environmental policy, and the ability to generate added credibility to the effort. The benefits Amoco brought to the environmental groups was technical knowledge and a cooperative industry posture. By acknowledging their common goals, these unlikely allies found that they could do together what they could not do alone.

This outreach effort was not restricted to environmental groups, however. In cooperation with the government, Amoco joined EPA's voluntary Green-Lights Program and the Industrial Toxics Emissions Reduction Program, commonly referred to as the 33/50 program. As a result of this latter program, Amoco reduced emissions of seventeen priority chemicals by 33 percent through mid 1992 and achieved a further 50 percent reduction by 1995.

Finally, the company developed industry-specific alliances through its membership in six prominent programs. In 1989, the Amoco Chemical Company joined the CMA's Responsible Care Program, and in 1990, the Amoco Oil and Production Companies joined the API's STEP program. Next, seeking broader exposure, Amoco joined the Global Environmental Management Initiative in 1992 and the Public Environmental Reporting Initiative in 1993. And finally, stretching Amoco's focus toward international environmental affairs, Amoco endorsed the International Chamber of Commerce Charter for Sustainable Development in 1991 and joined both the World Environment Center and the U.S. Council on International Business in 1993. Through membership in these groups, Amoco hoped to gain advance insights into international environmental developments and possibly gain a voice in their formation. Yet executives grew concerned over overlapping programs. As one EH&S executive put it, "With so many programs out there that were vying for our endorsement, [the EH&S vice president] adopted the attitude that 'you can't be Catholic and Protestant at the same time.'"

In summation, these external efforts were part of an overall transformation of the Amoco organization. Much like an invading virus, Amoco's environmental management responsibilities were diffusing through the company by the end of 1993. The thrust of the company's environmental efforts went in two directions, internal cultural change and external institutional change. But as this diffusion continued, the company found itself at a unique threshold, forced to make decisions regarding the function of its EH&S department and the objectives of the firm as a whole. Chapter Eight considers the ramifications of this threshold, based on the trajectory of the institutional evolution that preceded it.

THE INSTITUTIONAL DEFINITION OF CORPORATE ENVIRONMENTALISM, 1988–1993

By the end of 1993, the environmental issue had been completely redefined for corporations. What had previously been conceptualized by industry alone was now conceptualized by a wide array of strategic constituents. This expansion of the field surrounding the environmental issue was accompanied by an expansion of the scope of the issue. As Figure 6.13 shows, the issue grew steadily in complexity, from one defined largely in terms of air and water issues to one that included hazardous wastes, waste site remediation, toxics, and, for the oil industry, oil spills. But, for the chemical industry, a new component had been added outside the legislative framework established by the early 1980s—proactive management through the Responsible Care program.

But even more important than the expansion of the scope of the environmental issue was the evolution in how it was perceived within the

Figure 6.13. Media Perception of the Environmental Issue, 1988–1993.

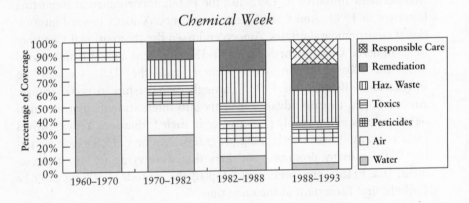

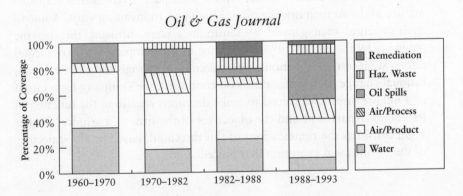

organization. As Figures 5.3 and 5.4 show, the primary focus of environmental activities had been shifting steadily toward a more industry-directed perspective since 1982. Corresponding to this internalized focus, the issue was now strongly perceived in terms of internal management considerations (see Figure 6.14). The predominance of the issue as a regulatory and compliance issue was now on the wane.

This was reflected within the corporation by environmental structures and strategies aimed at internal management goals and programs. Corporate environmentalism had evolved to again become an issue defined by industry, but this time it was defined in concert with the con-

Figure 6.14. Organizational Perception of the Environmental Issue, 1988–1993.

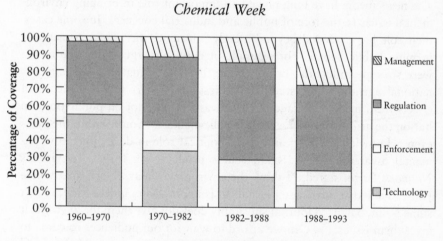

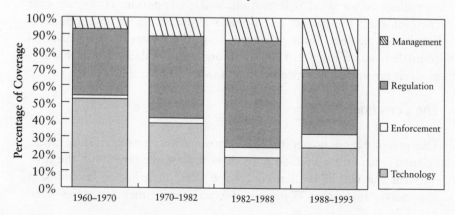

cerns, perspectives, and input of a wide ranging field of actors. In the history just told, this field included activists, the government, investors, competitors, and insurance companies.

But as stated in Chapter Two, the data sources employed to create this history are systematically exclusive. Although legal data reveal the formation and evolution of ties among certain institutional actors, it restricts the search to more formal and confrontational forms of institutional interactions while remaining blind to organizations that employ other forms of institutional influence such as protests or cooperative interaction. It restricts observation to discrete forms of institutional ties, thereby overlooking more diffuse forms of institutional influence. It would be appropriate at this point to consider who some of these other actors might be.

The Press

The news media have long played an important role in bringing environmental issues to the fore of public and industrial concerns. In some cases, their role has extended beyond merely informing the public, to actually forming public debate. For example, it is widely argued that the media were strongly influential in projecting the Love Canal disaster onto the national agenda.[41] One study by Protess and others found evidence of effects from media coverage of toxic waste issues, not on public opinion but on the attitudes and agendas of policymakers.[42] Some within the press even acknowledge taking an active, political role in developing environmental awareness. Teya Ryan, senior producer of Turner Television's *Network Earth,* stated, "I think the environment may be one area where you can say that advocacy journalism is appropriate, indeed vital. . . . At some point, balanced journalism simply does not give them the answers, it gives them issues. . . . Can we afford to wait for our audiences to come to its conclusions? I think not."[43] Whether this is the norm in environmental journalism is not what is important; what is important is the fact that environmental journalism has become a differentiated and influential member of the field. Noting that milestone, the Society of Environmental Journalists was formed in 1990 as an organization dedicated to this specialty; it presently has a membership of over eight hundred.

The Consumer

The presence and power of the environmental consumer is a much-debated issue. Public opinion polls show that people care about the environment and will allow that concern to affect their buying decisions. A 1989 survey found that 77 percent of Americans say that companies' environmental reputation affects what they buy.[44] However, it is widely believed that consumers will not pay a premium price for environmental attributes. The best that most marketers can expect is that when goods are comparably priced, environmental attributes can break the tie. As a result, companies are using environmentalism as a marketing point to an increasing extent. Up from only 3 percent in 1988, the number of new products using environmentalism in their marketing campaigns reached 12 percent in 1991 and has remained at that level since. If environmental certification programs such as the Green Seals Program in Europe gain acceptance in the United States, this practice can be expected to grow.

Companies such as Ben & Jerry's, Patagonia, the Body Shop, and Tom's of Maine are some of the more prominent examples of firms that have gained a competitive advantage by employing environmental marketing strategies. In another area, by capitalizing on growing public skepticism toward modern food production systems that employ pesticides, growth hormones, and unsustainable harvesting practices, the popularity of organic foods has grown rapidly. Sales nearly doubled in five years, from $3.9 billion in 1989 to $7.6 billion in 1994. Sales of bottled water have nearly tripled since 1984, from 933 million gallons to 2.87 billion gallons in 1995. In 1991, there were 195 health food supermarkets across the country; by the end of 1994, there were 650.[45]

And finally, those that "regularly recycle" bottles and cans rose from 46 to 58 percent from 1990 to 1992, and those that recycle newspapers rose from 26 to 43 percent.[46]

Financial Institutions

Although mainstream investors largely dismiss environmental concerns because they are seen as moral issues outside their realm, there exists evidence that this is changing.[47] First, in 1992 the United Nations Environment Programme (UNEP) coordinated the creation of a declaration of environmental commitment for the banking industry; it now has twenty-eight signatories. Bankers are beginning to accept that under certain circumstances they can be held responsible, through the legal system, for the environmental mistakes of their borrowers. To limit that risk, they are beginning to include environmental considerations in their lending decisions. Linking environmental implications to the likelihood of success for an economic venture, banks are equating poor environmental performance with high financial risk.

Insurers are likewise worrying that climate change could cause substantial losses in the years ahead. In November 1995, the insurance industry followed the banking industry with a UNEP environmental agreement of its own. Some insurers now argue that their interests are contrary to those who sell carbon-based fuels or use them in large quantities, due to climate change implications. One view now gaining support in the industry is that insurers should lobby for policies that reduce the risk of creating climate change.[48]

International Aspects

Environmental issues are rapidly crossing national boundaries to become international in scope and influence. The environmental side agreements to the North American Free Trade Agreement (NAFTA), the environmental accords of the European Community, and the International Standards Organization (ISO14000) are facilitating the spread of institutional norms across national borders.

And beyond specific regulatory programs, activists and others are striving to make environmental standards that are accepted in one country become accepted in others. For example, in June 1996 a class-action lawsuit was filed in New York against the Texaco Corporation for damages to the Ecuadoran rain forest ten years earlier. In what amounts to the transfer of Superfund liability across international borders, lawyers representing Ecuador's Amazon Indians and settlers are seeking compensation of more than $1 billion for alleged cancer risks, diseases, and loss of land. The company had drilled for oil in the region in the past but has since handed the wells over to Petroecuador, Ecuador's state-run oil company. At issue are wastewater pits that have been allowed to overflow into the local rivers, on which the inhabitants rely for water and fish.[49]

The Local Community

Two movements are changing the way companies assess development decisions. Each is linked to the empowerment of local communities concerning the kind of industrial activity that takes place in their midst. The first is the movement for environmental justice, which is often tied to the question of environmental racism. Particularly in urban areas, local communities are empowered by an integration of environmental and civil rights issues. Industrial activity in urban centers unfairly affects the poor (who generally inhabit these areas), and as a result they are gaining a stronger voice in deciding the fate of such developments.

The second movement is the "not in my backyard" (NIMBY) syndrome, which some say is now more accurately described as NOPE ("not on planet earth"). Much like the environmental justice movement, this is a movement of empowered local citizens deciding what kind of development will take place in their community. They can stall expensive investments and cripple corporate portfolios. For example, in the late 1980s, Clean Harbors, Inc., spent over $13 million to site a hazardous waste incinerator in Braintree, Massachusetts. A powerful NIMBY movement blocked issuance of the permit, and as a result the company's stock dropped from 25 to $4\frac{7}{8}$.[50] As this is not a unique example, most companies now consider community sentiment in their development decisions.

Others

This list need not end here. Any actor with a degree of influence on a firm can alter the organizational norms regarding environmental management. For example, suppliers and end users are increasingly integrating environmental concerns into their purchasing and ordering decisions.[51] Consultants, as well, are a conduit through which rules, norms, and beliefs are transferred. Though environmental management was long the exclusive venue of engineering consulting firms (such as Camp, Dresser & McKee, Environ, and CH2M Hill), management consulting firms (such as McKinsey & Company and Arthur Anderson) are trying to get into the business. Through these new channels, "best industry practices" will diffuse within and across industries to create new institutional perspectives on environmental management.

Generational Shifts

Underlying all of this, there is a fundamental generational shift occurring. How society views the environmental issue today is far different than how society viewed it just ten years ago. The Conference Board notes that the drivers of environmental responsibility today come from within the corporation, "as younger managers and their families begin making demands on top management that previous generations would never have dared to do."[52] This environmental awareness is being fostered in the new workforce by a growing number of environmental courses being offered at business schools,[53] engineering schools,[54] and journalism schools.[55]

This shift is reflected in other parts of society as well. Bringing environmentalism into the realm of religious morals, the Assisi Accord was endorsed by the world's major religions as an acknowledgment of the importance of environmental concerns. In turn, the Presbyterian Church decided in 1991 to place environmental concerns into the church canon, making it a sin to "threaten death to the planet entrusted to our care."[56]

And the following year, the Catholic Church added environmental concerns to its new catechism.[57]

Today's youth are being educated on the environment in ways that are far different from how their parents and grandparents were taught. Just watch children's Saturday morning television today. The volume of the environmental messages children are barraged with is overwhelming. And in some states, courses on environmental protection or the conservation of natural resources are becoming a mandatory requirement for elementary and secondary school students. Just as we may view the environmental norms, standards, and practices of yesterday's generation as primitive and naive, future generations will look in wonder at the wasteful environmental practices we maintain today. Societal cultural change is in motion and is not likely to stop. This change process has altered the past and present norms by which corporations have had to act, and it will alter how those firms will have to act in the future.

PART THREE

THE SUM OF INSTITUTIONAL CHANGE

7

THE PROGRESSION OF ENVIRONMENTALISM AND CORPORATE CHANGE

IN A MATTER OF THREE SHORT DECADES, the concept of corporate environmentalism was born and subsequently redefined through successive stages. Pressure on corporations for environmental management evolved from industry-based pressure to government regulation and finally to pressure from environmental activists, investors, insurance companies, and competitors. In response, the industrial organization shifted from reactively resisting environmental concerns in the 1960s to actively managing them in the 1990s. The corporate environmental management function grew from a small subsection of the engineering department to a large department operating independently. The media focus on this department's purpose expanded from air and water issues to include such concerns as hazardous waste disposal, remediation, toxics, communities' "right to know," ozone depletion, global warming, acid rain, solid waste disposal, chlorine phase-out, and environmental racism. The environmental management department's early focus on technological solutions made room for important managerial considerations. And in the technological component that persisted, the issue evolved from one handled at the end of the pipe to one that considered changes in product and process design. Fundamentally, corporate environmentalism evolved from an ancillary aspect of corporate operations driven by industry considerations to a central aspect of corporate strategy driven by a core business constituency. The heresy of the 1960s became the dogma of the 1990s.

In explaining these changes, we return to the point where we began, with these two questions: How did industry move from a posture of environmental resistance to one of proactive environmental management? And why did this transformation occur? In answering these questions, let's first revisit the initial idea raised in Chapter Two. Could one simply argue that since regulations and costs have continued to rise, this historical evolution is the result of industry's attempt to preempt further regulation and regain control of capital and operating expenditures? Is the threat of regulatory penalties and punitive damages the primary motivation for corporate change? While such an explanation appears quite reasonable, it is not by itself complete. The history of corporate environmentalism has, in fact, been marked by shifts and characteristics that bear little relation to the trajectory of costs or regulation.

First, corporate attention to environmental issues has not followed the linear trends in regulation and expenditures shown in Figures 2.1 and 2.2, but rather the cyclical trend of public opinion. Shown in Figure 7.1, research shows that public concern for environmental issues developed dramatically in the late 1960s and reached a peak with the first Earth Day in 1970. It declined considerably in the early 1970s and then more gradually over the rest of the decade, but it remained substantial. The 1980s saw a significant and steady increase both in public awareness of the seriousness of environmental problems and in public support for environmental protection, with the result that by the twentieth anniversary of Earth Day in 1990, public concern for environmental quality had reached unprecedented levels.[1] This progression in public opinion perfectly

Figure 7.1.　Trends in Public Concern over Environmental Issues.

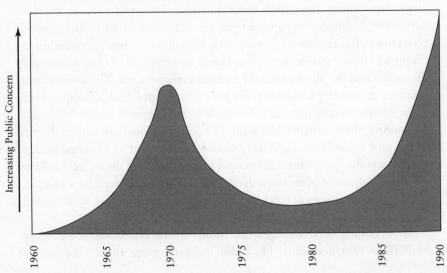

matches the trends in corporate attention depicted in Figures 6.6 and 6.9. It thus appears a more plausible explanation that industry attention to environmentalism follows the ups and downs of the public's concern over environmental issues rather than the upward trend of environmental regulations and expenditures.

Second, if costs or regulations were the primary drivers of corporate action, one might expect a commonality in corporate technical expenditures mandated by law but less commonality in organizational shifts outside the regulatory realm. Yet as this history reveals, industries have made organizational shifts in relative unison. For example, most corporations in the 1970s established environmental management departments with the same structure, purpose, and organizational power: they were organized along medium lines (for example, air and water); their central purpose was not operating improvements but regulatory compliance; and they were structurally separate from the rest of the organization, designed to buffer the operating core from the distractions of environmental regulation.[2] Later, in the mid 1980s, new organizational norms made it common practice for companies to establish the position vice president of environmental affairs,[3] and pollution prevention and waste minimization became the new focus. And in the early 1990s, the norms shifted yet again to include the establishment of board-level environmental management committees,[4] the public pronouncement of corporate environmental ethics by prominent executives,[5] the publication of annual environmental reports,[6] and the initiation of formal industrywide environmental programs.[7]

In short, firms have behaved in a clannish fashion, evolving through waves of commonly accepted organizational trends. Since regulations are traditionally technology (or performance) based, the connection between regulation and such organizational innovation is, at best, tenuous. Other signals from the organizational environment must be at play. Furthermore, if costs were to drive such organizational developments, it is difficult to explain why a marginal cost increase in one period should precipitate a particular industrywide shift in organizational structure rather than a marginal cost increase in another period. Again, history points to explanations for corporate environmental change that are more socially based than costs and regulations can provide alone.

Third, the content and purpose of these organizational trends suggest that they are not driven by individual cost structures and attempts at greater efficiency but rather by the social influence of external actors. More than common timing, these shifts focus on similar objectives that may or may not bear on the particular needs of all adopting firms. For example, in the development of industrywide environmental programs, the 1989 Chemical Manufacturer's Association (CMA) and the 1990 American Petroleum Institute (API) programs were nearly identical in wording and purpose. Yet as shown in Figures 7.2 and 7.3, the environmental cost structures in these two industries were quite different. While environmental expenditures for the chemical industry rose steadily through the 1980s, those for the oil industry remained flat from 1982 to 1989 and rose dramatically in 1990 because of the Clean Air Act amendments' requirements.

If industry action were based completely on costs, it would be more plausible to expect the API rather than the CMA to have initiated its own industrywide principles, in direct response to the oil industry's dramatic cost increases in 1990. This industry should have felt a direct threat from the sudden increase in costs and designed an independent program tailored to its specific needs and capabilities. Instead, API effectively copied the CMA program verbatim. This would suggest that, rather than responding to cost structures and regulatory demands in pursuit of increased organizational efficiency, organizations (either at the level of a trade association or the individual firm) are looking to other organizations for examples of how best to respond to environmental demands. As a result, organizational action would appear to be highly influenced by the actions of others.

Rather than choosing from a wide array of possible organizational responses, organizational behavior appears to be influenced by social forces, both explicit and implicit, that originate beyond the firm's boundaries. Simply put, these examples of corporate environmental behavior are inconsistent with purely rational economic explanations, which should see different industries, as well as different firms within those industries, reaching autonomous organizational decisions based on their own cost structures and strategic objectives. The commonality in the timing, type, and group acceptance of these organizational responses suggests the presence of other signaling mechanisms that rational-actor models based on direct resource ties are not sufficient to fully explain. These signals originate within the institutional environment.

THE POWER OF THE INSTITUTIONAL METAPHOR AND MODEL

Conceptualizing the origins of corporate environmental action as originating within the institutional environment shifts the lens of analysis from the individual firm to the entire system of which that firm is a part. This shift makes it possible to understand dynamics of organizational change that are

Figure 7.2.   Petroleum Industry Environmental Expenditures, 1973–1992.[8]

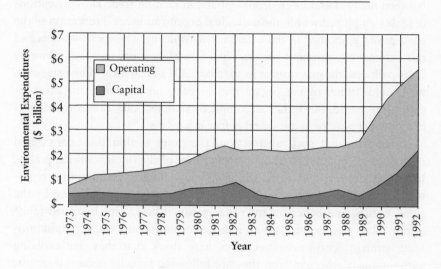

Figure 7.3.   Chemical Industry Environmental Expenditures, 1973–1992.[9]

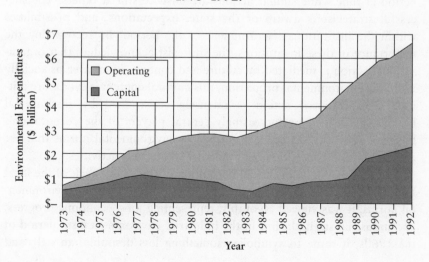

not readily visible through the lens of direct economic and resource constraints. It calls attention to the presence of social controls. The boundaries between the firm and its environment are, in fact, blurred. The conceptions of reality employed within the individual organization are a reflection of the conceptions embodied in the external environment. The social influence of this external environment becomes like a swirling soup, in which common ideas permeate the practices of its members. Or as Harrison White suggests, we should "think of the organizational field, not as some tidy atom or embracing world, but rather as complex striations, long strings rotating as in a polymer goo, or in a mineral before it hardens."[10]

Moving beyond such abstraction, the point is that the institutional environment, in large part, defines the range of the organizational reality. In setting strategy and structure, firms may choose action from a repertoire of possible options. But the range of that repertoire is bound by the rules, norms, and beliefs of the organizational field. This bounded range affects all its member firms with a degree of uniformity such that, in initiating strategy, corporate executives may think that they are evolving autonomously when, in fact, they are following broadly universal trends. These trends can be defined explicitly, or they can evolve implicitly. Whether it is the focus on regulatory compliance in the 1970s, the creation of pollution prevention or waste minimization programs in the 1980s, or the formation of a board-level environmental management committee in the 1990s, firms have been moving in relative unison in both strategy and structure.

Reframing the same point in an action rather than reaction perspective, this makes it clear why certain organizational actions are successful at one period in time while similar actions are unsuccessful at others. The successful strategist is aware of the state, expectations, and possibilities within the institutional environment of the period. By recognizing the importance of these institutions, the strategist acknowledges that organizational action is mediated by culture and context. In an area as socially visible as environmental protection, this cultural context is ever more critical. Organizational action is intensely constrained by institutional bounds, as defined by increasingly central players of the corporation's business networks. As such, it is not just environmental norms that are altered but also conceptions of fundamental business activities.

Take, for example, the social perception of the smokestack of the local factory. In the 1950s, prior to the advent of institutionalized environmental norms, it was viewed favorably, representing jobs, economic progress, and industrial strength. But in the industrial environmentalism period of the 1960s, it came to symbolize something less desirable, an ugly and smelly nuisance. In the regulatory environmentalism of the 1970s, it represented the need for government controls. In the social responsibility period of the 1980s, it became the source of toxic pollution, hazardous to the health of the community. And finally, in the strategic environmentalism of the 1990s, it has come to symbolize wasted resources.

No longer a "necessary evil" or a "cost of doing business" defined by government regulation, environmentalism is now becoming part of the "rules of the game," defined in the 1990s by a widening group of institutional constituents. For better or for worse, environmentalism has become a part of the business environment. This, in itself, is not a profound conclusion. It is drawn from a history that chronicles not how society views the firm's environmental responsibility but rather how industry views what the environmental issue "means" and what its role is in responding to it. But by looking deeper at the process by which this occurred and the subtleties of the institutional model used to explain that process, more profound observations can be drawn both about the organizational change process in general and about corporate environmental management in particular.

ENVIRONMENTAL HISTORY AT THE STRUCTURAL LEVEL

In a nutshell, the fact that the institutional framework exists means that corporate environmental management cannot be viewed in an isolated context. It must be understood within the context of the institutional environment. The firm and its organizational field are tightly linked. A shift in the field's constituency will yield a restructuring of the field's institutions, which in turn will be reflected in the structure and culture of the firm. Summarized in Figure 7.4, the structural history presented in the previous four chapters reveals the extent to which these connections have existed and how they have evolved.

As this history has explained, from 1960 until 1970, *industrial environmentalism* was the dominant conception of corporate environmental management. Industry existed alone in the organizational field, defining environmental management according to its own perspectives. Accordingly, it was seen as an ancillary problem to mainline operations, one to be dealt with on an ad hoc basis.

But in 1970, that conception was replaced by *regulatory environmentalism*. From 1970 until approximately 1982, government (in the form of the EPA) became the legitimate arbiter of what constituted acceptable corporate environmental management. Because the EPA possessed the power

Figure 7.4. A Structural History of Corporate Environmentalism.

	1960–1970 Industrial Environmentalism	1970–1982 Regulatory Environmentalism	1982–1988 Environmentalism as Social Responsibility	1988–1993 Strategic Environmentalism
Organizational Field	 *Industry-Focused:* Industry is alone in the organizational field.	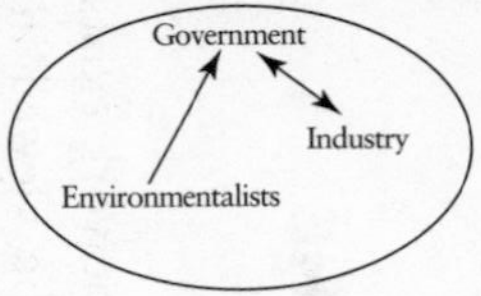 *Government-Focused:* The government dominates the organizational field. Industry influence declines.	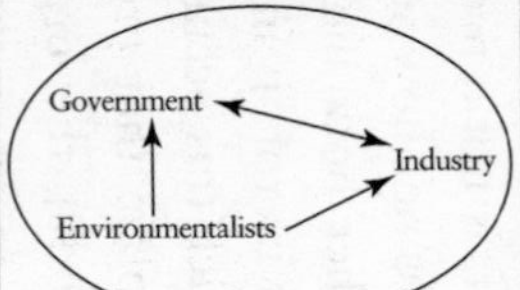 *Socially Focused:* Environmentalists pressure industry directly. Industry influence begins to rise.	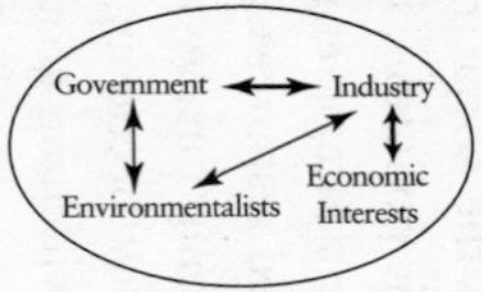 *Strategically Focused:* Economic interests enter the field. Industry continues to rise.
Dominant Institutions	*Industry Is the Solution:* Self-reliance and technological optimism	*Government Is the Solution:* Confrontation	*Industry and Government Are the Solution:* Cooperation	*The Organizational Field Is the Solution:* Institutional-reliance and technological optimism
Organizational Structure and Culture	*Problem Solving:* Considered an ancillary aspect of conducting business, it is handled primarily as an operating-line function.	*Technical Compliance:* Although elevated to a separate corporate department, it remains an ancillary role with low organizational power, focused strictly on legal requirements.	*Managerial Compliance:* Moving beyond mere technical responses, managerial structures are developed to achieve compliance based on internal constraints. Environmental responsibilities begin to diffuse throughout the organization.	*Proactive Management:* Organizational boundaries blur, allowing direct influence by external interests. The environmental department reaches new levels of organizational power. Environmental considerations begin to be pushed across functional lines and back down into the line operations, integrating them into both process and product decisions.

to define the issue, it became the battleground on which environmental groups and industry fought over the definition of responsible business practice. However, it did not define the issue per se; rather, with one constituent on either side, the agency mediated the institutional negotiation between them and established the definition of acceptable environmental management practices based on their opposing interests. Acknowledging EPA's central role in the organizational field, industry organized special departments based on the framework that the agency established. The role of these departments, organized around various segmented media (such as air and water), became the management of regulatory compliance, not environmental affairs.

From approximately 1982 until 1988, corporate environmentalism was again redefined, this time in terms of *social responsibility*. EPA's legitimacy had been undermined by Ann Burford Gorsuch's attempts to cripple the agency, and as a result, mere regulatory compliance no longer represented environmental legitimacy for the corporation or society. Environmental groups began to challenge industry directly, and industry began to seek cooperation with the government to find internally based solutions to environmental problems. As a result, within the organization, environmental management became more integrated into corporate operations. Firms sought to achieve environmental compliance by developing their own management structures.

Finally, from about 1988 until 1993, *strategic environmentalism* became the dominant conception of environmental management. The organizational field expanded with the entrance of investors, insurance companies, and competitors. The introduction of these traditional strategic constituents into the field of environmental concerns pushed industry to begin adopting a proactive strategy toward environmental management. Firms continued to move beyond the objectives of regulatory requirements and set environmental objectives based even more on internal management processes. Environmental responsibilities began to diffuse into departments throughout the organization. Economic competitiveness and environmental management were beginning to occupy common realms of concern within the corporation.

ENVIRONMENTAL HISTORY AT THE INSTITUTIONAL LEVEL

This structural history explains the nuts and bolts of what has happened over the past thirty-five years. But by going beyond this structural presentation and framing the history in the context of Scott's institutional pillars,[11] we can uncover a deeper meaning behind what has happened. The history of corporate environmentalism is a story of institutional negotiation over corporations' rules, norms, and, ultimately, beliefs regarding legitimate environmental management. Through successive stages, these institutions evolved in their scope and expanded their relevant constituency. In so doing, their institutional primacy reached increasing depths within the institutional hierarchy and the corporate mindset (see Table 7.1).

In 1960, the cultural beliefs within the oil and chemical industries were predicated on the idea that advances in engineering improved the quality of life for all humankind. Industry remained firm in its belief that environmental problems could be solved independently through its own technological prowess. This was a cultural remnant of what Florman called the "golden age of engineering,"[12] an age that environmentalism was helping to bring to a close. Such remnants were manifested in the cultural typifications or symbolism of the industry-dominated organizational field. Corporations denied the existence of serious environmental problems, because such an acknowledgment would contradict the beliefs on which their identity was based. Industry saw itself as a positive force in the development of human society. Environmentalism challenged this self-image, initiating a clash between the taken-for-granted beliefs within industry and society's emerging questions regarding the validity of those beliefs. The 1962 publication of Silent Spring[13] and the 1969 Santa Barbara oil spill were touchstones of that clash. As environmentalism grew from the mid 1960s through 1970, a growing mainstream appreciation for environmental protection increasingly challenged the nature of legitimate corporate behavior.

For the moment, at least, industry acquiesced to these growing concerns. At this time, environmental management was largely a matter of aesthetic controls on wastewater and air emissions. Dirty smokestacks were as yet just an ugly nuisance, a minor problem that industry felt could be handled independently with minimal technological adjustments. Such a simple framing was not seriously tangential to the orthodoxy of business management. Although resistant to the idea of increased regulation, the emerging logic of adding the necessary additional emission controls was accepted.

This acceptance is historically important, however, in that it marked the initial formation of the organizational field. This formation witnessed an increase in environment-related interactions among organizations in the field, the information load with which these organizations had to contend, and a mutual awareness among the participants that they were involved in a common enterprise.[14]

Table 7.1. An Institutional History of Corporate Environmentalism.

	1960–1970 Industrial Environmentalism	1970–1982 Regulatory Environmentalism	1982–1988 Environmentalism as Social Responsibility	1988–1993 Strategic Environmentalism
Institutional primacy	Cognitive	Regulative	Normative	Cognitive
Institutional support	Normative, regulative	—	Regulative	Normative, regulative
Field constituency	Industry	Industry, government, activists	Industry, government, activists	Industry, government, activists, investors, competitors, insurance companies
Basis of legitimacy	Culturally supported	Legally sanctioned	Morally/ethically governed	Culturally supported
Logic	Orthodoxy	Instrumentality	Appropriateness	Orthodoxy
Cultural carrier	Typifications, symbolism	Rules, laws	Values, expectations	Typifications, symbolism
Structural carrier	Identities	Governance system	Regimes	Identities
Routines	Scripts	Protocols	Conformity	Scripts

Once established, this field grew steadily in strength throughout the rest of the 1960s. Federal, state, and county governments began to develop environmental regulations, each attempting to define the legitimate expectations of their constituency. As these standards began to proliferate, industry did not challenge their legitimacy but rather accepted the inevitable outcome and sought a unifying body of environmental regulation. The formation of the EPA reflected the overlap between public and industry conceptions of proper corporate environmental responsibility. And so corporate environmentalism moved from cognitive denial of the problem to acceptance of regulatory constraints and requirements.

This first major institutional shift was met with little opposition from industry. President Nixon's decision to form the EPA signified to both industry and society a legitimate, regulatory representation of the cognitive beliefs that each held about the environment. However, it was not the conceptual definition of corporate environmental management that was institutionalized with the formation of the EPA. Rather, it was the boundaries determining how that definition would be negotiated and contested that were institutionalized. Environmental protection was now justified as a legitimate corporate concern in the context of external interests. Environmental groups and industry fought over the definition of legitimate environmental management practice, with the EPA serving as adjudicator. Industry accepted agency definitions and appeased the development of regulatory institutions for reasons of expedience and instrumentality. Internal governance systems and protocols were developed based on the rules and laws defined by the government.

However, as victories began to accrue to environmentalists throughout the 1970s, these rules and laws began to move away from industry's culturally supported conceptions of what was fair and reasonable. From 1970 until 1982, the institutional framing of environmental management was established through a wide body of regulations covering air, water, toxics, pesticides, hazardous wastes, drinking water, and so on.

By 1980, the regulative aspects of environmental legislation were sufficiently far from the cognitive beliefs of industry that tensions were near the boiling point. President Reagan saw these tensions and, with the aid of Ann Burford Gorsuch, challenged the formal rules, attempting to deinstitutionalize[15] the EPA's conceptions of corporate environmentalism by arguing that they were inconsistent with the values and cognitive beliefs of society. The public and political reaction to Gorsuch's attempts to derail the EPA forced Reagan to back down, however.

Both Reagan's and Nixon's actions represent a contrast between what could be called compromise and survival in institutional negotiation. In compromise, negotiators of conflict have intersecting spheres of reference and a stable set of framing. They acknowledge each other as legitimate partners for discourse with legitimate concerns to be considered. In survival, these spheres of reference are distinct from one another. One or both of the parties sees the other as illegitimate and therefore not one whose concerns are to be considered seriously. In institutionalizing the EPA, Nixon saw the former. In his attempt to deinstitutionalize the agency, Reagan saw the latter. Reagan's miscalculation of the cognitive consensus supporting environmental protection was met with protest and political backlash. The result was an exposure of the cognitive beliefs of society and a realization within industry that environmentalism would not go away, it had broad public support, industry's efforts must reflect that support, and regulatory compliance no longer represented environmental legitimacy to society.

With the removal of Gorsuch (as well as James Watt and Rita Lavelle), the contestation between industry and environmentalists was returned to a common realm based on compromise, not survival. In the process, the field was restructured, redefining the relationship between industry and environmental groups as existing within the same organizational field. The two protagonists would now negotiate over institutional norms directly. And with this new structure came a new institutional context for framing the issue of environmental management. Corporate environmentalism was now accepted within the normative institutional realm. It became ethically (and, for some, morally) appropriate to initiate controls that went beyond regulatory requirements as a matter of social obligation. The dominant values and expectations of the period drove firms to conform to the dominant logics of pollution prevention and waste minimization.

The next institutional break came in 1988, when insurance companies, competitors, and investors entered the organizational field, engaging in institutional contestation over a redefinition of appropriate conceptions of environmental management. This shift was facilitated by the large number of prominent environmental events that occurred almost simultaneously at this time, thereby inflaming societal and market sensitivities to environmental concerns. Environmentalism, previously a social issue, now became a strategic issue. And in so doing, it reached new levels of cultural primacy within the organization.

Examples of corporate environmentalism going regulatory compliance were now prominent,[16] and rhetoric reflecting the competitive aspects of corporate environmentalism was increasingly common.[17] For example, in 1990, the Carrier Corporation, a division of United Technologies, announced that it had invested $500,000 to eliminate the use of toxic solvents in cleaning copper and aluminum parts in the manufacture of air conditioners. By the end of one year, the company claimed to have recouped $1.2 million in reduced manufacturing costs.[18] In 1991, DuPont announced a $500 million capital improvement plan at three North and South Carolina chemical plants, which it claimed would reduce air emissions by 60 percent while increasing production by 20 percent.[19] The "win-win" scenario replaced pollution prevention and waste minimization as the dominant rhetoric and logic. In a 1995 Times Mirror poll, 69 percent of Americans believed that environmental protection and economic development could work together.[20]

Some suggested that environmentalism had thus reached the level of a cognitive institution. In 1991, Riley Dunlap wrote that "environmental protection has become a consensual issue in U.S. society, a basic value that no major bloc of voters opposes. . . . Anti-environmental values have no legitimacy in the public debate."[21] This may be strongly stated, but the existence of a culturally supported belief in some degree of corporate environmental responsibility is undeniable. That companies would no longer dump hazardous wastes in the "back forty" could safely be considered a given. If a company did choose to undertake such an activity, it would do so with the full knowledge that it was deviating severely from existing legal and ethical institutions. Similarly, no company would now look to billowing smokestacks as a proud example of economic progress, as was the case in the 1950s. They were now a sign of corporate irresponsibility and wasted resources.

Regardless of what meaning an organization places on a given object or action, institutional conceptions will predominate. Yet the extent to which these conceptions have penetrated the cognitive realm is unclear. What is clear is a trajectory to this institutional history that suggests at least the beginning of that penetration. It depicts the transitional path from one corporate reality to another, from one conception of environmental practice to another. The institutions surrounding environmental management evolved from a cognitive set of arrangements in the 1960s (at time t_1) through the regulative and normative institutional realms to emerge in the 1990s (at time t_2) with a new set of cognitive arrangements. Since this latter cognitive reality is fundamentally different than the former, the process is depicted as a spiral (see Figure 7.5). With these new institutional arrangements come new institutional relationships both inside and outside the company.

When institutions exist within the cognitive realm, core organizational functions are triggered as a response. In the 1960s, firms groped with the cognitive challenge of environmental management by handling it through a core operating function, as was then deemed necessary. Since the issue was perceived primarily as technological in nature, that core was engineering. In the 1990s, firms are again groping with the cognitive challenge

Figure 7.5. The Transition from One Cognitive Frame to Another.

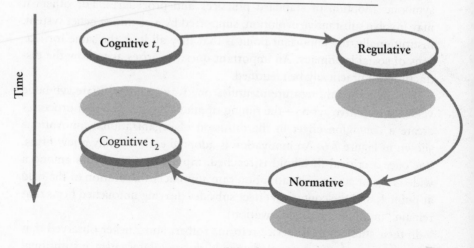

of environmental management, and again they are turning to core operating functions. But the issue is now seen as strategic and managerial as well as technological in nature. Therefore, in this new cognitive context, operating cores throughout the organization are being tapped: law, advertising, strategy, the executive board, investor relations, and so on.

When institutions reach the cognitive level, it is more than internal responses that change. External interpretations of those responses also change. Firms are judged externally by a new set of criteria and with increased scrutiny. No longer the sole venue of environmentalists, rating corporate environmental performance becomes the concern of mainstream business as well.[22] But the criteria for judgment is far from accurate, and the perception of environmental performance can be as important as the substance. In attempting to represent cognitive conformity, firms are now trapped into incorporating public relations campaigns into their environmental strategy. For some this is a genuine reflection of internal values. For others it is *greenwashing*, or symbolic action.

GREENWASHING: SYMBOLIC VERSUS SUBSTANTIVE ACTION

While conformance to institutional rules and norms becomes a necessary aspect of the demands on organizational life, the emerging necessity of conformance to cognitive institutions is a complex challenge. Companies may resemble one another in their visible adoption of evolving organizational trends, but their adoption of underlying values can vary greatly. For some companies, regulatory and normative compliance may involve the symbolic adoption of standard practices and procedures. For others it may involve substantive evolution, supported by a cognitive belief system. Institutionally, the important point is that they all look the same for reasons of social legitimacy. An important question arises as to how the distinction can practically be identified.

The institutional literature identifies one way to differentiate symbolic versus substantive action—the timing of adoption. Institutional processes create a contagion effect in the diffusion of organizational innovations shown in Figure 7.6. An innovation is adopted early by only a few firms. But once a critical threshold is reached, rapid adoption occurs among a wide range of actors. The adoption rate approaches saturation of the field at point 1, and the contagion effect subsides (leaving untouched firms that remain "immune" to the innovation).

In their study of civil service reform, Tolbert and Zucker observed that late adopters of institutional demands did not internalize institutional imperatives but rather mimicked the cultural artifacts of early adopters' actions without integrating the underlying values and norms that supported them.[23] As a result, early adopters developed structural changes that were consistent with the institutional norms of the field and the cultural norms of the firm. Followers of institutional shifts adopted for symbolic reasons and created structures without organizational support.

Similar to the contagion model in Figure 7.6, such institutional adoption creates a distribution curve, shown in Figure 7.7. Organizational innovation is adopted initially by only a few firms, but at a critical threshold, mass diffusion occurs, followed by a gradual decrease in adoption as the field is penetrated by the innovation. In this presentation, the presence of leaders and followers becomes more visible. By studying successive adoption curves, it should become clear whether certain firms are continual facilitators of institutional trends, thereby revealing possible symbolic adopters of institutional trends.

The strategic premise behind symbolic action is that institutionalized rules and norms need not be sustained. Therefore, in times of breakdown, such as the economic difficulties for the oil industry in the late 1980s, late adopters are able to abandon the weakly supported institutional structures, while early adopters find the structures integrated into their overall organizational structure to a level not easily extracted. The risk is that the firm develops a culturally inconsistent structure, built from artifacts and espoused values that vary significantly from the underlying beliefs that guide employee action. This can create organizational drag and decrease efficiency should institutionalized rules and norms be sustained.

Figure 7.6. "Contagion" Model of Organizational Diffusion.

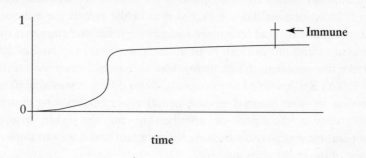

Figure 7.7. Adoption of Organizational Innovations.

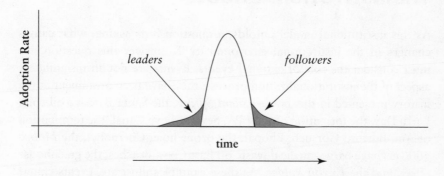

On the other hand, the benefits of being an early adopter can help a firm react quickly to anticipated changes in the institutional environment. Strategically, it can also allow a firm the potential to direct those changes, creating a standard others must follow. Not all firms possess the power to alter institutional arrangements, and among those that do, not all possess it to the same degree.[24] The relative size and legitimacy of an organization gives it differential power to influence the actions of others and shape social fields.[25] In this study, the most highly cited companies for both lawsuits and journal coverage were Exxon and Dow. What gives these companies power and what that power means is beyond the scope of this study; the fact that they are disproportionately influential in the environmental organizational field is what is of importance here.

Through coercive force, powerful members of the field can direct the formation of institutional norms that are consistent with their own objectives and needs. Or powerful members can find voluntary cooperation possible, based on the degree to which all members benefit from the formation of stable rules governing legitimate actions in the field.[26] For example, in the 1980s, Dow Chemical conducted public surveys around its Canadian plants to find out at what geographic distance from the plants its reputation did not exceed that of the rest of the industry. The disturbing answer was only three kilometers. It became clear that the firm could not stand out as clean in an industry that was perceived as dirty. To correct this problem, the company was able to influence the creation of the CMA's Responsible Care Program. By so doing, it was able to institutionalize its own internal environmental programs, making compliance with them a condition of membership for the trade association. Cooperation was possible because the program was a way to improve the image of the industry as a whole.

THE ROLE OF EVENTS IN THE INSTITUTIONAL MODEL

As this institutional model unfolds, a question begs asking: what causes changes in the institutional environment? To answer this question, we must consider the role of external events. Events are not an insignificant aspect of the institutionalization process; they have been prominent in the history presented in this book—*Silent Spring,* the Santa Barbara oil spill, Earth Day, the formation of the EPA, Seveso, Love Canal, the termination of Ann Burford Gorsuch, Bhopal, the ozone hole, Chernobyl, the *Mobro 4000* garbage barge, medical waste on East Coast beaches, the greenhouse effect, and the *Exxon Valdez.* As these examples illustrate, events can at times initiate a restructuring of the institutional environment. On the other hand, at other times events can have no effect at all. In either case, their presence is important, for both theoretical and practical reasons.

First, most theories of organizational behavior neglect the physical or "natural" environment as socially inert and therefore organizationally insignificant. Resource dependence theory, for example, places value in the physical environment only insofar as it creates a source of power for the social actor who controls it.[27] The physical environment, itself, is seen as having no value save that placed on it by the social environment. But the institutional evolution of corporate conceptions of environmental management is profoundly affected by the direct influence of the physical environment through external events. Institutional processes can be interrupted by the emergence of an environmental jolt or crisis, which can precipitate the entrance or exit of new institutional members or the alteration of existing power balances. Such shifts throw the established rules and norms into flux, out of which form a new set of institutional arrangements.

Events, by themselves, do not negotiate in the formation of organizational fields. They empower social actors to negotiate while directing the form and the focus of their strategy. Given the need for social surrogates, they become dependent on social interpretation. Whether they are reacting to scientific data, a sudden disaster, or a political maneuver, social actors are responsible for both the initial acknowledgment and the subsequent interpretation of the event and then for using that interpretation for negotiating change within the institutional environment. To elaborate further, two questions must be considered. What makes an event an event— why is it noticed? And what affect does an event have on institutional systems once it is noticed?

First, why are some events noticed while others are not? For example, one glaring omission from this history occurred on June 22, 1969, when Ohio's Cuyahoga River caught fire, causing $50,000 in damages to two wooden railroad bridges southeast of Cleveland. A sensational event, it empowered environmentalists and the public in gaining passage of major environmental legislation in the early 1970s.[28] But neither *Chemical Week* nor *Oil & Gas Journal* acknowledged its occurrence. This omission provides a revealing insight, for the history presented in these trade journals is not intended to be complete in the broad sense; rather, it reveals what is perceived to be relevant by the chemical and petroleum industries. That this seminal event was not noticed indicates that the level of its influence within these industries was negligible. All events are not critical, and all need not be acknowledged. For the business manager, the challenge becomes knowing which are critical (and thus demand a response) and which are not.

This differentiation becomes clearer through the institutional model. Events and their interpretation are context-specific. William Shakespeare wrote in *Romeo and Juliet* that "a rose by any other name would smell as sweet"; the institutional model might add that it depends on when the rose is smelled and by whom. An object or event is not objectively defined. How they are perceived is a direct reflection of when they were perceived and by whom. They are both time- and context-specific.

In comparing the environmental histories of the chemical and petroleum industries, it becomes clear that the chemical industry was much more open and aware of external events than was the oil industry. *Chemical Week* wrote a total of ninety-four articles on events, ranging from the publication of *Silent Spring* (1962) to the first Earth Day (1970), the *Exxon Valdez* (1989), and the Earth Summit in Rio (1992). Issues ranged from biodegradable detergents (1965) to ocean incineration (1978) and environmental racism (1993). Events in *Oil & Gas Journal* were primarily focused on oil spills such as the *Torrey Canyon* (1967), the Santa Barbara platform (1969), the *Amoco Cadiz* (1978), the Pemex spill (1979), the *Exxon Valdez* (1989), and the Kuwait oil well fires (1991).

In addition to the differences in who was viewing these incidents, context was also important. In both cases, a common trend was observed. Event-related articles progressively moved away from a company-specific focus and toward an emphasis on industrywide effects, suggesting an increasing sense of joint ownership of the environmental problem. This was observed most cryptically in the *Chemical Week* coverage of the Seveso (1976), Love Canal (1978), and Bhopal (1984) disasters and the *Oil & Gas Journal* coverage of the Santa Barbara (1969), *Amoco Cadiz* (1978), and *Exxon Valdez* (1989) oil spills. In both journals, the earlier incidents were reported in reactive fashion, emerging not at the time of the incident but rather at the time of government action in response to it. Further, the focus of the articles was on the specific companies involved and the government action against them. Coverage of the more contemporary catastrophes emerged immediately, and the articles dealt first with the potential and later with the actual impact of the incident on the industry as a whole.

But to understand the full institutional aspects of event interpretation, we must acknowledge that industry is not alone in determining the presence or meaning of an environmental incident. That determination falls to the organizational field. Take *Silent Spring* as an example. Rachel Carson did not discover the problems associated with DDT and the ecosystem. She performed no research studies nor any technical analyses. She was not even the first person to write about it. The problems of DDT had been well documented since World War II. What was critical about Carson's book (aside from her literary style) was the time in which she chose to write it. It emerged at a time when people were receptive to such a message. Much as the situation creates a leader, the context creates an issue. Had Carson written her book even five years before, it would not likely have caused the same level of controversy. It may not have made any sense given the dominant logics of the time. In fact, reflecting that perhaps she was just a little ahead of her time, most magazines turned down her initial proposals to write articles on the topic, forcing her to resort to writing a book. And after the book was completed, the *New Yorker* magazine faced legal threats and the withdrawal of advertising revenue for agreeing to serialize parts of the volume.

In another example, if it weren't for institutional context, it is not likely that Love Canal would have been noticed when it was. In the words of

Hugh Kaufman, the EPA official who helped expose the story, "Love Canal was a catastrophe but it wasn't the worst catastrophe in the country, or in New York state, or even in Niagara County." But, he says, "it was Love Canal, Hooker Chemical and Niagara Falls, honeymoon capital of the world. Editors all over the country had orgasms. So Love Canal became catastrophic, not any of the other 10,000 hazardous dump sites across America."[29] This became a landmark opportunity, empowering environmental activists to wage institutional "war," given the conveniently sensational participants, the emerging awareness of something called hazardous waste sites, and the event's coincidental timing with Jimmy Carter's presidential campaign.

In one final example, the cultural context defined the *Exxon Valdez* oil spill. This was by no means the first nor the worst oil spill in U.S. waters. As shown in Table 7.2, it ranks as the thirteenth largest spill in history and the second largest in the United States (the *Burmah Agate* spilled six hundred thousand more gallons on Texas shores in 1979). Yet in terms of notoriety and punitive damages inflicted, it ranks at the top. The reason for this dubious honor was not the scale of the accident as much as the timing. Oil spills occurring in 1969, 1979, and 1989 each were viewed differently depending on the makeup of the field and the accepted standards of the time. The Santa Barbara oil spill of 1969 represented an aesthetic concern for the beautiful beaches in that affluent community. Executives at Amoco acknowledge that the *Cadiz* spill in 1978 was handled largely as a maritime issue. The context of 1969 and 1978 allowed such conceptions. The context of 1989 would not allow Exxon the same. More than just perception, the appropriate censure and response to the incident also varied with the context. The notion of inflicting punishment on Union Oil for the Santa Barbara spill at the scale it was inflicted on Exxon would have made no sense for the time. The institutional norms would not have supported such a proposal.

The upshot of this first point is straightforward. The specific scientific and ecological "facts" surrounding a particular environmental disaster are secondary in determining the attention that incident receives. What is more important is when the event occurs, who is observing it, and what is the institutional context. In other words, the scope, the scale, and, ultimately, the notability of an environmental disaster is institutionally negotiated. The firm is not free to define it alone. Therefore, rather than focusing strictly on internally derived "facts" regarding toxicity and risk, the business executive who faces an environmental accident must remain aware of and, where possible, manage the institutional environment.

Table 7.2.   The World's Largest Oil Spills (by Volume).

1. 88.2 million gallons	July 19, 1979	Collision of *Atlantic Empress* and *Aegean Captain* in the Caribbean off Trinidad and Tobago
2. 73.5 million gallons	August 6, 1983	Fire aboard *Castillo de Bellver* off Cape Town, South Africa
3. 65.6 million gallons	March 16, 1978	Grounding of Amoco *Cadiz* near Portsall, France
4. 34.9 million gallons	March 18, 1967	Grounding of *Torrey Canyon* off Land's End, England
5. 33.8 million gallons	December 19, 1972	Collision of *Sea Star* in Gulf of Oman
6. 29.4 million gallons	May 12, 1976	Grounding of *Urquiola* at La Coruña, Spain
7. 29.1 million gallons	February 25, 1977	Fire aboard *Hawaiian Patriot* in the northern Pacific Ocean
8. 26 million gallons	January 5, 1993	Grounding of *Braer* off Shetland Islands, England
9. 19 million gallons	February 15, 1996	Grounding of *Sea Empress* at St. Ann's Head, Wales
10. 18 to 29 million gallons	March 20, 1970	Collision of *Othello* in Tralhavet Bay, Sweden
11. 13.5 million gallons	June 13, 1968	Hull failure of *World Glory* off South Africa
12. 10.7 million gallons	November 1, 1979	Collision of *Burmah Agate* off Galveston Bay, Texas
13. 10.1 million gallons	March 24, 1989	Grounding of *Exxon Valdez* in Prince William Sound, Alaska

Whether it is derived from the local, regional, national, or international institutional environment, the importance of an event is dependent on the perceptions of those outside the firm.

Once this is acknowledged, then, what effect will an event have on institutional structures? This too is defined by the institutional environment. Or, more to the point, the institutional environment can become redefined by the event. Events can either facilitate institutional change consistent with existing institutional arrangements or effect an alteration in those arrangements to reflect new institutional conceptions. The first is more politically derived. The second is more sudden and catastrophic in its impact.

In the first case, events serve as a *catalyst*. In the thermodynamic sense, a catalyst is a compound that, through its mere presence, facilitates a more rapid chemical reaction. It does not force a reaction that would not occur otherwise. In the same way, events can serve to hasten the development of the institutional issue of the moment without causing it to form. For example, consider the 1976 incident at Seveso, Italy, described earlier, in which a toxic cloud of dioxin was accidentally released from a chemical plant. At that time, the banning of carcinogenic substances such as DDT was the topical focus of environmental regulation in this country. As a result, Seveso served as a catalyst for the banning of dioxin. Ten years later, a cloud of methyl isocyanate was accidentally released from the Union Carbide plant in Bhopal, India. At that time, the topical policy focus was corporate disclosure of chemical contaminant information to employees and local communities. Therefore, the result of this incident was the development of several community "right to know" (RTK) laws, including the Toxics Release Inventory, which required that firms report all releases of contaminants from their plants to the public. These events did not cause the dioxin ban or the establishment of RTK legislation. They catalyzed their institutional development.

In this way, they can almost be viewed as politically convenient. Had they not occurred when they did, it is conceivable that another incident could have fulfilled the same purpose. Consider the formation of the Valdez Principles by the Coalition for Environmentally Responsible Economies. The *Exxon Valdez* spill empowered their emergence, but as Joan Bavaria, one of CERES's founders, acknowledges, "Valdez was really a matter of convenience. It was a tragedy that moved a cause. Environment as an investor issue really started up in 1981. It was in the early part of 1988 that things really heated up when we had Bhopal, dirty beaches, and the big media press.... We were really a reflection of changes going on within the environment."[30] Although the *Valdez* spill catalyzed the formation of CERES, it would have likely happened later as the result of another triggering event. Moving down the chain of institutional development, CERES itself was a catalyst for change.

This example describes a particular actor capitalizing on an external event. It suggests that institutional outcomes are clear and predictable. But they are not. The catalyzing process can come from the most unpredictable of sources and can have results far from what was intended. For example, President Reagan's decision to challenge the legitimacy of the EPA in 1981 proved to be a decisive moment in the evolution of corporate environmentalism. Hardly considered a staunch environmentalist, Reagan catalyzed the initiation of an institutional shift, whereby corporations adopted new forms of environmental responsibilities that just two years before they were resisting. In the words of Sierra Club conservation director Carl Pope, President Reagan "reinvented the environmental movement by his contempt for it."[31] As in each of the examples cited, events can act as catalysts, facilitating the progression of institutional evolution. But if this were the only role events played, the model might suggest a politically determined path dependence to the institutionalization process.

But events can also highlight breakdowns or failures of existing institutional arrangements, thereby creating chaotic shifts in the trajectory of institutional development. They can identify new areas of concern that existing institutional rules or norms do not properly address. For example, once identified, the Love Canal disaster profoundly changed the institutional face of environmentalism in this country. For the first time, an environmental incident emerged as a sudden and unpredictable disaster from as innocuous a place as one's own backyard. Prior to Love Canal, the notion of a hazardous abandoned waste site had no meaning within the institutions of corporate management. Although previously seen, it had yet to be defined and categorized as a major environmental concern. Had it not been for the institutional impact of Love Canal, the highly publicized incidents that followed—at Times Beach, the Stringfellow Acid Pits, and the Valley of the Drums—would not have had contextual meaning.

Furthermore, as a result of the ensuing negotiation among environmental groups, business, and the government, the institutional face of corporate environmentalism was also profoundly changed with the passage of the Comprehensive Environmental Response Compensation and Liability Act, or Superfund, in 1980.[32] With this legislation, industry was now assigned a responsibility for these sites, and it was held liable for actions that were legal when they were undertaken. Such a notion was previously inconceivable. Worse yet, a company could also be held fiscally liable for an entire cleanup, regardless of its level of involvement in the contamination. Love Canal profoundly changed the institutional conceptions of corporate environmental management.

Whether as a catalyst or as an institutional change agent, events alter institutional development. Those who are affected by the institutionalization process can view them as either threats or opportunities. Events can precipitate new institutional structures that place further constraints on the organization—new regulatory demands on the firm, new budgetary restrictions on the government agency, new membership constraints on the activist group. However, sudden events or crises can also permit a sharp end to what had seemed to be locked in by institutional pressure.[33] Whereas hard-won organizational success breeds resistance to change, sudden events plunge the organization and the field into unfamiliar circumstances, legitimating unorthodox experiments that revitalize them.[34] The flux created by a sudden event can allow institutional entrepreneurs to influence new institutional outcomes. New structures and strategies can be designed that can be either directly or indirectly introduced into the institutional environment.

RECOGNIZING THAT FIRMS EXIST WITHIN MULTIPLE ORGANIZATIONAL FIELDS

Putting together the model thus far, corporate conceptions of environmental management emerge from the negotiated interests of the organizational field. As the field shifts in its constituency, so too do the institutional rules, norms, and beliefs that guide the formation of organizational structure and strategy. Such shifts can be initiated by the emergence of external events that alter institutional arrangements. But there awaits one final piece of the puzzle to be considered, the complexity of the institutional environment.

The institutional environment is not monolithic. Organizations can exist within multiple fields, each with its own cultural rules, some of which may be at odds with those of others. A firm may face one organizational field in terms of human resources, for example, while it faces another in terms of environmental management and yet another in terms of manufacturing protocols. Firms can respond to this field multiplexity by either interacting with each field through separate functional departments employing differentiated attention, attempting to merge field interests into one cohesive strategy, or superseding the interests of one field with the interests of another. While the middle option may often be beyond the firm's control, the other two are within organizational control. Yet each has its costs and benefits.

The first option, differentiated attention, may cause inconsistency in organizational action. The EH&S or operations level may profess proactive environmental management in response to the field with which it interacts (regulatory agencies, activists, suppliers, customers), and the government affairs department may lobby Congress for regulatory rollbacks in response to the field with which it interacts (government legislators). Different fields employ different routes of influence into the organization, triggering different organizational routines and responses. The challenge for the organizational executive is to mediate among field interests and coordinate coherent organizational responses. The challenge for the activist and the regulator is to strive to create institutional uniformity that will minimize the possibility of conflicting institutional demands.

But even with consistency of fields, different departments within a single firm can act unilaterally and respond with autonomous and inconsistent action. Each department employs its own set of routines for both interpreting and reacting to institutional pressure. Much like the old adage, "if the only tool you own is a hammer, all your problems look like nails," government affairs may always respond to environmental pressures with lobbying efforts. At the same time, operations may always respond by altering process parameters, and EH&S may always respond by developing environmental management protocols. Each department can respond to the pressure as it seems appropriate. In the end, what is deemed appropriate is subjectively defined.

As firms face these multiple fields, they can also choose the third option of supplanting the interests of one field with those of another. At times, the expectations of one field overlap with or interfere with the expectations of another. The firm then responds to the field demands to which it is most attuned or that it values to the greatest extent. Clearly, economic survival would supersede environmental survival in the organizational agenda.

The history told in this book provides a prominent example, the period in 1990 when the proactive optimism of the chemical industry was not shared by the oil industry. Several fields began to compete with the oil industry's environmental institutions. The first interfering field was economic. The norms of corporate profitability were in conflict with the norms of proactive environmental responsibility. For one thing, the U.S. average wellhead price for crude oil had been on a rocky decline since the early 1980s, such that by the early 1990s it was (in constant dollars) roughly equivalent to the price in 1970.[35] As Figure 7.8 shows, this price decline was directly related to industry profits, which dropped significantly in 1990.

The overlap between economic institutional demands and those of environmental protection occurred around the issues of acid rain and

Figure 7.8.   Industry Profit Index.[36]

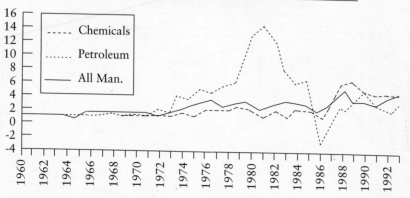

Note: Baseline: 1960 = 1.

global warming.[37] Air issues have always been more prominent for the oil industry. (Over the period 1960 to 1993, sixty-six percent of the oil industry's capital expenditures were spent on air projects, compared to only 37 percent for the chemical industry.)[38] The air issue, as Figure 7.9 shows, drove environmental capital costs up by over 300 percent through the Clean Air Act amendments of 1990. (Ironically, this increase merely raised industry costs to levels that matched what the chemical industry had long been spending—roughly 9 percent of overall capital expenditures.) The global warming issue, through proposed intervention, threatened to push them even higher. Discussion of carbon taxes both nationally and internationally would impose serious economic constraints on the production and sale of petroleum products. In the end, the fields of environmental protection and corporate competitiveness were in direct opposition. Economic concerns superseded.

The second field restricting oil industry attention to environmental issues was technical. While the normative possibilities for pollution prevention within the chemical industry were somewhat flexible, those for the petroleum industry were far more limited. Oil companies faced no significant possibilities for changing its raw materials, product, or processes—the three primary options for pollution prevention measures. Although work was being done on compressed natural gas and liquefied natural gas, gasoline remained the only feasible product. Although gasoline can theoretically be processed from other sources such as shale or coal, crude oil remained the only economically viable raw material. And finally, the processes used to transform the raw material to the product,

Figure 7.9.   Environmentalism as a Percentage of Total Capital
Expenditures.[39]

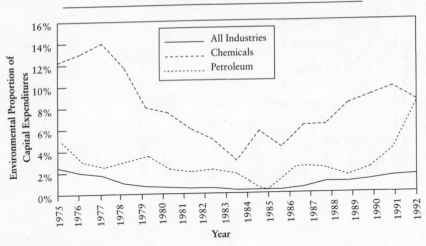

such as catalytic cracking, hydrogenation, and distillation, were unquestioningly defined and open to only limited modification. Substitutions in acids and catalysts were possible, but their impact was slight.[40] The field related to technology stifled that of environmental concerns, and the industry responded by rejecting the demands of the environmental organizational field.

Summing up this framework, then, we can describe what we have been witnessing over the past three decades as the product of political negotiation and institutional evolution. The institutional history of corporate environmentalism is a product of the co-evolution of *institutions* outside the firm and *the structures and strategies* inside the firm. Both have been continually evolving as new events or crises call attention to the need for new forms of broadly accepted values and practices. The status of corporate environmental management is explained as the historical product of this external examination, the result of what is described as a negotiation among the internal members of the firm and external members of the *organizational field*: primarily the government, other firms sharing similar technological and political constraints, and external environmental interests.

EXPANDING THE INSTITUTIONAL MODEL

For the organizational theorist, this argument is more than an application of institutional theory. As stated at the outset, environmental management is a unique phenomenon for elaborating on the processes of corporate change. It allows us to identify new triggers of organizational action and elaborate on the implications of these triggers. As such, it also presents an expansion of the institutional model, bringing it closer to a realistic understanding of the behavior of the firm. It does this by elaborating on two neglected questions in the institutional literature:

1. From where do organizational fields emerge?
2. What happens when they change?

To fill the gap, this analysis goes beyond the institutional literature to borrow ideas and conceptions from related sociologists (predominantly Pierre Bourdieu, Harrison White, and Neil Fligstein)[41] and expands on the traditional institutional model in three ways: it challenges the predominate institutional focus on isomorphism, it acknowledges political dynamics in the institutionalization process, and it provides a role for agency in the institutional environment.

A central aspect of this analysis is that it attempts to reestablish links between the "old" and "new" institutional framework.[42] The schism between "old" and "new" institutional theory is an unfortunate circumstance. Though they present different views of institutions and their characteristics, these views need not be mutually exclusive. They can be combined to provide a clearer understanding of the dynamics of institutional phenomena.

In the "old" institutional perspective, institutions are the product of political processes. Powerful actors within the field negotiate, form alliances, and make political trade-offs to foster an environment that constrains or co-opts individual interests.[43] The origins and evolution of such institutions come about by design and satisfy the interests of the most powerful actors within the field. The field, therefore, is formed and evolves to serve the interests of powerful elites. While this explanation allows for the political influence of vested interests in the formation and evolution of fields and institutions, it fails to explain how organizational fields guide the underlying beliefs of individuals. Organizational legitimacy represents the agreed-on institutions that align with individual and collective interests. But it misses the influence of taken-for-granted beliefs that lie beyond the control of individual actors, focusing more on regulative and normative control.

In the "new" institutional perspective, institutions are more subtle. They represent pervasive cultural beliefs that are beyond individual control and perception. They guide individual interests and drive organizations toward isomorphic structures. The membership of the field then becomes more ambiguous, going beyond resource ties to include sources of cognitive influence[44] around which generalized belief systems are developed.[45] While this approach explains how organizational fields influence underlying motivations for action, it lacks a satisfactory explanation of the dynamics of institutional change.[46] Organizational legitimacy becomes a fixed asset, never challenged, and granted to those who conform to institutional norms. Isomorphism and institutional stability become the key focus. In explaining the dynamics of institutional change, an integration of key concepts within each theoretical tradition—isomorphism from the "new" institutional literature and political contestation from the "old" institutional literature—can provide the foundation for a more persuasive model.

Isomorphism as an Empirical Question

For better or for worse, isomorphism has become the most widely recognized conceptualization of institutional phenomena.[47] Since institutions are constructs of the mind, phenomena that "we cannot see, feel, touch, or even measure,"[48] isomorphism becomes an easily identifiable construct for labeling institutional phenomena. Yet it need not always be so. A preoccupation with isomorphism directs attention away from the source of institutional action (institutions and the organizational field) and focuses on one possible outcome (organizational homogeneity). In actuality, the degree of isomorphism becomes an empirical question. It should not be taken for granted as always being present. And if present, it need not reflect the presence of taken-for-granted beliefs. Such thinking often results in the concept becoming a tautology. We define an organizational field when we have observed that isomorphism exists. Then we argue that the isomorphism was caused by the organizational field. The mere acknowledgment of coercive mechanisms for institutional isomorphism suggests a lack of consensus in identity and meaning systems.

The analysis in this book focuses instead on institutional change as a source of organizational action. Rather than trying to ask why organizations are alike, this analysis asks what the reasons for the present structure and culture of the firm are and why it evolved to this point. Isomorphism is an implication of this process, but the central conception is institutional change and the resultant cultural and organizational evolution.

Institutionalization as Political Negotiation

By going beyond isomorphism, this account explains the genesis and evolution of dominant institutions as the outcome of political contestation and a struggle over legitimacy, not only at the level of organizational practice but also at the level of the organizational field. The neoinstitutionally restricted focus on the taken-for-granted aspects of the *cognitive* realm overlooks the political aspects of the *regulative* and *normative* realms (when they are operable). Scott's three pillars compose the whole of the institutional reality and, as such, exist simultaneously. While their relative prominence and levels of primacy may vary over time, they exist in interrelated and mutual dependence. Although the cognitive level of institutions may remain unchallenged, the regulative and normative levels of institutions are "the products of human design, the outcomes of purposive action by instrumentally oriented individuals."[49] Contrary to "new" institutional assumptions, institutions at these levels are susceptible to political processes.

Once a rule or norm has become institutionalized within the regulative or normative realm, then it can be contested among the field's participants. Institutionalization at these levels sets consensus on the boundaries of negotiation, and it then becomes a fight among institutional actors to establish the specifics of particular ideas and conceptions. As rules or norms become less contested through enduring persistence, a truncation of alternative options for organizational action takes place. These accepted rules and norms predominate the field of legitimate behavior. They become established as an accepted part of the social structure and begin to be established as taken-for-granted beliefs at the cognitive institutional realm. The form of the prevailing corporate conceptions of legitimate behavior then becomes similar to what Fligstein calls "conceptions of control"[50] or what White calls "styles or disciplines."[51] These constructs are more clearly tied to the positions of various institutional actors than the general embeddedness of a cognitive institutional belief.

A Role for Individual Agency in Institutional Arguments

With the conceptual introduction of political negotiation and institutional interests comes an implicit acknowledgment of power and agency in the institutional argument. As integral members of the field, corporate decision makers have the power either to resist or to rapidly respond[52] and the power to initiate shifts in the institutional environment.[53] Firms can diverge from the normative and coercive institutions of the field. But in so doing, they become aware that their actions run counter to the dominant logic that is directing corporate action. This requires an elevated level of institutional power, purposeful effort, and an acceptance of risk. In an example of institutional resistance, the Exxon Corporation was reluctant to acknowledge responsibility or take remediation action in the critical hours immediately following the *Valdez* shipwreck of 1989. The power of the firm to resist institutional pressures is exemplified by its ability to ignore activist protests, endure public condemnation, and pay the resulting penalties. Executives of rival oil companies admit they could not have resisted such pressure nor paid the resultant fines, which could have bankrupted their organizations.

Although neoinstitutional approaches do not acknowledge the role of agency and power (for which they have often been criticized), these considerations are receiving increasing attention. Oliver has developed a typology of strategic responses to institutional pressures that vary according to the degree of active agency and resistance exerted by the organization.[54] She provides theoretical predictors to strategic responses, based on the willingness and ability of organizations to conform to their institutional environments as well as the characteristics of the institutional forces being applied. However, this model describes a sharp distinction between the firm and its field. While there is an empirical necessity to separate the two constructs, such a mechanistic description of organization–organizational field interaction creates some of the same pitfalls as rational choice theory.

Instead, organizational action should be viewed as both the result of and source of institutional action. As an integral part of the organizational field, an organization's strategic response will likely yield a reformation of the field's institutions, while through feedback loops the firm will again be influenced by the resultant field. In this way, the firm can not only lag behind or lead institutional pressures, it can also influence (both by design and by accident) their ultimate formation. In the Exxon case, the company's resistance empowered interest groups and the government to push through the Oil Pollution Act of 1990, further increasing the regulatory restrictions on all crude oil shipping. This resistance also empowered a jury to inflict a record $5 billion judgment against the company. These outcomes have increased institutional pressure toward homogeneity by coercing Exxon individually to improve its environmental practices and expanding the standard by which all firms should behave. The process of institutional interaction becomes recursive, as social structure becomes both the "medium and outcome of the reproduction of practices. Structure enters simultaneously into the constitution of social practices and 'exists' in the generating moments of this constitution."[55]

For example, Dow Chemical's ability to institutionalize its own internal environmental programs as a condition of membership in the CMA demonstrates one way in which social practices are generated. It thus reflects the origins of coercive and mimetic isomorphism as a strategic activity. Dow initiated institutional forces to gain legitimation and strategic benefits for actions already undertaken, actions that would have yielded negative benefits if undertaken alone but yielded positive benefits when undertaken in unison with the rest of the population.

Since institutional theory has largely been applied to nonprofit organizations such as schools[56] and municipalities,[57] this type of result would not likely be observed, since there exists little incentive for these types of organizations to force others to follow. However, in the case of corporate greening, where firms may be seeking burden reduction in response to exogenous shocks, institutional forces may be created as a strategic activity to gain legitimation for reactive responses. As a result, firms have tremendous incentive to coerce others to follow.

Institutional Change as "Dynamic Isomorphism"

Each of these expansions on institutional theory culminate in a model of institutional change. As "new" institutional theory focuses on institutional stability—targeting how institutions result in isomorphic behavior—and "old" institutional theory focuses on the stability of political control and the institutionalized interests of powerful elites, fundamental issues remain unresolved: Where do these social structures come from? How do they evolve? And what happens when they do?

Rather than existing in a static, steady state, this argument represents a field that evolves in its makeup and power balances among broad groups of social actors, each of which possesses particular vested interests. With the establishment of a particular field configuration, institutional norms and rules become set. Isomorphism sets in. But with the advent of a precipitating event, the field shifts, and the corresponding institutional structures are reset to reflect the political interests of the newly formed field. This new set of institutional members becomes both motivator and marker of the precipitation of a new set of modified institutional arrangements.[58] In effect, the field and its dominant institutions move through stages of stability, punctuated by sudden and dramatic shifts in the institutional environment.[59] I label this phenomenon *dynamic isomorphism*.

8

ENVIRONMENTALISM, SUSTAINABLE DEVELOPMENT, AND INSTITUTIONS

A Prognosis

THE INSTITUTIONAL HISTORY of corporate environmentalism reveals not only a set of mechanisms for explaining organizational change but also a trajectory for how that change has progressed. This trajectory can be projected into the future to provide insights into where we are headed and what that means for the corporate enterprise. Such prophesying always has its risks, resting the credibility of the model on the accuracy of its predictions. And as the history in the preceding chapters shows quite clearly, history is prone to sudden and unpredictable turns of events. What I want to present in this chapter, then, is not a precise template for the future but rather the trajectory of possible outcomes revealed by the lens of institutional theory, based on the course now set. In particular, I want to consider two separate aspects of the future of corporate environmentalism. First, what does this institutional history reveal for the individual constituents in the field? And second, what does it tell of the future of corporate environmentalism? The first question focuses on individual strategy within the institutional context as it is now unfolding. The second question addresses a broader topic—how that institutional context fits into the wider historical scheme and what future forms it may take.

THE INSTITUTIONAL FUTURE FOR INSTITUTIONAL CONSTITUENTS

First, an overriding message for all constituents to take from this book is that there is no such thing as "a green company." While many professionals, academics, policy analysts, and activists struggle to pinpoint a concise definition of a green company, such a goal will remain forever elusive. As long as interpretations of human impacts on the ecosystem continually evolve, conceptions of corporate environmental management will remain in flux. Regardless of any alleged certainty in scientific data, it is the social and institutional interpretation of what those data mean that will drive continued environmental change. Under such circumstances, the best one can do is to describe how companies "are going green," not what "is green." Given this as a backdrop, let us consider how policymakers, environmental activists, and business managers will evolve within this steadily changing institutional context.

Implications for the Policymaker

What is the role of policy in an era where corporations are seeking greater regulatory flexibility to pursue internal measures of environmental performance? First, this emerging industry posture is not a signal for dismantling the regulatory structure already in place, as some within industry are suggesting. The fact that cognitive institutions are being triggered and can be triggered further does not lead to the conclusion that regulative or normative institutions are no longer necessary. The three levels of institutions form the whole of the institutional environment. Each supports the other, and each is a critical component of the entire system. To tamper with one component would result in an alteration of the system as a whole. Regulative and normative institutions form what might be considered a baseline on which cognitive institutions can crystallize and form. To remove or reduce this supporting baseline would destroy the cultural foundations on which cognitive institutions develop. Future regulation instead should focus on establishing new forms of institutional pressure, without upsetting the balance of the institutional fabric.

In contemporary corporate environmental management, the problem is that cognitive institutions have evolved but regulative institutions have not. Regulations have institutionalized a system of thought and behavior based on the framework of the 1970s, which is segmented by media, channeled by command-and-control structures, and based on adversarial relations. Much of this institutional format is now inconsistent with the cognitive institutions being formed and is therefore becoming obsolete, limiting rather than stimulating organizational innovation and organizational change. But rather than breaking down the current regulatory structures, efforts must focus on bringing the regulative and cognitive institutions back in line.

In an attempt to accomplish this task, the current discourse on environmental policy, particularly within economic circles, is focused on dismantling the current command-and-control structure of regulation in favor of market incentives that push firms to further their own economic interests through protecting the environment. These may include deposit-refund systems, effluent taxes, or tradable permit schemes. In effect, these constitute an attempt by the EPA to link environmental protection to the strategic interests of the firm, thereby removing environmental concerns from the regulative and normative levels and installing them at the profit-seeking, cognitive level of the firm.

But this approach does not give proper attention to the institutional dynamics of organizational action. It continues to treat the state as the sole adjudicator of organizational legitimacy.[1] It overlooks that the state is but one player—albeit a more powerful one—in the complex institutional fabric. The present form of corporate environmental management is the product of the influence of a variety of institutional actors, each triggering its own form of organizational response. Direct government regulation stimulates one type of organizational innovation and as such is limited in its scope of influence. To initiate new forms of organizational innovation, new triggers from the organizational field must be stimulated. As we have seen, regulatory pressures from 1970 to 1982 yielded compliance-based responses. But following 1988, environmental pressures from investors or insurance companies, rather than the government, stimulated organizational responses closer to the core of the organization.

As long as market incentives originate from government, one-dimensional organizational responses will result. Whether it is market incentives or strict technology standards, regulatory scripts will be enacted within the organization. This has been born out in the recent trading of marketable sulfur dioxide permits under the Clean Air Act amendments of 1990.[2] Economic models predict that utilities with a greater potential to reduce emissions will do so, collect the permits for their overcompliance, and sell them to other utilities to make additional profits. However, what companies are doing instead is overcomplying with the regulations and stockpiling the permits in anticipation of using them later to keep their aging plants open when standards become more stringent. The market price for a ton of sulfur dioxide has fallen steadily from $250 in 1992 to $140 in 1995 to a mere $68 in 1996.[3] Rather than devising new organizational routines for dealing with this innovative regulatory format, firms retrace standard routines historically enacted for responding to regulation.

Using the institutional framework to regulatory advantage, policy should focus on the secondary effects of regulatory programs.[4] It should design regulation to facilitate the increasing development of institutional structures from fields other than those associated directly with environmental regulation. This can both trigger new types of organizational responses and eliminate competing institutional pressures from other organizational fields. This has worked in the past, with powerful results.

For example, the Toxics Release Inventory of 1986 mandated that companies publish environmental release data for public dissemination. This information empowered communities and environmental activists to apply new forms of pressure for increased environmental controls, based on actual documentation of environmental discharges. Both industry and communities became more aware of the volume of pollution being emitted and, by inference, more aware of the responsibility of corporations to reduce it. Thomas Lefferre, operations vice president for Monsanto, wrote in 1990, "All of us are caught up in the myth of compliance.... If for example, you file a Title III report that says your plant emits 80,000 pounds of suspected carcinogens to the air each year, *you* might be comforted by the fact that you're in compliance with your permit. But what if your plant is two blocks from an elementary school? How comfortable would you be then?"[5]

Regulatory efforts should strive to do more of the same. Policies should begin to move away from a focus on direct, marginal, and incremental mechanisms for bringing about individual corporate change. Instead, they should start to focus on changing the organizational field to stimulate both direct and indirect pressures for industrywide change. Specifically, policy must attempt to change the organizational fields of other core business networks, such as financial markets, international regimes, and consumer demands. The involvement of these external interests facilitates an alteration of the entire social system and goes to the source of organizational action.

Implications for the Environmental Activist

Given this emerging backdrop, where is the future of environmental activism headed? Some suggest it will suffer a decline. Mark Dowie writes that the environmental movement is "courting irrelevance," dominated by national organizations who are more concerned with fund-raising and cooperative relationships with government and industry than with listen-ing to vast constituencies or staunchly supporting key environmental issues.[6] Supporting this prognosis, the membership and funding of the major environmental groups declined for the first time in 1992, with a concurrent drop in public opinion toward environmental issues. It is time for environmental activists to rethink their goals and their methods for achieving them.

Specifically, what role does the environmental activist have in a world where corporations are searching for environmental answers in response to institutional pressures more central to their organizational networks (such as insurance companies, investors, and competitors)? There emerge two primary roles. The first is that of the *consultant*. The second is that of the *militant*. The first requires a close relationship with industry and gov-ernment. The second requires isolation from the isomorphic forces of mainstream thought, leaving the activist on the periphery where the sources of change and innovation generally originate.[7] As it has become clear, no single agent can assume both roles. But as may also be clear, both roles are needed for the future development of the environmental agenda. The consultant deals with promoting institutional change in the present. The militant sets an agenda and drafts a road map for institutional change in the future.

The consultant has a direct route to influencing change within the corporation, thereby creating institutional pressure for innovations to become institutionalized in the broader field. For example, while CERES has been unable to gain widespread formal adoption of its Valdez Principles, it has been highly successful in changing the norms of business practice by utilizing the institutional routes into the corporation of the annual board meeting and the stockholder proxy. Today, the innovations introduced by CERES (which include environmentalists on executive boards, board-level EH&S committees, and the distribution of public disclosure reports) have taken root throughout the increasingly complex system that drives corporate environmental change. Like the ripple of a stone dropped in a still pool of water, those now joining CERES in pres-suring for further acceptance of these changes are growing: the World Business Council for Sustainable Development (WBCSD), Japan's Keidanren, Europe's growing array of green business networks (for exam-ple, BAUM, Business in the Environment), the United Nations Environ-ment Programme, the Global Environmental Management Initiative, the Global Tomorrow Coalition, and, most notable, the ISO14000 standards.

By actively targeting large companies or industry leaders for coopera-tive work, the activist working as a consultant can effect widespread change by channeling the power of institutional change. Toward this end, several environmental groups have begun to develop joint alliances with corporations to mutually develop solutions to environmental problems. The Environmental Defense Fund (EDF) was the first to enter such a joint alliance, forming a joint comprehensive waste reduction task force with the McDonald's Corporation. Expanding on its success, EDF (in conjunc-tion with the Pew Charitable Trusts) has embarked on a new project called the Alliance for Environmental Innovation, which works with indi-vidual companies to find optimal solutions to environmental problems. To maximize its institutional impact, the Alliance works only with market leaders and companies toward the end of the value chain. Such companies have the power to initiate the formation of institutional norms that other firms must follow. Although acting as a consultant in the technical sense, the Alliance does not accept payment for its services. This sets the group apart from other types of consultants, allowing the group to resist co-optation and remain true to its baseline goals of environmental protection rather than turning to the goal of profit maximization.

Corporations need not be the only target for environmental consultancy. Activist consultants can also form alliances with or disseminate informa-tion to nontraditional partners (such as the health care industry, finance institutions, or the general public), thereby triggering institutional change through new organizational fields. In this way, the consultant can reduce field inconsistency and create a more uniform institutional environment for the firm. One area of particular note is the field of accounting. Accounting is the language of business and as yet remains somewhat disconnected from the corporate changes imposed by environmentalism. The World Resources Institute, for one, is trying to bridge this gap with its Total Cost Accounting Project. The goals of the project are to assess better internal data collection and analysis practices for identifying environmental costs.

In acting as consultants, however, activists risk tacit co-optation. Through steady interaction with business concerns, they can begin to align more with those they are trying to influence than with the cause to which they were originally attached. In 1962, Robert Michels called this phenomenon the "iron law of oligarchy," where the leaders of a social movement gradually become detached from the masses and cause that they originally represented.[8] As activists become integrated into the orga-nizational field and their gradual acceptance by industry and government as cooperative working partners allows them a stronger voice in influenc-ing institutional change, the concurrent convergence in structure and strategy they experience will likely cause a loss of relative identity. That identity lies in their differences with these industries, and any convergence in tactics will result in pressure toward convergence in purpose. A likely consequence is that they will be viewed by external supporters as co-opted, thus obscuring their purpose and decreasing membership and contributions (as is presently happening).

The activist's militant role can help to avoid this fate while also charting new directions in corporate environmental management. The militant remains outside the influence of the organizational field, searching for answers away from the taken-for-granted beliefs, myths, prejudices, and clichés that restrict mainstream thought. Several environmental groups have chosen this route (such as EarthFirst!), preferring to follow ideals that are rigidly structured within an internal set of norms and beliefs. However, as EarthFirst! illustrates, the militant risks offending those they are trying to change, thereby damaging their legitimacy. Without acceptance, the activist risks being marginalized and thus faces collapse.[9]

Not all periphery thinking need be extreme in nature. Other environmental groups can credibly study difficult environmental issues away from institutional influences. One area that may need more input from the periphery rather than the mainstream is that of *sustainable development*. At present, the term is extremely vague. As it begins to develop, environmentalists may wish that it does so away from the isomorphic pressures of the organizational field, in much the same way that the present environmental movement grew in relative isolation during the 1960s. The new ideology of sustainable development could germinate within a new group of institutional stakeholders that lies in the periphery, away from the distractions of the organizational field. From there it can generate the necessary critical mass and strength of convictions to create the tension necessary to foster institutional change. If it emerges too early, however, it may become susceptible to co-optation and control by political influences.

Implications for the Corporate Manager

For the corporate manager, the present state of environmental management includes an expanding field of constituents and a bewildering array of new conceptions—"pollution prevention," "total quality environmental management," "industrial ecology," "life cycle analysis," "sustainable development," and "environmental justice," to name just a few. Things that were unthinkable only ten years ago have now become standard business practice today. But this increasing institutional complexity has translated into organizational uncertainty. The institutional framework offers a model for understanding the uncertainty firms now face. While corporate environmentalism has increased in institutional complexity, it has done so through the expansion of the organizational field.

The shape of the field helps determine the appropriate organizational response. In the 1970s, regulatory environmentalism necessitated a segmented corporate response. An autonomous and isolated EH&S department was organizationally efficient. In the 1980s, with corporate environmentalism redefined as social responsibility, this segmented structure could be perpetuated. However, with strategic environmentalism in the 1990s, firms must adopt a more integrated structure for responding to the myriad external institutional pressures they face. Just as the environmental management practices of the 1970s were a reflection of their cultural context, so too are the environmental management practices of today. And just as managers cannot judge the practices of the 1970s by the standards of today, they likewise cannot decide corporate strategy today based on the institutional standards of thirty, ten, or even five years ago. Contemporary corporate decision makers who remain fixed on trends or shifts in public opinion or political agendas will find such measures an inaccurate reflection of the future form of environmental practice. The institutional model provides a framework that is more complex, constituting the interests of a vast array of constituents through channels that are more implicit and complex than simple regulation or costs.

This new set of institutional constituents have redefined the environmental issue into terms that reflect their own interests, terms with which the organization is already familiar. In effect, environmentalism is becoming less and less an environmental issue. As insurance companies apply environmental pressure on firms, environmental management ceases to be an environmental issue per se and becomes instead a risk-management issue. As competitors apply environmental pressure, it becomes an issue of competitive strategy. With investors, it becomes an issue of shareholder value. The firm's business channels are being altered to bring environmentalism to organizational attention through avenues related to marketing, accounting, finance, and so on.

It becomes evident that the business manager need not believe in the validity of environmental issues to take them seriously as a business concern. What matters is that key business constituents possess that concern and are translating it through core business channels. As shown in Figure 8.1, environmental management is really a composite of core organizational functions. In each case, the firm already has a structure and language with which to conceptualize the issue and formulate a response. By realizing this "fit," firms can begin to see environmental issues as something internally manageable rather than externally directed.

Figure 8.1. The Institutional Reframing of Corporate Environmentalism.

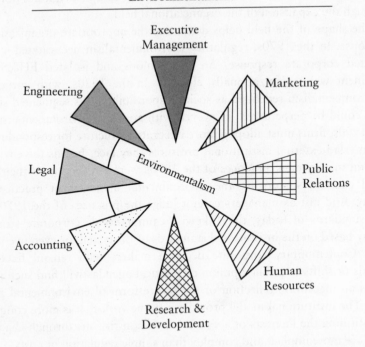

IMPLICATIONS FOR THE EH&S DEPARTMENT As firms seek to accommodate the environmental interests of the expanding institutional environment, they will be forced to push environmental responsibilities to the functional levels best equipped to handle them. As the issue of the environment gets larger, so too will its individual components. Looking back at Figure 8.1, while the environmental circle gets larger, so do the functional slices. And as a percentage, the environmental proportion (falling to the EH&S department) will diminish. Environmentalism will diffuse throughout the organization, affecting nearly every facet of its structure. As this diffusion process continues, there will be less need for an exclusive corporate environmental affairs department and more reliance on an environmental management structure that integrates the skills of all operating and support departments.

This can be observed already in the historical progression of the environmental organization. The evolution from end-of-the-pipe treatment in the 1970s to waste minimization in the 1980s to pollution prevention in the 1990s involved a progressive shift in the departmental knowledge base away from the environmental departments and toward engineering and management departments. This can be seen as the inevitable result of the

EH&S department's origin, purpose, and function. It is, in effect, the natural outcome of the maturation of corporate environmentalism.

The role of the corporate environmental management function is a transitional one, facilitating the evolution from the disconnected environmental ignorance of the mid 1960s to the integrated environmental awareness of the coming century. In effect, environmental managers have been destined to eventually work themselves out of a job. Although EH&S's role will not disappear as long as environmental regulations continue to be written, the prominence of its role and the relevance of its function to corporate practice will continue to diminish. The more important environmental work will fall to the broadly diffused management staff in the pursuit of internally defined environmental goals.

Taken to its extreme outcome, environmentalism should ultimately disappear into the cultural foundations of the corporation, just as the drive for greater profits or quality has. It will be implicit in the organizational structure and individual roles of each of the firm's members. No profitable company must overtly remind its employees that the corporate objective is to make a profit. Likewise, a company that has achieved a reputation for first-class quality need not overtly advise its employees to perform their duties with quality in mind. These concerns become ingrained into the everyday practices of the firm; they disappear from the conscious and become part of the unconscious.

IMPLICATIONS FOR CAREER DEVELOPMENT Given this trajectory, those seeking a career in environmental management will need to craft a careful marketing strategy. Firms will begin to look less for environmental specialists and more for environmental generalists; they will look not for people who know only environmental affairs but for people who can articulate environmental issues in the language of finance, accounting, and marketing. The converse will also ring true. Those seeking a career in other areas of business management will find that knowledge of environmental management has become a necessary prerequisite, an attribute integral to the conceptual framework of their decision-making process.

In fact, many firms today are adding environmental performance to the list of performance measures considered at promotion and bonus time. And many executives are finding that tenure in environmental management is an important step in their promotion path and a necessary step toward understanding the full range of issues facing the corporation. Similarly, many business schools today include environmental considerations in their degree programs, either through specific course offerings or by "infusing" environmental topics into standard course requirements.[10]

In this way, students are taught environmental management not simply as an adjunct to their management studies but as an integral component of accounting, finance, marketing, strategy, process design, and product development courses. Just look in any newspaper today. The environment is no longer the strict venue of the environmental writer, delegated to the science or government policy pages. It is now found in the business, marketplace, and investment pages, with stories written by the business, international affairs, and economics correspondents.

IMPLICATIONS FOR CORPORATE ENVIRONMENTAL STRATEGY The crux of the implications for the corporate manager is that the firm is approaching a new threshold. In trying to develop the most efficient and effective response to environmental demands, it will push environmental responsibilities up to the executive level, down to the operating line, and across functional lines. For both cultural and institutional reasons, this will prove a difficult challenge. Firms must break down the organizational structures and beliefs that have been built up over the past three decades and set new norms and values to replace them. This organizational change cannot be performed in a vacuum, however. It must include a consideration for managing its institutional environment. In the first place, the firm must break down or shield the organization from the institutional forces that sustain organizational inertia. Second, the firm must attempt to influence the development of institutional norms in a direction that supports internal organizational efforts. In short, a two-pronged focus will be critical, one that considers change in both the internal and the external context. Looking at the closing chapter of Amoco's organizational evolution reveals how one company is groping with this challenge.

By 1993, EH&S at Amoco found its internal status raised, not only through the promotion of its departmental manager to an upper-level position but also through the passage of upwardly mobile managers through the department on their way up the corporate ladder. Two upper-level refinery managers recently moved into the EH&S department; one continued on to become general manager of crude oil operations for the pipeline company. His stint in EH&S proved an asset in his career progression. One executive believes that this kind of career development is inevitable for two reasons: environmental insights are becoming increasingly important at the upper levels, and, "You merely have to do a statistical test. In the past there simply weren't many environmental jobs for people to move through. Now that the department has grown, people start to float in. It's kind of a chicken and egg thing."

This is also seen as a way to integrate operating perspectives into EH&S and, when transfers occur in the opposite direction, to help integrate environmental concerns into operations. This move, however, remains a tough sell in many parts of the company. One chemical plant manager explains, "I think that today, it's very beneficial, particularly at a young age, to get EH&S background and then rotate back into the line. We are always trying to get people to do that. Some line people are reluctant, however, because they think EH&S is a dead end. We're trying to change that."

In managing external relations, the company has gone far beyond acknowledging stakeholder interests. It is attempting to gain competitive advantage through its outreach programs. First, in 1992 an internal competitor analysis program focusing on environmental performance was initiated. Interestingly, this new program focused not only on oil companies (such as ARCO, Chevron, Mobil, Occidental, Shell, BP, Exxon, Sun, Texaco, and Unocal) and chemical companies (such as Dow, DuPont, Eastman-Kodak, Goodrich, Monsanto, Quantum, and Rohm & Haas) but also on nontraditional competitors (such as AT&T and General Electric).

But for Amoco as well as other companies, environmental benchmarking is far from perfected as a management tool (one executive describes it as "driving by the rearview mirror"). As one analyst explains:

> The problem with environmental benchmarking is that it is difficult to normalize these factors to a dollar figure. What management wants is for us to try to measure the dollar impact being avoided by expending EH&S costs. Ideally, what we would like is to be able to do a cost-benefit curve and see the intersection where costs equal benefits and stop there. But the environment can't be thought of that way. There aren't direct economic trade-offs. The nature of the business is that you could have a disaster at any minute, and the costs will shoot through the roof. We've been trying to figure out what is the proper stance to take with respect to the environment. We believe that if you are successful, you stay in business. If you stay in business long enough, you will have an accident. So, given that it will occur, what kind of a reputation do you want to have when it does? Do you want to be on CNN touting your greenness the night before your tanker crashes? I think we've already decided that the answer to that is no.

Clearly the disaster aspect of environmental management complicates its analysis. In describing who he thinks is today's industry environmental leader, a senior environmental manager cites environmental accidents as a clear factor: "Dow Chemical is far and away the environmental leader. They had to survive the damage of the napalm and agent orange experiences. They learned to do certain things well and set the standard. They set the pace by which others have to move. No one wants to be the laggard. If you are first, you've learned and established yourself. It will cost followers more to meet your standard, and when they get there, you've moved ahead. They control their own destiny. You don't want the public to see you as a laggard."

It is not merely through measuring its performance with competitors that Amoco intends to gain strategic advantage. Programs are being developed that the company hopes will allow it to be the one to "set the standard." For example, in 1993 the company was instrumental in launching the Public Environmental Reporting Initiative (PERI) as an alternative to signing the CERES Valdez Principles.[11] According to a July 13, 1993, management presentation, "public environmental reports are important vehicles for increasing the public's perception of a company's social responsibility. Investor fund managers specializing in responsible or 'green' companies are similarly influenced by open reporting. A leader in this arena can not only reap the benefits arising from a satisfied public and 'green' investors but can also put considerable pressure to catch up on the competition." Ten major corporations have joined the initiative, which will soon be expanded to Europe. And since the formation of PERI, the number of companies preparing public environmental disclosure reports has risen dramatically.[12]

But the most dramatic effort of this type was a partnership with the EPA to study pollution reduction possibilities at the company's Yorktown refinery in 1990. To add credibility to the effort, the environmental research group, Resources for the Future, was commissioned for external peer review. The idea that an oil company would allow both a regulating agency and an environmental group access to one of its major refineries was a bold step. Many inside the firm (and inside the industry) speculated that this would expose Amoco to increased enforcement and activist scrutiny. Amoco executives feel vindicated by the results, however.

At a cost of $2.3 million (of which Amoco paid 70 percent and the EPA paid 30 percent), Amoco discovered that greater regulatory flexibility would allow them opportunities for greater emissions reduction while at the same time reducing costs. Specifically, they could achieve the same level of emissions reductions as the Clean Air Act required but at one-quarter of the cost ($10 million versus $40 million), if they were allowed to choose where the money should be spent. This could be achieved by enlisting the help of process engineering in finding more creative solutions to environmental goals. The EH&S vice president believes that, rather than responding to EPA-dictated technology and performance standards, "if you give this company a mark on the wall and tell them to go for it, I have no doubt as to their capability to achieve it." A former refinery manager agrees: "When we push for more flexible options, I'm taking a lot on faith. I have to believe that we have engineers who know our processes a lot better than some twenty-five-year-old [EPA] engineer in Cincinnati or at Research Triangle Park."

In terms of direct benefit, however, the Yorktown project appears unsuccessful on the surface. Explains a senior corporate lobbyist, "In direct terms, Yorktown was a failure. It created no benefit for the plant itself. We gained nothing economically. We still had to comply with the regulations that were coming about. Other companies were, and are, saying we were crazy for doing that project. Other plants within Amoco don't want to do this kind of project again. They just don't have the budget for doing this kind of a study. . . . But overall, we would not at all consider it a failure. The public relations benefits alone raise the integrity of Amoco, and that is quantifiable."

But the individual benefits of such a program are limited. He acknowledges a field ownership of the environmental problem which cannot be escaped: "We are still an oil company, and we still have to live with the sins of our brothers. We were doing fine until Exxon spilled all that oil. Then we were painted with the same brush as them. Now we have OPA–90. In this business, your environmental integrity is based on your lack of problems with the other members of your industry." He stresses that with the Yorktown effort, "Now it's time to bring in other players. We had to prove to other stakeholders that this was worth fighting, but we don't have the clout to stop something in Washington. Anything we did alone could be stopped by Exxon or a group of other companies."

Toward that end, in 1992 the Yorktown project evolved into the Environmental Innovations Program (EIP), a direct advocacy program focused on gaining greater acceptance of more flexible regulatory mechanisms by gaining both industry and government support. However, creating internal change can be just as difficult a challenge as changing the opinions of industry and government. States the founder of the EIP program, "Finding out what everyone wants is very difficult. What essentially it boils down to is that we've spent twenty-five years perfecting the command-and-control response. It's hard to get people to switch from what they know best." In effect, what the company is attempting to do is to unlearn the institutional and cultural rules, norms, and beliefs that have become established over the past three decades of the modern environmental movement. To do so, it must effect change both internally and externally. The environmental strategy of institutional change requires both.

THE INSTITUTIONAL FUTURE OF CORPORATE ENVIRONMENTALISM

The implications thus far focus on environmental management as it is presently conceptualized. But this conceptualization may not remain the dominant one for long. New forms of environmental problems are emerging, accompanied by calls for new forms of corporate action. Moving beyond the future strategies of institutional constituents, it is time to consider the future trajectory of corporate environmentalism in general. How did it get to where it is today, and what does that tell us about where it is going?

In 1972, another researcher chanced a similar analysis. In a well-cited article, Anthony Downs utilized the "issue-attention" cycle to predict that the intensity of public environmental interest was about to inexorably decline.[13] His model described "a systematic cycle of heightened public interest and then increasing boredom with major issues,"[14] which moved through five stages:

1. The issue receives initial concerned attention.

2. The issue enjoys growing widespread enthusiasm.

3. The true costs of significant progress become apparent.

4. In response, public interest declines.

5. The issue is replaced by another issue in the public eye.

Obviously, history has proven Downs's prognosis wrong. But the more important question is, why? The answer lies in the institutional evolution of environmentalism. Through the introduction of new constituents and new institutional conceptions, environmentalism has been continually redefined. What he called "ecology" in 1972 has evolved successively into environmental management, waste minimization, and pollution prevention. These evolving conceptions of corporate environmentalism are the product of new perspectives on environmental problems and an expanding institutional constituency that defines both how to view these problems and what the appropriate solutions should be.

The institutional model tells a story of political negotiation over the form and function of new corporate behavior. The concept of corporate environmental management has evolved and continues to evolve through the influence of the multilevel institutional structure. The presence of all three levels—regulative, normative, and cognitive institutions—creates a permanent and encompassing connection between the firm and its field. With this connection in place, corporate environmental innovations will proliferate at a more rapid rate. But there is a problem here. With the three levels of the institutional structure established and in place, is future change only to be incremental? This model could suggest that corporate environmental management has reached its final generalized functional and strategic state. Are we witnessing the twilight of the history of corporate environmentalism?

This would be true only if environmental problems were static in their form *and* their interpretation. Such is not the case, however. On the horizon lies yet another conceptualization of environmental problems that will require new forms of corporate action in response. Historian Paul Kennedy, in his book *Preparing for the Twenty-First Century,* identifies "the dangers to our natural environment" as one of six general trends important for the coming century.[15] He states, however, that "the environmental crisis we confront is quantitatively and qualitatively different from anything before, simply because so many people have been inflicting damage on the world's ecosystem during the past century that the system as a whole—not simply its various parts—may be in danger."[16] In particular, he calls attention to the depletion of cropland topsoil, tropical rain forests, animal and plant species, and potable water supplies, as well as the increasing problems caused by global warming. Others are echoing his observations.[17] In short, a redefinition of environmental problems is under way, repositioning them in global terms and focusing on the protection and availability of the earth's resource base. In 1987, the UN report of the World Commission on Environment and Development (the Bruntland Report) termed the solution to these growing concerns as "sustainable development" and, more specifically, "meeting the needs of the present without diminishing the need of the future."[18]

Yet the future form of this newly emerging term is extremely uncertain. How will it be defined? How will it fit into the progression of corporate environmental history? What role will corporations be expected to fill in responding to it? The answer to each of these questions lies in the form and ideology of the field defining it and is both institutional and political in nature. What are the institutional aspects of its birth and growth? Is it emerging out of the organizational field dealing with environmental management, or is it emerging from a new field of actors? Does it represent a continuation of the institutional rules, norms, and values around which environmental management has been developed, or does it represent a significant departure in institutional thought? The fundamental question is whether the shift in institutional structures from environmental management to sustainable development represents a shift that is revolutionary or evolutionary. If evolutionary, the idea will emerge out of the institutional structures as presently arranged. If revolutionary, completely new structures will determine how the idea is defined and enacted. The answer can be found in the characteristics of the field defining it.

Presently, that central field of actors defining sustainable development has been heavily weighted toward industry. Corporations have seized on sustainability as an issue they can handle themselves, much like the industrial environmentalism of the 1960s. Corporations are developing task forces, establishing vice presidential positions, and joining government studies (such as the President's Council on Sustainable Development) to address the agenda and business implications of sustainability. Corporate executives are also going to the public and making proclamations about their perspective on sustainable development. Edgar Woolard, chairman of DuPont, writes, "Industry, as society's producer has a special role to play in creating sustainable development, and some of us in the industrial community are working on ways to make sustainability a characteristic of industrial programs."[19] Frank Popoff, CEO of Dow Chemical Company, writes, "If we view sustainable development as an opportunity for growth and not as prohibitive, industry can shape a new social and ethical framework for assessing our relationship with our environment and each other."[20] And the Monsanto Corporation has now adopted as its corporate strategy "Sustainable Development for the World's Future."

By taking an aggressive role in defining sustainable development, corporations are treating the issue as evolutionary in nature, emerging out of the institutions surrounding environmental management as they presently conceive of them. In much the same way that corporations defined industrial environmentalism in the 1960s based on their own cognitive structures, they are now defining *industrial sustainability* in the 1990s based on an equally insular field.

But the field that is responsible for such future definitions is not so singular. Dominant institutional conceptions are subject to the interpretation of the entire organizational field, as well as emerging constituents outside of it. In fact, contrarian views to the industry-conceived definitions of sustainability are developing within new institutional constituents, which include international environmental organizations and governing bodies and a newly vocal and notably absent constituent in the environmental management field—academia.[21] These actors argue that sustainable development is a revolutionary change, representing a significant departure from the institutional arrangements presently constructed. The evolutionary concept of sustainability as defined by industry, they argue, allows governments and industry to "embrace environmentalism without commitment."[22] Industrial sustainability is being treated as a tool or mechanism, they contend, merely a set of actions, a selective set of strategies driven by the existing institutional norms of corporate practice.[23]

Instead, they argue that sustainable development represents a new institutional framework that challenges not only existing institutions on environmental management but also underlying assumptions of the market economy. In challenging both, sustainable development calls into question the social and physical autonomy of the firm, the profit motive as a singular objective, the prominence of technology in solving environmental problems, and the necessary imperative of economic growth.[24]

To some, this extensive a challenge points to the need for a complete breakdown and restructuring of existing social structures to bring about a new institutional framework, or what Thomas Kuhn referred to as a "paradigm shift."[25] But a change as dramatic as the paradigm shift would be historically inconsistent. A more credible and evolutionary explanation can be found in the institutional framework.

In studying the evolution of scientific thought, what Kuhn refers to as a paradigm is similar to what this book refers to as an institutional or social structure—the organizational field and its dominant frameworks of rules, norms, and beliefs by which reality is understood. In depicting paradigmatic change, Kuhn describes the progression of science as being a series of transitions from *normal* science to *revolutionary* science. A phase of normal science begins when a new theory emerges, becomes dominant, and becomes the "paradigm." It is the role of normal science to undertake the "mopping up," as Kuhn calls it, of the existing facts to match the new theory. Paradigmatic theories are overturned when anomalies emerge, and revolutionary science commences as scientists try to discover more about this anomaly. This paradigmatic shift is marked by scientific uncertainty and ends when another scientific theory becomes dominant and then becomes the new paradigm. So one might argue that as population, natural resource, and environmental problems expose anomalies in the dominant logic of corporate environmental management, institutional uncertainty will result, only to be resolved when a new social structure emerges and becomes dominant.

But in explaining social change, the paradigm shift is overly simplistic. Old institutions do not simply collapse and disappear; they become the building blocks of future institutions. Just as existing institutions are the products of their historical past, future institutions will be built on the remnants of those existing today. Social organization, as a result, is perpetually the product of history. The institutional framework provides greater depth to Kuhn's explanation by allowing political dynamics to guide the evolution process. The richness of the regulative, normative, and cognitive construction of reality is that it helps explain the realities of social paradigms in a more precise fashion. All three levels exist and are changing at the same time. When one predominates or when they all align, a stable paradigm can emerge. But when they are not in alignment or when no one level predominates, there is confusion, tension, and paradigmatic uncertainty. In resolving this uncertainty, individual actors can impose their own interests and try to direct institutional or paradigmatic processes in a direction that serves their interests.

Looking over time, we can see the shifting paradigms of institutional evolution. In the early part of the century, for example, overuse of the country's natural resources led to the emergence of the "conservation" movement. Under the administration of President Theodore Roosevelt and through the efforts of naturalist John Muir and forester Gifford Pinchot, this era saw the creation of great federal agencies for managing public parks, forests, soils, water, and wildlife.[26] This paradigm of environmentalism was relatively stable until a new awareness of environmental problems led to the initiation of the history told in this book. The conservation movement did not disappear but rather was subsumed within the ecology movement, which was later subsumed within the environmental movement. And in turn, the environmental movement will likely be subsumed within the sustainable development movement. History continually builds on itself, creating new structures to explain newly emerging anomalies in our conceptions of reality.

Modern corporate environmentalism, thus far, has focused on the environmental implications of the waste outputs from corporate activities. Sustainable development incorporates new concerns over environmental degradation and takes the concept of environmental management one step further. It focuses not just on waste outputs but also on process inputs and product development. It considers not only the damages that the byproducts of industrial activity inflict on the environment but also the damages that all human activity inflicts on the resource base that both present and future generations will rely on. As such, the overall shift will be revolutionary in scope but will emerge in an evolutionary fashion out of the building blocks of the institutional structures as they presently exist. The dynamics by which this transformation will take place have been illustrated in this history of corporate environmentalism.

Opposing conceptions of sustainability are developing in distinct spheres of influence. Industry views are central to the organizational field, and therefore they presently dominate the emerging conceptualization. Alternative views are developing outside the mainstream organizational field, however, and given this separation, they will form in isolation from the isomorphic forces of the industry field. Eventually what will result will be an institutional "war" to relieve the mounting tension created by oppositional conceptions of sustainable corporate development. If industry wins this war, the shift from environmental management to sustainable development will involve an evolutionary shift built on the institutional structures that are presently constructed. If oppositional views prevail, the shift will be revolutionary in nature. The field will be restructured, and new forms of institutional structures will precipitate. New regulative and coercive institutions will be laid on the existing institutional framework.

What will determine when this war will take place and who will win it will be the interjection of external events. The sustainable development equivalent of Love Canal or Earth Day can legitimate the political positions of individual constituents in the field, creating institutional power to force opposing institutional constituents into a common realm of contestation. The kind of outcome is largely dependent on the type of event that starts the process. Three possibilities present themselves.

First, opposing conceptions of sustainable development could be thrust into the organizational field by the force of an unpredictable event, one that highlights the inconsistencies in the existing institutional framework, such as the Bhopal incident in 1984. In this instance, institutional constituents will have little control over the time and form of the ensuing institutional negotiation. The event will force it on them, the outcome will be extremely uncertain, and the process will be chaotic.

Second, the peripheral perspectives of sustainable development could force themselves into the dominant organizational field by a catalyzing event that empowers their developing perspective. In this scenario, peripheral institutional constituents will opportunistically capitalize on the event, having had the time to develop the credibility necessary to sustain an institutional confrontation. Thus they will possess some control over the time and form of this institutional negotiation, much like the institutional restructuring that accompanied the celebration of the first Earth Day in 1970. The outcome in this case will be more predictable and the process more organized, reflecting the interests of the individual constituents.

There is, of course, the third possibility, that a lack of external events will leave alternative views of sustainable development unsupported, a critical mass of thought and institutional power will not be reached, and the movement will subside. It will fail to reach maturity and will not achieve permanence within the institutional structures. However, in all likelihood, as long as the political and environmental signals for sustainable development continue, support for institutional change will be maintained, either by empowering new institutional constituents or by strengthening existing ones.

In sum, the historical outcome will depend in large part on uncertain external events and the institutional interpretation of them. For alternative conceptions of sustainable development to become institutionalized, events must cause the existing organizational field to accept the entrance of new institutional constituents or to alter the power relationships among existing constituents. This will allow the introduction of a new set of institutional rules, norms, and beliefs that include concerns for sustainable development. A stable new institutional paradigm will not be achieved until this happens. These new institutional arrangements will either take the form of an evolutionary alteration of the cognitive institutions through negotiated compromise, or they will take the form of a revolutionary alteration of the regulative and normative institutions through confrontation. This latter option will force one member of the field (industry) to accommodate the interests of other members of the field. By its present actions, this is clearly an outcome that industry is trying to preempt, by taking an aggressive position early.

CONCLUSION

In the end, whether it is environmental management or sustainable development, the final legitimate form of corporate environmental behavior cannot be considered in an isolated context, conducted in a vacuum, or developed on an autonomous basis. All organizational action is mediated by the history, culture, and context of the institutional environment. Moving from conservation to ecology, environmental management, and finally sustainable development, this book has presented an institutional framework for understanding corporate environmentalism in the chemical and petroleum industries. Extending this framework to other industries is an exercise left to the reader. However, finding institutional connections and parallels between this and other histories should not prove a difficult task. The institutional demands of insurance, investors, and government transcend industrial boundaries. It is only the extent of this transcendence, as it is sustained or blocked by industry-specific events, that varies.

But regardless of the peculiarities of each industry's development, the institutional model remains a valuable tool for understanding the external influences on the behavior of firms. Firms have been pushed and pulled along by the institutions of their organizational field and have developed internal structures to reflect its demands. In its most recent manifestation, corporate environmentalism has begun to reach the strategic level of a cognitive institution. To profess, as many do, that this means that industry is finally seeing the light is to argue that the light has always been there to see. In fact, it has not. How companies define their responsibility toward the environment is a direct reflection of how society views the environmental issue and thus of how the organizational field defines the role of business in responding to it. Evolving perspectives of what constitutes heresy and what constitutes dogma in a given industry depend not just on costs and regulation but on the full social, political, and economic system of which the industry is a part.

APPENDIX A: DATA SOURCES

CENTRAL TO THE HISTORY presented in this book are three key variables: the organizational field, dominant institutions, and organizational structure and culture. Three data sources corresponding to each variable were utilized: federal case law, industry trade journals, and an organizational case study. Although each variable was developed from a separate data source, each is cross-referenced with the others and with supporting data to provide a consistent history. The information from these sources permitted a range of analyses, from company-specific to industrywide.

This material reflects a diverse range of perspectives from which to view the evolution of corporate environmental practice, creating certain advantages in both building and testing a credible model of the phenomenon. They offer glimpses into the various levels of organizational behavior, from macro to micro. Likewise, they utilize a range of quantitative and qualitative methods, both in the collection and the presentation of the data. Such diversity allows triangulation of the resultant model from several perspectives, thereby increasing the credibility of its conclusions. Such triangulation also allows for a clearer and richer presentation of the model and its related information.

FEDERAL CASE LAW

In an attempt to characterize the relative influence and power of the constituents of the organizational field, a statistical review of all environment-related federal case law from 1960 through 1993 was conducted. From cases argued in the U.S. Supreme Court, U.S. courts of appeals, district courts, bankruptcy courts, courts of federal claims, tax courts, military courts, and related federal and territorial courts, data were collected using the Westlaw system known as FENV-CS. These data characterize the evolution of the organizational field, identifying both the emergence of new members and the shifting power relationships among them, as revealed by the volume of cases filed by and against the various institutional interests.

The environmental law database contains documents that relate to regulation of the natural environment. Included are documents on pollution control, radioactive and toxic waste management, the National Environmental Policy Act, and conservation of natural resources. (A document is a case—a decision or order—decided by one of the courts listed above.)

Key words for extracting the applicable cases fell into five categories:

1. *Environmental Groups:* The Sierra Club, the Natural Resources Defense Council, the Environmental Defense Fund, the Audubon Society, the National Wildlife Federation, Friends of the Earth, Public Interest Research Groups, the Wilderness Society, Defenders of Wildlife, Citizens for a Better Environment, the Izaak Walton League, Greenpeace, National Parks and Conservation, Environmental Action, the Environmental Policy Institute, the Nature Conservancy, the Conservation Foundation, EarthFirst!, the World Wildlife Fund, the Conservation Fund, Clean Water Action

2. *Community, Labor, and Insurance Groups:* Union, Brotherhood, Insurance

3. *Government:* The Environmental Protection Agency, William Ruckelshaus, Russell Train, Douglas Costle, Ann Burford Gorsuch, Lee Thomas, William Reilly, Carol Browner, the Council for Environmental Quality, the Department of the Interior, the Department of Agriculture, the Department of Health, Education and Welfare

4. *Chemical Industry:* The Chemical Manufacturers Association, Dow Chemical, DuPont, Union Carbide, Monsanto, W. R. Grace, Ethyl, Procter & Gamble, Pfizer, Johnson & Johnson, Unilever, Merck, Hoechst Celanese

5. *Petroleum Industry:* The American Petroleum Institute, Exxon, Mobil, Chevron, Amoco, Shell, Texaco, ARCO, Occidental, Phillips, Sun

The total number of citations collected under this search scheme was 5,588. After duplicates were eliminated, the database numbered 3,572 citations. Defendants and plaintiffs were then individually characterized as either environmentalists, government, industry, or other, with these further subclassifications:

Environmentalists: Community groups, employee groups, environmental groups, insurance companies, other

Government: City, state, DOA, DOI, EPA, other federal agency

Industry: Chemical company, petroleum company, other company, chemical trade group, petroleum trade group, other trade group

With plaintiffs and defendants so classified, case law could be sorted and analyzed according to the respective influential parties, and analyses could be conducted as to the evolution of the organizational field.

This legal data offer a balance to the trade journal data while providing greater depth on the prominent institutional members: environmentalists, community groups, employees, insurers, industry, and the government. The institutional connectedness uncovered in this analysis is more objectively based than that revealed by the trade journal analysis. In this way, a comparison between the trade journal analysis and that of the federal case law provided an opportunity for triangulation, testing the observed phenomena from two disparate sources.

TRADE JOURNAL STUDY

A historical content analysis of the trade journals *Chemical Week* and *Oil & Gas Journal* provided both quantitative and qualitative data in characterizing the evolution of the dominant institutions. Content analysis was used for making inferences by systematically and objectively identifying specified characters within the text.[1] These inferences provided information about the sender of the message, the audience of the message, or the message itself.[2] They could reveal the focus of individual, group, institutional, or societal attention to a specific issue or groups of issues.

By directing this type of analysis toward trade journals, an extemporaneous log of internal industry views was uncovered, not only on the actions undertaken but also on the motivations behind those actions. The role that trade journals play in the institutionalization process is twofold. First, they act as a common source of information, aiding in the normalization of industry perspectives. Second, they act as a historical record of the key actors, the activity undertaken, the motivations behind this activity, and the events that initiated that action.

Three characteristics were of particular importance in choosing the specific journals to be analyzed. The particular journals had to be of sufficient circulation to be considered representative of industry attitudes, of particular focus to represent distinct industry segments, and of particular direction to target business and technical management audiences. Finally, the two journals had to be comparable in size and frequency of publication, so as to allow direct comparison of the resulting data. Given that the intent of this research is to study the chemical and oil industries specifically, seven trade journals were identified as possible subjects for analysis (see Table A.1).

Although *Chemical Engineering* and *Chemical & Engineering News* enjoy the highest circulation, they were ruled out for analysis due to their focus. *Chemical Engineering* targets issues pertinent to both the chemical and petroleum industries. This would disallow a distinction between the two for comparative analysis. *Chemical & Engineering News* not only covers the chemical and petroleum industries but also targets academic and government audiences. In terms of meeting the objective criteria, *Chemical Week* and *Oil & Gas Journal* were perfectly matched. They have comparable circulations (46,440 and 42,500, respectively). They are reasonably distinct in their industry specialization. They both target business and technical management. And they are both weekly publications.

Having chosen the journals for analysis, each issue from 1960 until 1993 was then reviewed. First, articles that focused on environmental issues were identified through the table of contents. Environmental articles were defined as any article dealing with the protection or preservation of natural resources, the political and social aspects of environmental protection, the technological or management concerns related to both regulatory compliance and pollution control, or any business aspects of environmental regulation or pollution control. Issues regarding radiation and nuclear waste were excluded as a separate and distinct issue. This provided the first variable for analysis, the fundamental level of environmental concern exhibited within the industry.

Once identified, each specific article was reviewed in more depth for five attributes related to its focus: the media, the agent, the action undertaken, the type of technology described (if applicable), and the motivation

Table A.1.   Trade Journals Considered for Analysis.

Journal	Frequency	Circulation
Chemical & Engineering News	Weekly	138,574
Chemical Engineering	Monthly	70,205
Chemical Week	Weekly	46,440
Oil & Gas Journal	Weekly	42,500
Chemical Marketing Reporter	Weekly	17,000
National Petroleum News	Weekly	12,797
Oil & Gas Investor	Monthly	6,500

for its use or development (if applicable). Figure A.1 depicts the coding sequence applied. Under each attribute, listed along the top, articles were assigned to various classifications and subclassifications. For example, an article could be classified under "media/air," "agent/industry/trade association," or "action/advertising." If the action were technology, the specific type of motivation would also be characterized. In addition to articles, editorials were reviewed to deepen the understanding of the characteristics and motivations of the institutional evolution.

AMOCO CORPORATION CASE STUDY

The first two data sources provided an overview of the development of the organizational field and industrywide institutions. A case study of Amoco provides a glimpse into the evolution of organizational structure and strategy within a single corporation while providing illustrative examples of the influence of the organizational field on this firm's evolution, the influence of this corporation on the development of the organizational

Figure A.1.   Content Analysis Coding Sequence.

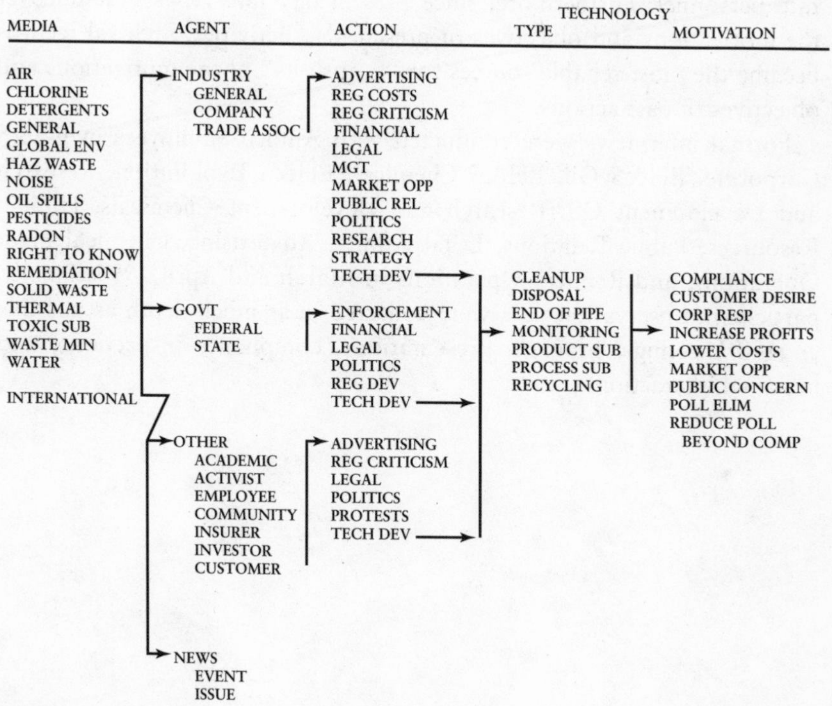

field, and the influence of external events in the evolution of both the organization and the organizational field.

This segment of the research involved a variety of sources, which can be subsumed under the headings external archival data, internal archival data, ethnographic interviews, and participation observation. The intent was to collect longitudinal data to determine how and when Amoco progressed through its environmental development. The formal research methodology was negotiated and approved by senior Amoco executives in the Environmental Affairs and Safety Management Committee in Chicago on February 3, 1994.

External archival data reviewed included computerized literature search sources, journal and newspaper articles, and all annual reports, 10–K reports, and company environmental statements from 1960 to 1993. Internal archival data reviewed included internal communication documents, committee minutes, organizational charts, company newsletters, and formal reports to outside agencies. The objectives of this literature review was to uncover the background information on corporate objectives, markets and technologies, environmental compliance records, and release and emissions history, as well as the progression of organizational change and notable environmental and corporate milestones and advances. These formed a basis for more in-depth discussions with corporate personnel. Furthermore, since present-day interviews best uncover the motivations and objectives of present-day activities, archival records became the most reliable sources for "snapshots" of the motivations and objectives of past actions.

Formal interviews were conducted with Amoco employees in EH&S Corporate, EH&S Oil, EH&S Chemical, EH&S Exploration, Research and Development Oil, Research and Development Chemicals, Human Resources, Public Relations, Legal Affairs, Advertising, Chemical Plant Operations, and Refinery Operations in March and April 1994. Finally, participant observation data were collected in as much depth as possible at staff meetings, program presentations, compliance inspections, and informal interactions.

APPENDIX B: STATISTICAL TABLES

Table B.1. Chow Test[1] for a Structural Break (Industry-Focused Articles).

Data Set	Year of Break	Chow Test	F-Value
Chemical Week	1982	6.35***	9.67***
Oil & Gas Journal	1982	20.95***	1.10

*** p " .001

Table B.2. Linear Regression Trend Analysis (Industry-Focused Articles).

Date	Slope	y-Intercept	r^2	F-Value
		Chemical Week		
1960–1982	–0.01**	19.41**	0.37	12.35**
1982–1993	0.02**	–34.00**	0.46	8.46**
		Oil & Gas Journal		
1960–1982	–0.01***	27.63***	0.55	25.23***
1982–1993	0.03***	–64.75***	0.75	29.09***

** p " .01, *** p " .001

NOTES

PREFACE (PP. XVII–XXIV)

1. Stein, J. (1979). *College Dictionary.* (New York: Random House).

2. Professor and director of the global environment program, Leonard N. Stern School of Business, New York University.

3. Gladwin, T. (1993). "The meaning of greening: A plea for organizational theory." In Fischer and Schott (Eds.), *Environmental Strategies for Industry: International Perspectives on Research Needs and Policy Implications.* (Washington, DC: Island Press), p. 47.

4. Renewing Organizational Theory, Stanford Conference on Organization Research at Asilomar, Pacific Grove, California, April 21–23, 1996; see also Stern, R., & S. Barley (1996). "Organizations and social systems: Organization theory's neglected mandate." *Administrative Science Quarterly, 41,* 146–162.

5. Professor of industrial engineering and engineering management, Stanford University, and editor of *Administrative Science Quarterly.*

6. Carson, R. (1962). *Silent Spring.* (Boston: Houghton Mifflin).

7. Florman, S. (1976). *The Existential Pleasures of Engineering.* (New York: St. Martin's Press).

8. Allison, G. (1971). *Essence of Decision.* (New York: HarperCollins).

9. Ibid., p. 259.

10. Ibid., p. 260.

11. Ibid.

12. For example, see Gottlieb, R. (1993). *Forcing the Spring: The Transformation of the American Environmental Movement.* (Washington DC: Island Press); Scheffer, V. (1991). *The Shaping of Environmentalism in America.* (Seattle: University of Washington Press).

13. See, for example, Capra, F., & P. Gunter (1995). *Steering Business Toward Sustainability.* (Tokyo: United Nations University Press); Smart, B. (1992). *Beyond Compliance.* (Washington, DC: World Resources Institute); Schmidheiny, S. (1992). *Changing Course.* (Cambridge, MA: MIT Press); Cairncross, F. (1992). *Costing the Earth.* (Boston: Harvard Business School

Press); and Hirschorn, J., & K. Oldenberg (1991). *Prosperity Without Pollution.* (New York: Van Nostrand).

14. Lightman, A. (1996). *Dance for Two.* (New York: Pantheon Books), p. 6.

CHAPTER ONE (PP. 3–23)

1. Friedman, M. (1970, September 13). "The social responsibility of business is to increase its profits." *New York Times Magazine,* pp. 32–33, 122, 124, 126.

2. Lund, L. (1974). *Corporate Organization for Environmental Policy-Making.* (New York: Conference Board).

3. U.S. Environmental Protection Agency (1993). *U.S. EPA Oral History Interview #1: William D. Ruckelshaus.* (Washington, DC: U.S. Government Printing Office).

4. Porter, M., & C. van der Linde (1995, September-October). "Green and competitive: Ending the stalemate." *Harvard Business Review,* pp. 120–134.

5. Morrison, C. (1991). *Managing Environmental Affairs: Corporate Practices in the U.S., Canada and Europe.* (New York: Conference Board).

6. Popoff, F. (1991, December 30). "Pollution prevention: No longer a pipe dream." *Business Week,* p. 90.

7. Lefferre, T. (1990, May). "The decade of the environment." *Chemtech,* p. 262.

8. Woolard, E. (1992, Spring). "An industry approach to sustainable development." *Issues in Science and Technology,* pp. 29–33.

9. Kennedy, R. (1991, Third Quarter). "Achieving environmental excellence: Ten tools for CEOs." *Prism,* pp. 79–88.

10. Gottlieb, R. (1993). *Forcing the Spring: The Transformation of the American Environmental Movement.* (Washington, DC: Island Press); Dowie, M. (1995). *Losing Ground: American Environmentalism at the Close of the Twentieth Century.* (Cambridge, MA: MIT Press).

11. Portnoy, P. (1990). *Public Policies for Environmental Protection.* (Baltimore: Johns Hopkins University Press).

12. Scheffer, V. (1991). *The Shaping of Environmentalism in America.* (Seattle: University of Washington Press).

13. Downs, A. (1972). "Up and down with ecology: The issue-attention cycle." *Public Interest, 28,* 38–50; Dunlap, R. (1991). "Trends in public opinion toward environmental issues: 1965–1990." *Society and Natural Resources, 4,* 285–312.

14. U.S. Department of Commerce (1973–1992). *Current Industrial Reports: Abatement Costs and Expenditures.* Report Nos. MA200(73)-1 through

MA200(92)-1, Economics and Statistics Administration. (Washington, DC: U.S. Government Printing Office).

15. Weick, C. (1979). *The Social Psychology of Organizing.* (New York: Random House).

16. U.S. Environmental Protection Agency (1992). *1990 Toxic Release Inventory.* Report No. 700-S-92–002. (Washington, DC: U.S. Government Printing Office).

17. Erskine, H. (1971). "The polls: Pollution and industry." *Public Opinion Quarterly, 36*, 263–280.

18. Cambridge Reports/Research International (1992). *Corporate EQ Scores 1992: Americans Rate Corporate Environmental Performance.* (Cambridge, MA: Cambridge Reports/Research International).

19. U.S. Department of Commerce, op. cit. (1973–1992); U.S. Census Bureau (1980–1993). *Statistical Abstracts of the United States.* (Washington, DC: U.S. Government Printing Office).

20. "Getty's Berg calls EPA U.S. oil's worst enemy." (1979, October 22). *Oil & Gas Journal*, p. 38.

21. Walter Quanstrom holds a doctorate in zoology from the University of Oklahoma.

CHAPTER TWO (PP. 24–43)

1. The exact magnitude of industrial environmental expenditures has varied quite widely among various sources. The Department of Commerce cites a figure of $26 billion in 1992, but the Bureau of Economic Analysis places the figure at $102 billion, and the EPA places it at $135 billion. See Palmer, K., W. Oates, & P. Portney (1995). "Tightening environmental standards: The benefit-cost or the no-cost paradigm?" *Journal of Economic Perspectives, 9*(4), 119–132. However, regardless of these differences, the point here is not to argue the magnitude but the trend, which has been steadily rising in each case.

2. Ausubel, J., & H. Sladovich (1989). *Technology and Environment.* (Washington, DC: National Academy of Engineering).

3. U.S. Department of Commerce (1973–1992). *Current Industrial Reports: Abatement Costs and Expenditures.* Report Nos. MA200(73)-1 through MA200(92)-1, Economics and Statistics Administration. (Washington, DC: U.S. Government Printing Office).

4. Katz, D., & R. Kahn (1978). *The Social Psychology of Organizations.* (New York: Wiley), pp. 23–30.

5. Scott, W. R., & J. Meyer (1992). "The organization of societal sectors." In Meyer & Scott (Eds.), *Organizational Environments: Ritual and Rationality.* (Thousand Oaks, CA: Sage), pp. 129–154.

6. Hyson, J., & W. Bolce (1983). *Business and Its Environment*. (St. Paul, MN: West), p. 167.

7. Olson, M. (1965). *The Logic of Collective Action: Public Goods and the Theory of Groups*. (Cambridge, MA: Harvard University Press).

8. Latham, E. (1952). *The Group Basis of Politics*. (Ithaca, NY: Cornell University Press).

9. Hahn, R., & R. Stavins (1991). "Incentive-Based Environmental Regulation: A New Era from an Old Idea." *Ecology Law Quarterly, 18*(1), 1–42.

10. The latter, commonly marked by the NIMBY ("not in my backyard") syndrome, are increasingly characterized by the NOPE ("not on Planet Earth") syndrome.

11. For basic texts on institutional theory, see Thomas, G., J. Meyer, F. Ramirez, & J. Boli (1987). *Institutional Structure: Constituting State, Society, and the Individual*. (Thousand Oaks, CA: Sage); Zucker, L. (1988). *Institutional Patterns and Organizations*. (New York: Ballinger); Powell, W., & P. DiMaggio (1991). *The New Institutionalism in Organizational Analysis*. (Chicago: University of Chicago Press); and Meyer, J., & W. R. Scott (Eds.) (1992). *Organizational Environments: Ritual and Rationality*. (Thousand Oaks, CA: Sage).

12. Orru, M., N. Biggart, & G. Hamilton (1991). "Organizational isomorphism in East Asia." In Powell & DiMaggio (Eds.), *The New Institutionalism in Organizational Analysis*. (Chicago: University of Chicago Press), pp. 361–389.

13. DiMaggio, P., & W. Powell (1991). "Introduction." In Powell & DiMaggio (Eds.), *The New Institutionalism in Organizational Analysis*. (Chicago: University of Chicago Press), pp. 1–38.

14. Russo, J., & P. Shoemaker (1989). *Decision Traps*. (New York: Doubleday).

15. Bazerman, M. (1994). *Judgment in Managerial Decision Making*. (New York: Wiley), p. 17.

16. DiMaggio, P. (1983). "State expansion and organizational field." In Hall & Quinn (Eds.), *Organizational Theory and Public Policy*. (Thousand Oaks, CA: Sage), pp. 147–161.

17. Scott, W. R. (1991). "Unpacking institutional arguments." In Powell & DiMaggio (Eds.), *The New Institutionalism in Organizational Analysis*. (Chicago: University of Chicago Press), pp. 164–182.

18. DiMaggio, op. cit. (1983).

19. Diagram from Lounsbury, M. (1996, April 21–23). "Garbage can institutionalism: Symbolic conflict and the interfield diffusion of contending models." Paper presented at Renewing Organizational Theory, Stanford

Conference on Organization Research at Asilomar, Pacific Grove, California.

20. Meyer, J., J. Boli, & G. Thomas (1987). "Ontology and rationalization in Western cultural account." In Thomas and others (Eds.), *Institutional Structure: Constituting State, Society, and the Individual.* (Thousand Oaks, CA: Sage), pp. 12–38.

21. Orru, M., N. Biggart, & G. Hamilton, op. cit. (1991).

22. Scott, W. R. (1995). *Institutions and Organizations.* (Thousand Oaks, CA: Sage).

23. Ibid., p. 52.

24. Ibid.

25. Kennedy, J. F. (1962). Commencement address at Yale University, June 11, 1962. In *Public Papers of the Presidents.* (Washington DC: U.S. Government Printing Office), pp. 470–475.

26. White, H. (1992). *Identity and Control: A Structural Theory of Social Interaction.* (Princeton, NJ: Princeton University Press).

27. Pfeffer, J. (1981). *Power in Organizations.* (Boston: Pitman).

28. Thomas, R. (1994). *What Machines Can't Do: Politics and Technology in the Industrial Enterprise.* (Berkeley: University of California Press).

29. Perrow, C. (1970). "Departmental power and perspectives in industrial firms." In Meyer and Zald (Ed.), *Power in Organizations.* (Nashville, TN: Vanderbilt University Press).

30. Fligstein, N. (1990). *The Transformation of Corporate Control.* (Cambridge, MA: Harvard University Press).

31. Ibid.

32. DiMaggio, P., & W. Powell (1983). "The iron cage revisited: Institutional isomorphism and collective rationality in organizational fields." *American Sociological Review, 48,* 147–160.

33. Zucker, L. (1987). "Normal change or risky business: Institutional effects on the 'hazard' of change in hospital organizations, 1959–79." *Journal of Management Studies, 24,* 671–701.

34. Leibniz, G. (1866). "Second éclaircissement du système de la communication des substances." In Janet (Ed.), *Œuvres Philosophiques* (Paris: Ladrange).

35. Thomas, G., J. Meyer, F. Ramirez, & J. Boli, op. cit. (1987); see also Morgan, G. (1986). *Images of Organization.* (Thousand Oaks, CA: Sage).

36. Schein, E. (1985). *Organizational Culture and Leadership.* (San Francisco: Jossey-Bass); Schein, E. (1990). "Organizational culture." *American Psychologist, 45,* 109–119.

37. Hoffman, A. (1994). "Organizational Change and the Greening Process: A Case Study of the Amoco Corporation." *Total Quality Environmental Management, 4*(1), 1–21.

38. King, A. (1993). *Directed Organizational Stability and Undirected Evolution: Environmental Regulation in the U.S. Printed Circuit Fabrication Industry.* Unpublished doctoral dissertation, Sloan School of Management, Massachusetts Institute of Technology, Cambridge.

39. Lund, L. (1974). *Corporate Organization for Environmental Policy-Making.* (New York: Conference Board).

40. Holusha, J. (1992, September 20). "Dow Chemical's czar unlocks the gates." *New York Times,* p. 5.

41. Schein, E., op. cit. (1990).

42. Ibid.

43. Morgan, G., op. cit. (1986).

44. Schein, E., op. cit. (1990).

45. Giddens, A. (1984). *The Constitution of Society.* (Berkeley: University of California Press).

CHAPTER THREE (PP. 47–63)

1. Pillar, C. (1991). *The Fail-Safe Society: Community Defiance and the End of American Technological Optimism.* (Berkeley: University of California Press), p. 5.

2. Inaugural address of John F. Kennedy, January 20, 1961.

3. "Men of the Year" (1961, January 2). *Time,* pp. 40–46.

4. Florman, S. (1976). *The Existential Pleasures of Engineering.* (New York: St. Martin's Press).

5. "Antimerger law is archaic." (1961, January 28). *Chemical Week,* p. 5.

6. "What price federal regulation?" (1961, May 13). *Chemical Week,* p. 5.

7. "Sanity on food additives." (1961, February 25). *Chemical Week,* p. 5.

8. "Who pays the piper?" (1961, January 14). *Chemical Week,* p. 5.

9. Carson, R. (1962). *Silent Spring.* (Boston: Houghton Mifflin).

10. "Nature is for the birds." (1962, July 28). *Chemical Week,* p. 5.

11. "The chemicals around us." (1962, July 14). *Chemical Week,* p. 5.

12. "Scientist-spokesman tells industry's pesticide story." (1962, November 10). *Chemical Week,* pp. 28–29.

13. "Better off than we expected." (1966, January 29). *Chemical Week,* p. 5.

14. "'68 can be a rewarding year." (1967, December 30). *Chemical Week,* p. 5.

15. "AEC, then NASA, now NWC?" (1966, July 9). *Chemical Week*, p. 5.

16. "Who wields the billy club?" (1969, January 18). *Chemical Week*, p. 5.

17. "Wanted: One set of rules." (1968, October 5). *Chemical Week*, p. 5.

18. "The government approach to smog." (1969, March 15). *Chemical Week*, pp. 54–60.

19. "Converting the critics." (1969, January 11). *Chemical Week*, pp. 68–69.

20. "Meet the pollution managers." (1968, June 29). *Chemical Week*, pp. 54–60.

21. "It's going to be a great world—if . . ." (1970, May 13). *Chemical Week*, p. 5.

22. "Pollution control occupies him on three fronts." (1970, June 24). *Chemical Week*, p. 60.

23. "Golden opportunity for leadership." (1970, November 18). *Chemical Week*, p. 5.

24. Ibid.

25. "Now oil must concern itself with pure air." (1960, June 20). *Oil & Gas Journal*, p. 71.

26. "Leaded gasoline poses no threat to public health." (1961, December 25). *Oil & Gas Journal*, pp. 171–172.

27. Although the absolute number of environmentally related articles was similar in the two journals, the number of environmentally related articles as a percentage of the total was quite disparate between them. Throughout the study, *Chemical Week* averaged a fairly consistent 220 overall articles per quarter, while *Oil & Gas Journal* averaged 450. There were an average of thirty-four environmentally related articles per year for each, or 9 percent of the total for *Chemical Week* and 3 percent for *Oil & Gas Journal*. These figures should not detract from the research results, as it is trends in this evolution that are of interest.

28. "Oilmen oppose lead rush—but does Washington know?" (1970, April 27). *Oil & Gas Journal*, p. 35.

29. "Automotive pollution: Time for a decision." (1970, January 26). *Oil & Gas Journal*, p. 79.

30. "Air pollution curbed, profits hiked." (1964, August 24). *Oil & Gas Journal*, pp. 92–93.

31. "Why oil needs new social techniques." (1967, November 20). *Oil & Gas Journal*, p. 117.

32. "Oil's new look in public relations." (1968, March 11). *Oil & Gas Journal*, p. 43.

33. "Calm appraisal is needed to end Santa Barbara hysteria." (1969, February 17). *Oil & Gas Journal*, p. 35.

34. "Correcting industry's image has become everyone's job." (1969, November 24). *Oil & Gas Journal*, p. 47.

35. Goodwin, N. (Producer) (1993). "Rachel Carson's *Silent Spring.*" On *The American Experience.* (Boston: WGBH).

36. Scheffer, V. (1991). *The Shaping of Environmentalism in America.* (Seattle: University of Washington Press), p. 47.

37. Molotch, H. (1970). "Oil in Santa Barbara and power in America." *Sociological Inquiry, 40,* 131–144.

38. Yergin, D. (1991). *The Prize.* (New York: Touchstone), p. 569.

39. Gottlieb, R. (1993). *Forcing the Spring: The Transformation of the American Environmental Movement.* (Washington, DC: Island Press), p. 111.

40. Ibid., p. 107.

41. U.S. Environmental Protection Agency (1992). *The Guardian: Origins of the EPA.* (Washington, DC: U.S. Government Printing Office), p. 1.

42. Schwartz, I. (1973, February 14). "More of management moves into the environment picture." *Chemical Week,* p. 59.

43. Hopkinson, R. (1970). *Corporate Organization for Pollution Control.* (New York: Conference Board), p. 12.

44. Schwartz, I., op. cit. (1973, February 14), p. 59.

45. *Chemical Week* (1962, July 28).

46. Goodwin, op. cit. (1993).

CHAPTER FOUR (PP. 64–87)

1. U.S. Environmental Protection Agency (1993). *U.S. EPA Oral History Interview #1: William D. Ruckelshaus.* (Washington, DC: U.S. Government Printing Office).

2. Ibid.

3. Landy, M., M. Roberts, & S. Thomas (1990). *The Environmental Protection Agency: Asking the Wrong Questions.* (New York: Oxford University Press).

4. Novick, S. (1986, January). "The 20 year evolution of pollution law: A look back." *Environmental Forum,* pp. 12–18.

5. Myers, P. (1990). "The road we've traveled." *EPA Journal, 16*(5), 57–60.

6. The chemical and petroleum industries consistently followed these broader industry trends. In this case, the chemical and petroleum industries filed a mean of 6.71 lawsuits per year, with 97 percent directed at the EPA.

7. U.S. Environmental Protection Agency (1994). *Enforcement Accomplishments Report, FY 1993.* Report No. 300-R94–003. (Washington, DC: U.S. Government Printing Office).

8. "Ecology mows 'em down in chemical land." (1971, February 10). *Chemical Week,* pp. 8–9.

9. "Environmental disclosures: No problem so far." (1971, September 29). *Chemical Week*, pp. 42–44.

10. "Easing rules for Alaska crude oil." (1973, August 8). *Chemical Week*, pp. 25–26.

11. "Energy crisis makes pollution control job tougher." (1974, March 6). *Chemical Week*, p. 37.

12. "Outlook for modification of air standards is foggy." (1975, February 19). *Chemical Week*, p. 27.

13. "EPA: Just one more on that side of the question." (1975, December 3). *Chemical Week*, p. 5.

14. "The toxic substances limbo." (1975, October 29). *Chemical Week*, p. 5.

15. "It's time to start settling out of court." (1977, January 26). *Chemical Week*, p. 5.

16. "EPA flunks test in Science 1." (1977, March 30). *Chemical Week*, p. 15.

17. "Who's David and who's Goliath?" (1978, February 22). *Chemical Week*, p. 5.

18. "The coercive Utopians: Their hidden agenda." (1979, August 8). *Chemical Week*, p. 5.

19. "The confidentiality problem." (1980, December 10). *Chemical Week*, p. 5.

20. "He's giving the environment top priority." (1978, July 26). *Chemical Week*, p. 32.

21. "David, you've knocked off Goliath. Now what?" (1980, January 2). *Chemical Week*, p. 5.

22. "In terms of regulation, you ain't seen nuttin yet." (1980, January 23). *Chemical Week*, p. 5.

23. "St. Clair: Industry must enter the debate." (1980, February 6). *Chemical Week*, p. 5.

24. "CMA in $4 billion battle with regulation." (1980, June 25). *Chemical Week*, p. 54.

25. "1980: A year for learning." (1981, January 7). *Chemical Week*, p. 3.

26. "Environmentalists forcing energy crisis on nation." (1971, March 15). *Oil & Gas Journal*, p. 21.

27. "It's time to blow the whistle on run-away environmentalists." (1971, March 15). *Oil & Gas Journal*, p. 53.

28. "Bad auto-emission controls being forced on motorists." (1972, September 11). *Oil & Gas Journal*, p. 45.

29. "Environmental demands, oil supply on collision course." (1972, November 13). *Oil & Gas Journal*, p. 91.

30. "Getty's Berg calls EPA U.S. oil's worst enemy." (1979, October 22). *Oil & Gas Journal*, p. 38.

31. "Basic environmental law must be revamped in U.S." (1979, December 24). *Oil & Gas Journal,* p. 17.

32. "Congress near choice for nature and against man." (1980, August 4). *Oil & Gas Journal,* p. 17.

33. De Marchi, B., S. Funtowicz, & J. Ravetz (1996). "Seveso: A paradoxical classic disaster." In Mitchell (Ed.), *The Long Road to Recovery: Community Responses to Industrial Disaster.* (New York: United Nations University Press), pp. 86–120.

34. Ibid.

35. Hoffman, A. (1995). "An uneasy rebirth at Love Canal." *Environment,* 37(2), 4–9, 25–31; Hoffman, A. (1993). "Who loves Love Canal?" *Tomorrow,* 3(3), 58–64.

36. *Hazardous Waste Market: Handling, Storage and Disposal.* (1981). (New York: Frost & Sullivan).

37. U.S. Environmental Protection Agency (1990). *Superfund: Environmental Progress.* (Washington, DC: U.S. Government Printing Office).

38. "Real property." (1987, November 1). *ABA Journal,* p. 67.

39. Ibid.

40. Russell, M., W. Colglazier, & B. Tonn (1992). "The U.S. hazardous waste legacy." *Environment,* 34(3), 12–15, 34–39.

41. Lund, L. (1974). *Corporate Organization for Environmental Policy-Making.* (New York: Conference Board).

42. Hopkinson, R. (1970). *Corporate Organization for Pollution Control.* (New York: Conference Board).

43. Schwartz, I. (1973, February 14). "More of management moves into the environment picture." *Chemical Week,* pp. 59–61.

44. Hopkinson, R., op. cit. (1970).

45. Lund, L., op. cit. (1974), p. 2.

46. Ibid.

47. Ibid., p. 3.

48. "Product stewardship: Responsibility never ends." (1973, October 3). *Chemical Week,* p. 45.

49. This lack of concern was due in part to the low impact of Superfund on the oil industry relative to other industries. Although all were required to pay a tax on feedstocks to support the act, only eight of the top fifty companies named as Superfund potentially responsible parties (PRPs) were oil companies, while twenty-five were chemical companies. U.S. Environmental Protection Agency (1991). *Superfund Site Enforcement Tracking System.* Internal Database, U.S. EPA Region 1, Boston, Massachusetts.

CHAPTER FIVE (PP. 87–106)

1. Dunlap, R. (1991). "Trends in public opinion toward environmental issues, 1965–1990." *Society and Natural Resources, 4,* 285–312.

2. Myers, P. (1990). "The road we've traveled." *EPA Journal, 16*(5), 57–60.

3. Ruffner, F. G. (Ed.) (1993). *The Encyclopedia of Associations.* (Detroit: Gale Research).

4. U.S. Environmental Protection Agency (1994). *Enforcement Accomplishments Report, FY 1993.* Report No. 300-R94–003. (Washington, DC: U.S. Government Printing Office).

5. "EPA in disarray: Can it do the job industry expects?" (1981, October 21). *Chemical Week,* pp. 82–85.

6. "EPA passes test on RCRA." (1982, June 9). *Chemical Week,* p. 3.

7. "But first, define the problem." (1982, July 14). *Chemical Week,* p. 3.

8. "Deliberate speed on Superfund." (1982, November 3). *Chemical Week,* p. 3.

9. "EPA's new credibility crisis." (1983, February 16). *Chemical Week,* p. 3.

10. "The environmental activists: They've grown in competence and they're working together." (1983, October 19). *Chemical Week,* pp. 48–56.

11. "Nice guys may be back in style." (1984, September 12). *Chemical Week,* p. 3.

12. "CIIT: Happy 10th birthday—and many more." (1984, June 27). *Chemical Week,* p. 3.

13. "No, you're not paranoid." (1985, April 3). *Chemical Week,* p. 3.

14. "Killing the golden geese." (1985, April 10). *Chemical Week,* p. 3.

15. "Environmental law: More than compliance." (1987, April 8). *Chemical Week,* p. 3.

16. "Rethinking the backyard issue." (1989, August 23). *Chemical Week,* p. 5.

17. "A changing CMA at an unchanging Greenbrier." (1986, June 11). *Chemical Week,* p. 3.

18. "Better balance seems assured between energy and environment." (1981, March 16). *Oil & Gas Journal,* p. 25.

19. "Clean Air Act and regulations need big revamp to reflect reality." (1981, June 1). *Oil & Gas Journal,* p. 43.

20. "Clean air rules need overhaul for environmental and economic program." (1981, July 27). *Oil & Gas Journal,* p. 95.

21. "Lead phasedown should be among first targets in regulatory reform." (1981, August 24). *Oil & Gas Journal,* p. 47.

22. "U.S. environment, economy will lose if EPA issue is used for political gain." (1983, April 4). *Oil & Gas Journal,* p. 37.

23. "Environmental self-policing serves industry's best interests." (1981, December 21). *Oil & Gas Journal,* p. 19.

24. "Undue haste on Superfund risks marvelous mess, hurt industries." (1984, August 13). *Oil & Gas Journal,* p. 39.

25. "Bad Superfund bill can only get worse for oil industry." (1986, October 13). *Oil & Gas Journal,* p. 19.

26. "EPA jumps on right track with draft oil waste report." (1987, October 5). *Oil & Gas Journal,* p. 19.

27. "Clean Air Act deadline delay the right move for clean air." (1987, November 30). *Oil & Gas Journal,* p. 11.

28. "Concern over environment or economic obstructionism?" (1984, February 13). *Oil & Gas Journal,* p. 31.

29. "Balance needed in environmental values, national energy needs." (1985, November 4). *Oil & Gas Journal,* p. 39.

30. "Energy and environmentalism, 1: Environmentalism should acknowledge successes, failures." (1987, June 8). *Oil & Gas Journal,* p. 13.

31. Shrivastava, P. (1996). "Long-term recovery from the Bhopal crisis." In Mitchell (Ed.), *The Long Road to Recovery: Community Responses to Industrial Disaster.* (New York: United Nations University Press), pp. 121–147.

32. Ibid.

33. Ibid.

34. Shrivastava, P. (1992). *Bhopal: Anatomy of a Crisis.* (London: Chapman & Hall).

35. "A training post for DuPont top brass." (1982, June 16). *Chemical Week,* p. 40.

36. Ibid.

37. "Decentralizing environmental burdens." (1982, March 3). *Chemical Week,* p. 38.

38. Ibid., p. 37.

39. Ibid.

40. Ibid., p. 38.

41. Smith, T. (1987, September 16). "If you tread on me, let's talk about it." *Chemical Week,* p. 3.

42. Sarokin, D., and others (1985). *Cutting Chemical Wastes.* (New York: Inform, Inc.).

43. Ibid., p. 29.

44. Ibid., p. 32.

45. U.S. Office of Technology Assessment (1986). *Serious Reduction of*

Hazardous Waste. Report No. OTA-ITE-317. (Washington, DC: U.S. Congress, Office of Technology Assessment), p. 14.

46. Ibid., p. 25.

47. Todd, J. (1986, February). "Waste reduction: Industry's challenge." Paper given at the Lindbergh Symposium on Environment and Technology, Orlando, FL.

CHAPTER SIX (PP. 107–140)

1. Stavins, R. (1988). *Project 88: Harnessing Market Forces to Protect Our Environment.* Public policy study sponsored by Senators Timothy Wirth and John Heinz, Washington, DC.

2. Ibid.

3. Dunlap, R. (1991). "Trends in public opinion toward environmental issues, 1965–1990." *Society and Natural Resources, 4,* 285–312.

4. Buttel, F., A. Hawkins, & A. Power (1990). "From limits of growth to global change." *Global Environmental Change, 1*(1), 57–66.

5. Miller, R. (1989, January 2). "Earth is chosen as *Time*'s planet of the year." *Time,* p. 3.

6. U.S. General Accounting Office (1988). *Hazardous Waste: The Cost and Availability of Pollution Insurance.* (Washington, DC: U.S. Government Printing Office).

7. Interfaith Center on Corporate Responsibility (1989–1994). *The Corporate Examiner.* (New York: Interfaith Center on Corporate Responsibility).

8. Ruffner, F. G. (Ed.) (1993). *The Encyclopedia of Associations.* (Detroit: Gale Research).

9. U.S. Environmental Protection Agency (1994). *Enforcement Accomplishments Report, FY 1993.* Report No. 300-R94–003. (Washington, DC: U.S. Government Printing Office).

10. "Green line equals bottom line." (1990, November 21). *Chemical Week,* p. 5.

11. "Viewpoint." (1992, July 22). *Chemical Week,* p. 2.

12. "*Exxon Valdez* disaster leaves industry with much to repair." (1989, April 3). *Oil & Gas Journal,* p. 17.

13. "Winning the environmental lead." (1990, April 23). *Oil & Gas Journal,* p. 19.

14. "A good lesson from a bad year." (1990, December 31). *Oil & Gas Journal,* p. 19.

15. "API's O'Keefe: Environment still top issue for U.S. industry." (1991, May 6). *Oil & Gas Journal,* p. 140.

16. "Global warming, 2: Science casts doubt on alarmist theory." (1992, April 27). *Oil & Gas Journal*, p. 13.

17. "Global warming, 1: Politics of sacrifice obscuring science." (1992, April 20). *Oil & Gas Journal*, p. 23.

18. "Global warming, 4: Issue offers great potential for error." (1992, May 11). *Oil & Gas Journal*, p. 15.

19. "The U.S. gasoline revolution begins." (1992, October 26). *Oil & Gas Journal*, p. 17.

20. Maxwell, J., & S. Weiner (1993, Winter). "Green consciousness or dollar diplomacy? The British response to the threat of ozone depletion." *International Environmental Affairs*, pp. 19–41.

21. Marples, D. (1996). "The Chernobyl disaster: Its effects on Belarus and Ukraine." In Mitchell (Ed.), *The Long Road to Recovery: Community Responses to Industrial Disaster.* (New York: United Nations University Press), pp. 183–230.

22. Rathje, W., & C. Murphy (1992, August 22). "Poor, misunderstood garbage." *New York Times*, p. 21.

23. Lehmann-Haupt, C. (1992, July 9). "Books of the *Times:* Most of what people say about trash is rubbish." *New York Times*, p. C-19.

24. Veasey, D. (1992, August 16). "By land, sea and air, at war with pollution." *New York Times*, p. 1.

25. Veasey, D. (1992, August 9). "By land, sea and air, at war with floating debris." *New York Times*, p. 1.

26. Scheffer, V. (1991). *The Shaping of Environmentalism in America.* (Seattle: University of Washington Press), p. 182.

27. Davis, N. (1996). "The *Exxon Valdez* oil spill, Alaska." In Mitchell (Ed.), *The Long Road to Recovery: Community Responses to Industrial Disaster.* (New York: United Nations University Press), pp. 231–272.

28. Hoffman, A. (1996). "A strategic response to investor activism." *Sloan Management Review, 37*(2), 51–64.

29. De Boerr, H. (1992, June 17). "Green jobs at the top." *Financial Times*, p. 12.

30. Cahill, L., & S. Engelman (1993, Fall). "Bolstering the board's environmental focus." *Directors and Boards*, pp. 23–25.

31. Investor Responsibility Research Center (1992). *Compliance Index.* (Plainfield, NH: Investor Responsibility Research Center).

32. Cahill, L., & S. Engelman, op. cit. (1993, Fall).

33. Morrison, C. (1991). *Managing Environmental Affairs: Corporate Practices in the U.S., Canada and Europe.* (New York: Conference Board).

34. Ibid., p. 11.

35. Ibid.

36. Berenbeim, R. (1992). *Corporate Ethics Practices.* (New York: Conference Board).

37. Ibid.

38. Orti, L. (1995). *Environmental Alliances: Critical Factors for Success.* (New York: Conference Board), p. 7.

39. Ibid.

40. Hoffman, A. (1995, July 5/12). "The many faces of environmental stewardship." *Chemical Week,* pp. 63–65.

41. Hoffman, A. (1993). "Who loves Love Canal?" *Tomorrow, 3*(3), 58–64.

42. Protess, D., and others. (1987). "The impact of investigative reporting on public opinion and policy-making: Targeting toxic waste." *Public Opinion Quarterly, 51*(2), 166–185.

43. Lindzen, R. (1992). "Global warming: The origins and nature of alleged scientific consensus." *Regulation, 15*(2), 87–98.

44. Krupp, F. (1990). "Win/win on the environmental front." *EPA Journal, 16*(5), 30–31.

45. Burros, M. (1996, February 7). "A new goal beyond organic: Clean food." *New York Times,* pp. B-1, B-5.

46. Frankel, C., & W. Coddington (1994). "Environmental marketing." In Kolluru (Ed.), *Environmental Strategies Handbook.* (New York: McGraw-Hill), pp. 643–677.

47. Leggett, J. (1996). *Climate Change and the Financial Sector.* (Munich, Germany: Gerling Akademie Verlag).

48. Schmidheiny, S. (1996). *Financing Change.* (Cambridge, MA: MIT Press).

49. Goering, L. (1996, June 25). "Pollution test case pits Ecuadorans against U.S. firm." *Chicago Tribune,* pp. 1, 14.

50. Hoffman, A. (1992). *The Hazardous Waste Remediation Market: Innovative Technological Development and the Market Entry of the Construction Industry.* CCRE Working Paper No. 92–1. (Cambridge: Department of Civil and Environmental Engineering, Massachusetts Institute of Technology).

51. See Jablonski, J. (1994). *Prospering Through Environmental Leadership.* (Albuquerque, NM: Technical Publishing Consortium, Inc.); and Maxwell, J., L. Matysiak, J. Nash, & J. Ehrenfeld (1993, Summer). "Preventing waste beyond the company walls: P&G's response to the need for environmental quality." *Pollution Prevention Review, 3,* 317–333.

52. Morrison, C., op. cit. (1991), p. 18.

53. See Makower, J. (1993). "Business schools get in line." *Tomorrow, 3*(3), 50–53; Mangan, K. (1994, November 2). "The greening of the MBA."

Chronicle of Higher Education, pp. A19–A20; Pham, A. (1994, June 28). "Business schools see green." *Boston Globe,* p. 35.

54. See Wagner, B. (1994, March 21). "The greening of the engineer." *U.S. News & World Report,* pp. 90–91.

55. Friedman, S. (1996). "Teaching the beat: Rising interest in e-journalism reflected in academic option." *SEJournal, 6*(1), 1, 7.

56. "Presbyterians ratify teaching on sex, ecology." (1991, June 9). *Boston Globe,* p. 4.

57. Woodward, K., & R. Nordland (1992, November 30). "New rules for an old faith." *Newsweek,* p. 71.

CHAPTER SEVEN (PP. 143–175)

1. Dunlap, R. (1991). "Trends in public opinion toward environmental issues, 1965–1990." *Society and Natural Resources, 4,* 285–312.

2. King, A. (1993). *Directed Organizational Stability and Undirected Evolution: Environmental Regulation in the U.S. Printed Circuit Fabrication Industry.* Unpublished doctoral dissertation, Sloan School of Management, Massachusetts Institute of Technology, Cambridge.

3. De Boerr, H. (1992, June 17). "Green jobs at the top." *Financial Times,* p. 12.

4. Cahill, L., & S. Engelman (1993, Fall). "Bolstering the board's environmental focus." *Directors and Boards,* pp. 23–25.

5. For example, Popoff, F. (1991, December 30). "Pollution prevention: No longer a pipe dream." *Business Week,* p. 90; Lefferre, T. (1990, May). "The decade of the environment." *Chemtech,* p. 262; Woolard, E. (1992, Spring). "An industry approach to sustainable development." *Issues in Science and Technology,* pp. 29–33; Kennedy, R. (1991, Third Quarter). "Achieving environmental excellence: Ten tools for CEOs." *Prism,* 79–88.

6. Deloitte Touche Tohmatsu (1993). *Coming Clean.* (London: Deloitte Touche Tohmatsu International).

7. Hoffman, A. (1995, July 5/12). "The many faces of environmental stewardship." *Chemical Week,* p. 65.

8. U.S. Department of Commerce (1973–1992). *Current Industrial Reports: Abatement Costs and Expenditures.* Report Nos. MA200(73)-1 through MA200(92)-1, Economics and Statistics Administration. (Washington, DC: U.S. Government Printing Office).

9. Ibid.

10. White, H. (1992). *Identity and Control: A Structural Theory of Social Interaction.* (Princeton, NJ: Princeton University Press), p. 127.

11. Scott, W. R. (1995). *Institutions and Organizations*. (Thousand Oaks, CA: Sage), pp. 35, 52.

12. Florman, S. (1976). *The Existential Pleasures of Engineering*. (New York: St. Martin's Press).

13. Carson, R. (1962). *Silent Spring*. (Boston: Houghton Mifflin).

14. DiMaggio, P. (1983). "State expansion and organizational field." In Hall & Quinn (Eds.), *Organizational Theory and Public Policy*. (Thousand Oaks, CA: Sage), pp. 147–161.

15. Jepperson, R. (1991). "Institutions, institutional effects, and institutionalism." In Powell & DiMaggio (Eds.), *The New Institutionalism in Organizational Analysis*. (Chicago: University of Chicago Press), pp. 143–163.

16. See Schmidheiny, S. (1992). *Changing Course*. (Cambridge, MA: MIT Press); and Smart, B. (1992). *Beyond Compliance*. (Washington, DC: World Resources Institute).

17. See Walley , N., & B. Whitehead (1994, May-June). "It's not easy being green." *Harvard Business Review*, pp. 46–51; and Porter, M., & C. van der Linde (1995, September-October). "Green and competitive: Ending the stalemate." *Harvard Business Review*, pp. 120–134.

18. "Industrial switch: Some firms reduce pollution with clean manufacturing." (1990, December 24). *Wall Street Journal*, pp. 1, 17.

19. "DuPont to spend big to cut plant pollution." (1991, August 5). *Engineering News Record*, p. 22.

20. *The Environmental Two-Step*. (1995). (Washington, DC: Times Mirror).

21. Dunlap, R. (1991, October). "Public opinion in the 1980s: Clear consensus, ambiguous commitment." *Environment*, p. 12.

22. See Rice, F. (1993, July 26). "Who scores best on the environment?" *Fortune*, pp. 114–122.

23. Tolbert, P., & L. Zucker (1983). "Institutional sources of change in the formal structure of organizations: The diffusion of civil service reform, 1880–1935." *Administrative Science Quarterly, 28,* 22–39.

24. Fligstein, N. (1990). *The Transformation of Corporate Control*. (Cambridge, MA: Harvard University Press).

25. Fligstein, N. (1991). "The structural transformation of American industry: An institutional account of the causes of diversification in the largest firms, 1919–1979." In Powell & DiMaggio (Eds.), *The New Institutionalism in Organizational Analysis*. (Chicago: University of Chicago Press), pp. 311–336.

26. Ibid.

27. Pfeffer, J. (1982). "The external control of the organization." In Pfeffer

(Ed.), *Organizations and Organization Theory* (Boston: Pitman), pp. 178–207.

28. Opheim, T. (1993). "Fire on the Cuyahoga." *EPA Journal, 19*(2), 44.

29. Keating, B., & D. Russell (1992, July-August). "EPA yesterday and today." *E Magazine,* p. 33.

30. Hoffman, A. (1996). "A strategic response to investor activism." *Sloan Management Review, 37*(2), 51–64.

31. Keating, B., & D. Russell, op. cit. (1992, July-August).

32. Dower, R. (1982). "Hazardous wastes." In Portney (Ed.), *Public Policies for Environmental Protection.* (Washington, DC: Resources for the Future), pp. 151–194.

33. White, H., op. cit. (1992).

34. Meyer, A. (1982). "Adapting to environmental jolts." *Administrative Science Quarterly, 27,* 515–537.

35. Mack, T., J. Norman, H. Rudnitsky, & A. Tanzer (1994, February 28). "History is full of giants that failed to adapt." *Forbes,* pp. 73–78.

36. U.S. Council of Economic Advisors (1994). *The Economic Report of the President.* (Washington, DC: U.S. Government Printing Office).

37. U.S. Department of Commerce, op cit. (1973–1992).

38. Ibid.

39. Ibid.; U.S. Census Bureau (1980–1993). *Statistical Abstracts of the United States.* (Washington, DC: U.S. Government Printing Office).

40. U.S. Environmental Protection Agency (1991). *Industrial Pollution Prevention Opportunities for the 1990s.* Report No. 600–8-91–052. (Washington, DC: U.S. Government Printing Office).

41. Bourdieu, P. (1990). *The Logic of Practice.* Trans. R. Nice. (Stanford, CA: Stanford University Press); White, H. (1992). *Identity and Control: A Structural Theory of Social Interaction.* (Princeton, NJ: Princeton University Press); Fligstein, N. (1990). *The Transformation of Corporate Control.* (Cambridge, MA: Harvard University Press).

42. This distinction is outlined in the introduction to DiMaggio & Powell (1991). Others are trying to reestablish the links of this divided literature, such as Hirsch, P., & M. Lounsbury (1997). "Ending the family quarrel: Toward a reconciliation of 'old' and 'new' institutionalism." *American Behavioral Scientist, 40,* 406–418; Holm, P. (1995). "The dynamics of institutionalization: Transformation processes in Norwegian fisheries." *Administrative Science Quarterly, 40,* 398–422; Kraatz, M., & E. Zajac (1996). "Exploring the limits of the new institutionalism: The causes and consequences of illegitimate organizational change." *American Sociological Review, 61*(5), 812–836; and Greenwood, R., & C. R. Hinings (1996). "Understanding radical organizational change: Bringing together the old

and new institutionalism." *Academy of Management Review, 21,* 1022–1054.

43. See Selznick, P. (1949). *TVA and the Grass Roots.* (Berkeley: University of California Press); Selznick, P. (1957). *Leadership in Administration: A Sociological Interpretation.* (Berkeley: University of California Press).

44. Scott, W. R. (1991). "Unpacking institutional arguments." In Powell & DiMaggio (Eds.), *The New Institutionalism in Organizational Analysis.* (Chicago: University of Chicago Press), pp. 164–182.

45. Scott, W. R., & J. Meyer (1991). "The organization of societal sectors: Propositions and early evidence." In Powell & DiMaggio (Eds.), *The New Institutionalism in Organizational Analysis.* (Chicago: University of Chicago Press), pp. 108–140.

46. DiMaggio, P. (1988). "Interest and agency in institutional theory." In Zucker (Ed.), *Institutional Patterns and Organizations.* (New York: Ballinger), pp. 3–21.

47. DiMaggio, P., & W. Powell (1983). "The iron cage revisited: Institutional isomorphism and collective rationality in organizational fields." *American Sociological Review, 48,* 147–160.

48. North, D. (1990). *Institutions, Institutional Change and Economic Performance.* (New York: Cambridge University Press), p. 107.

49. DiMaggio, P., & W. Powell (1991). "Introduction." In Powell & DiMaggio (Eds.), *The New Institutionalism in Organizational Analysis.* (Chicago: University of Chicago Press), p. 8.

50. Fligstein, N., op. cit. (1991).

51. White, H., op. cit. (1992); see also Ocasio, W. (1994). "Political dynamics and the circulation of power: CEO succession in U.S. industrial corporations, 1960–1990." *Administrative Science Quarterly, 39,* 285–312.

52. See Oliver, C. (1991). "Strategic responses to institutional processes." *Academy of Management Review, 16,* 145–179; and Powell, W. (1991). "Expanding the scope of institutional analysis." In Powell & DiMaggio (Eds.), *The New Institutionalism in Organizational Analysis.* (Chicago: University of Chicago Press), pp. 183–203.

53. DiMaggio, P., op. cit. (1988).

54. Oliver, C., op. cit. (1991).

55. Giddens, A. (1979). *The Problems of Social Theory: Action, Structure, and Contradiction in Social Analysis.* (Old Tappan, NJ: Macmillan).

56. Brint, S., & J. Karabel (1991). "Institutional origins and transformations: The case of American community colleges." In Powell & DiMaggio (Eds.), *The New Institutionalism in Organizational Analysis* (Chicago: University of Chicago Press), pp. 337–360.

57. Tolbert, P., & L. Zucker, op. cit. (1983).

58. Holm, P. (1995). "The dynamics of institutionalization: Transformation processes in Norwegian fisheries." *Administrative Science Quarterly, 40*, 398–422.

59. Gersick, C. (1991). "Punctuated equilibrium: A multi-level exploration of revolutionary change theories." *Academy of Management Review, 16*, 10–36.

CHAPTER EIGHT (PP. 176–197)

1. This is a common conception of the government in institutional studies. See, for example, DiMaggio, P. (1991). "Constructing an organizational field as a professional project: U.S. art museums, 1920–1940." In Powell & DiMaggio (Eds.), *The New Institutionalism in Organizational Analysis.* (Chicago: University of Chicago Press), pp. 267–292; and Fligstein, N. (1990). *The Transformation of Corporate Control.* (Cambridge, MA: Harvard University Press).

2. Bailey, J. (1995, November 15). "Utilities overcomply with Clean Air Act, are stockpiling pollution allowances." *Wall Street Journal,* p. A8.

3. Bradley, J. (1996, July-August). "Buying high, selling low." *E Magazine,* pp. 14–15.

4. DiMaggio, P. (1983). "State expansion and organizational field." In Hall & Quinn (Eds.), *Organizational Theory and Public Policy.* (Thousand Oaks, CA: Sage), pp. 147–161.

5. Lefferre, T. (1990, May). "The decade of the environment." *Chemtech,* p. 262.

6. Dowie, M. (1995). *Losing Ground: American Environmentalism in the Twentieth Century.* (Cambridge, MA: MIT Press).

7. Powell, W. (1991). "Expanding the scope of institutional analysis." In Powell & DiMaggio (Eds.), *The New Institutionalism in Organizational Analysis.* (Chicago: University of Chicago Press), pp. 183–203.

8. Michels, R. (1962). *Political Parties.* (New York: Free Press).

9. Gamson, W. (1975). *The Strategy of Social Protest.* (Florence, KY: Dorsey Press).

10. Jubeir, J. (1995). "Educating environmental managers for tomorrow." *EPA Journal, 21*(2), 31–33.

11. Hoffman, A. (1996). "A strategic response to investor activism." *Sloan Management Review, 37*(2), 51–64.

12. Deloitte Touche Tohmatsu (1993). *Coming Clean.* (London: Deloitte Touche Tohmatsu International).

13. Downs, A. (1972). "Up and down with ecology: The issue-attention cycle." *Public Interest, 28*, 38–50.

14. Ibid., p. 39.

15. Kennedy, P. (1993). *Preparing for the Twenty-First Century.* (New York: Random House).

16. Ibid., p. 96.

17. See Brown, L., C. Flavin, & H. Kane (1996). *Vital Signs, 1996.* (New York: Norton).

18. World Commission on Environment and Development (1987). *Our Common Future.* (New York: Oxford University Press).

19. Woolard, E. (1992, Spring). "An industry approach to sustainable development." *Issues in Science and Technology,* p. 29.

20. Schmidheiny, S. (1992). *Changing Course.* (Cambridge, MA: MIT Press), p. 87.

21. See Jennings, P. D., & P. Zandbergen (1995). "Ecologically sustainable organizations: An institutional approach." *Academy of Management Review, 20,* 1015–1052; and Hart, S. (1995). "A natural resource based view of the firm." *Academy of Management Review, 20,* 986–1014.

22. Jacobs, M. (1993). *The Green Economy: Environment, Sustainable Development and the Politics of the Future.* (Vancouver, Canada: UBC Press), p. 59.

23. Colby, M. (1989). *The Evolution of Paradigms of Environmental Management in Development.* SPR Planning Paper No. 1. (Washington, DC: Strategic Planning Division, Strategic Planning and Review Department, World Bank).

24. See Gladwin, T., J. Kennelly, & T. Krause (1995). "Shifting paradigms for sustainable development: Implications for management theory and research." *Academy of Management Review, 20,* 874–907; Daly, H., & J. Cobb (1994). *For the Common Good.* (Boston: Beacon Press); and Daly, H. (1991). *Steady-State Economics.* (Washington, DC: Island Press).

25. Kuhn, T. (1970). *The Structure of Scientific Revolutions.* (Chicago: University of Chicago Press).

26. Scheffer, V. (1991). *The Shaping of Environmentalism in America.* (Seattle: University of Washington Press).

APPENDIX A (P. 199–204)

1. Stone, P., and others (1968). *The General Inquirer: A Computer Approach to Content Analysis* (Cambridge, MA: MIT Press).

2. Weber, R. (1985). *Basic Content Analysis.* (Thousand Oaks, CA: Sage).

APPENDIX B (P. 205)

1. Chow, G. (1960). "Test of equality between sets of coefficients in two linear regressions." *Econometrica, 28,* 591–605.

BIBLIOGRAPHY

Allison, G. (1971). *Essence of Decision.* (New York: HarperCollins).

Ausubel, J., & H. Sladovich (1989). *Technology and Environment.* (Washington, DC: National Academy of Engineering).

Bailey, J. (1995, November 15). "Utilities overcomply with Clean Air Act, are stockpiling pollution allowances." *Wall Street Journal,* p. A8.

Bazerman, M. (1994). *Judgment in Managerial Decision Making.* (New York: Wiley).

Berenbeim, R. (1992). *Corporate Ethics Practices.* (New York: Conference Board).

Bourdieu, P. (1990). *The Logic of Practice.* Trans. R. Nice. (Stanford, CA: Stanford University Press).

Bradley, J. (1996, July-August). "Buying high, selling low." *E Magazine,* pp. 14–15.

Brint, S., & J. Karabel (1991). "Institutional origins and transformations: The case of American community colleges." In Powell & DiMaggio (Eds.), *The New Institutionalism in Organizational Analysis* (Chicago: University of Chicago Press), pp. 337–360.

Brown, L., C. Flavin, & H. Kane (1996). *Vital Signs, 1996.* (New York: Norton).

Burros, M. (1996, February 7). "A new goal beyond organic: Clean food." *New York Times,* pp. B-1, B-5.

Buttel, F., A. Hawkins, & A. Power (1990). "From limits of growth to global change." *Global Environmental Change, 1*(1), 57–66.

Cahill, L., & S. Engelman (1993, Fall). "Bolstering the board's environmental focus." *Directors and Boards,* pp. 23–25.

Cairncross, F. (1992). *Costing the Earth.* (Boston: Harvard Business School Press).

Cambridge Reports/Research International (1992). *Corporate EQ Scores 1992: Americans Rate Corporate Environmental Performance.* (Cambridge, MA: Cambridge Reports/Research International).

Capra, F., & P. Gunter (1995). *Steering Business Toward Sustainability.* (Tokyo: United Nations University Press)

Carson, R. (1962). *Silent Spring.* (Boston: Houghton Mifflin).

Chow, G. (1960). "Test of equality between sets of coefficients in two linear regressions." *Econometrica, 28,* 591–605.

Colby, M. (1989). *The Evolution of Paradigms of Environmental Management in Development.* SPR Planning Paper No. 1. (Washington, DC: Strategic Planning Division, Strategic Planning and Review Department, World Bank).

Daly, H. (1991). *Steady-State Economics.* (Washington, DC: Island Press).

Daly, H., & J. Cobb (1994). *For the Common Good.* (Boston: Beacon Press).

Davis, N. (1996). "The *Exxon Valdez* oil spill, Alaska." In Mitchell (Ed.), *The Long Road to Recovery: Community Responses to Industrial Disaster.* (New York: United Nations University Press), pp. 231–272.

De Boerr, H. (1992, June 17). "Green jobs at the top." *Financial Times,* p. 12.

"Decentralizing environmental burdens." (1982, March 3). *Chemical Week,* p. 38.

Deloitte Touche Tohmatsu (1993). *Coming Clean.* (London: Deloitte Touche Tohmatsu International).

De Marchi, B., S. Funtowicz, & J. Ravetz (1996). "Seveso: A paradoxical classic disaster." In Mitchell (Ed.), *The Long Road to Recovery: Community Responses to Industrial Disaster.* (New York: United Nations University Press), pp. 86–120.

DiMaggio, P. (1983). "State expansion and organizational field." In Hall & Quinn (Eds.), *Organizational Theory and Public Policy.* (Thousand Oaks, CA: Sage), pp. 147–161.

DiMaggio, P. (1991). "Constructing an organizational field as a professional project: U.S. art museums, 1920–1940." In Powell & DiMaggio (Eds.), *The New Institutionalism in Organizational Analysis.* (Chicago: University of Chicago Press), pp. 267–292

DiMaggio, P., & W. Powell (1983). "The iron cage revisited: Institutional isomorphism and collective rationality in organizational fields." *American Sociological Review, 48,* 147–160.

DiMaggio, P., & W. Powell (1991). "Introduction." In Powell & DiMaggio (Eds.), *The New Institutionalism in Organizational Analysis.* (Chicago: University of Chicago Press), pp. 1–38.

Dower, R. (1982). "Hazardous wastes." In Portney (Ed.), *Public Policies for Environmental Protection.* (Washington, DC: Resources for the Future), pp. 151–194.

Dowie, M. (1995). *Losing Ground: American Environmentalism at the Close of the Twentieth Century.* (Cambridge, MA: MIT Press).

Downs, A. (1972). "Up and down with ecology: The issue-attention cycle." *Public Interest, 28,* 38–50.

Dunlap, R. (1991, October). "Public opinion in the 1980s: Clear consensus, ambiguous commitment." *Environment,* p. 12.

Dunlap, R. (1991). "Trends in public opinion toward environmental issues, 1965–1990." *Society and Natural Resources, 4,* 285–312.

"DuPont to spend big to cut plant pollution." (1991, August 5). *Engineering News Record,* p. 22.

The Environmental Two-Step. (1995). (Washington, DC: Times Mirror).

Erskine, H. (1971). "The polls: pollution and industry." *Public Opinion Quarterly, 36*(2), 263–280.

Fligstein, N. (1990). *The Transformation of Corporate Control.* (Cambridge, MA: Harvard University Press).

Fligstein, N. (1991). "The structural transformation of American industry: An institutional account of the causes of diversification in the largest firms, 1919–1979." In Powell & DiMaggio (Eds.), *The New Institutionalism in Organizational Analysis.* (Chicago: University of Chicago Press), pp. 311–336.

Florman, S. (1976). *The Existential Pleasures of Engineering.* (New York: St. Martin's Press).

Frankel, C., & W. Coddington (1994). "Environmental marketing." In Kolluru (Ed.), *Environmental Strategies Handbook.* (New York: McGraw-Hill), pp. 643–677.

Friedman, M. (1970, September 13). "The social responsibility of business is to increase its profits." *New York Times Magazine,* pp. 32–33, 122, 124, 126.

Friedman, S. (1996). "Teaching the beat: Rising interest in e-journalism reflected in academic option." *SEJournal, 6*(1), 1, 7.

Gamson, W. (1975). *The Strategy of Social Protest.* (Florence, KY: Dorsey Press).

Gersick, C. (1991). "Punctuated equilibrium: A multi-level exploration of revolutionary change theories." *Academy of Management Review, 16,* 10–36.

"Getty's Berg calls EPA U.S. oil's worst enemy." (1979, October 15). *Oil & Gas Journal,* p. 89.

Giddens, A. (1979). *The Problems of Social Theory: Action, Structure, and Contradiction in Social Analysis.* (Old Tappan, NJ: Macmillan).

Giddens, A. (1984). *The Constitution of Society.* (Berkeley: University of California Press).

Gladwin, T. (1993). "The meaning of greening: A plea for organizational theory." In Fischer & Schott (Eds.), *Environmental Strategies for Industry: International Perspectives on Research Needs and Policy Implications.* (Washington, DC: Island Press).

Gladwin, T., J. Kennelly, & T. Krause (1995). "Shifting paradigms for sustainable development: Implications for management theory and research." *Academy of Management Review, 20,* 874–907

Goering, L. (1996, June 25). "Pollution test case pits Ecuadorans against U.S. firm." *Chicago Tribune,* pp. 1, 14.

Gottlieb, R. (1993). *Forcing the Spring: The Transformation of the American Environmental Movement.* (Washington, DC: Island Press).

Hahn, R., & R. Stavins (1991). "Incentive-based environmental regulation: A new era from an old idea." *Ecology Law Quarterly, 18*(1), 1–42.

Hart, S. (1995). "A natural resource based view of the firm." *Academy of Management Review, 20,* 986–1014.

Hazardous Waste Market: Handling, Storage and Disposal. (1981). (New York: Frost & Sullivan).

Hirsch, P., & M. Lounsbury (1997). "Ending the family quarrel: Toward a reconciliation of 'old' and 'new' institutionalism." *American Behavioral Scientist, 40,* 406–418.

Hirschorn, J., & K. Oldenberg (1991). *Prosperity Without Pollution.* (New York: Van Nostrand).

Hoffman, A. (1992). *The Hazardous Waste Remediation Market: Innovative Technological Development and the Market Entry of the Construction Industry.* CCRE Working Paper No. 92–1. (Cambridge: Department of Civil and Environmental Engineering, Massachusetts Institute of Technology).

Hoffman, A. (1993). "Who loves Love Canal?" *Tomorrow, 3*(3), 58–64.

Hoffman, A. (1994). "Organizational change and the greening process: A case study of the Amoco Corporation." *Total Quality Environmental Management, 4*(1), 1–21.

Hoffman, A. (1995, July 5/12). "The many faces of environmental stewardship." *Chemical Week,* pp. 63–65.

Hoffman, A. (1995). "An uneasy rebirth at Love Canal." *Environment, 37*(2), 4–9, 25–31.

Hoffman, A. (1996). "A strategic response to investor activism." *Sloan Management Review, 37*(2), 51–64.

Holm, P. (1995). "The dynamics of institutionalization: Transformation processes in Norwegian fisheries." *Administrative Science Quarterly, 40,* 398–422

Holusha, J. (1992, September 20). "Dow chemical's czar unlocks the gates." *New York Times,* p. 5.

Hopkinson, R. (1970). *Corporate Organization for Pollution Control.* (New York: Conference Board), p. 12.

Hyson, J., & W. Bolce (1983). *Business and Its Environment.* (St. Paul, MN: West), p. 167.

"Industrial switch: Some firms reduce pollution with clean manufacturing." (1990, December 24). *Wall Street Journal,* pp. 1, 17.

Interfaith Center on Corporate Responsibility (1989–1994). *The Corporate Examiner.* (New York: Interfaith Center on Corporate Responsibility).

Investor Responsibility Research Center (1992). *Compliance Index.* (Plainfield, NH: Investor Responsibility Research Center).

Jablonski, J. (1994). *Prospering Through Environmental Leadership*. (Albuquerque, NM: Technical Publishing Consortium, Inc.).

Jacobs, M. (1993). *The Green Economy: Environment, Sustainable Development and the Politics of the Future.* (Vancouver, Canada: UBC Press), p. 59.

Jennings, P. D., & P. Zandbergen (1995). "Ecologically sustainable organizations: An institutional approach." *Academy of Management Review, 20,* 1015–1052

Jepperson, R. (1991). "Institutions, institutional effects, and institutionalism." In Powell & DiMaggio (Eds.), *The New Institutionalism in Organizational Analysis.* (Chicago: University of Chicago Press), pp. 143–163.

Jubeir, J. (1995). "Educating environmental managers for tomorrow." *EPA Journal, 21*(2), 31–33.

Katz, D., & R. Kahn (1978). *The Social Psychology of Organizations.* (New York: Wiley), pp. 23–30.

Keating, B., & D. Russell (1992, July-August). "EPA yesterday and today." *E Magazine,* p. 33.

Kennedy, P. (1993). *Preparing for the Twenty-First Century.* (New York: Random House).

Kennedy, R. (1991, Third Quarter). "Achieving environmental excellence: Ten tools for CEOs." *Prism,* pp. 79–88.

King, A. (1993). *Directed Organizational Stability and Undirected Evolution: Environmental Regulation in the U.S. Printed Circuit Fabrication Industry.* Unpublished doctoral dissertation, Sloan School of Management, Massachusetts Institute of Technology, Cambridge.

Kraatz, M., & E. Zajac (1996). "Exploring the limits of the new institutionalism: The causes and consequences of illegitimate organizational change." *American Sociological Review, 61,* 812–836.

Krupp, F. (1990). "Win/win on the environmental front." *EPA Journal, 16*(5), 30–31.

Kuhn, T. (1970). *The Structure of Scientific Revolutions.* (Chicago: University of Chicago Press).

Landy, M., M. Roberts, & S. Thomas (1990). *The Environmental Protection Agency: Asking the Wrong Questions.* (New York: Oxford University Press).

Latham, E. (1952). *The Group Basis of Politics.* (Ithaca, NY: Cornell University Press).

Lefferre, T. (1990, May). "The decade of the environment." *Chemtech,* p. 262.

Leggett, J. (1996). *Climate Change and the Financial Sector.* (Munich, Germany: Gerling Akademie Verlag).

Lehmann-Haupt, C. (1992, July 9). "Books of the *Times:* Most of what people say about trash is rubbish." *New York Times,* p. C-19.

Leibniz, G. (1866). "Second éclaircissement du système de la communication des substances." In Janet (Ed.), Œuvres Philosophiques (Paris: Ladrange).

Lightman, A. (1996). Dance for Two. (New York: Pantheon Books).

Lindzen, R. (1992). "Global warming: The origins and nature of alleged scientific consensus." Regulation, 15(2), 87–98.

Lund, L. (1974). Corporate Organization for Environmental Policy-Making. (New York: Conference Board).

Mack, T., J. Norman, H. Rudnitsky, & A. Tanzer (1994, February 28). "History is full of giants that failed to adapt." Forbes, pp. 73–78.

Makower, J. (1993). "Business schools get in line." Tomorrow, 3(3), 50–53.

Mangan, K. (1994, November 2). "The greening of the MBA." Chronicle of Higher Education, pp. A19–A20.

Marples, D. (1996). "The Chernobyl disaster: Its effects on Belarus and Ukraine." In Mitchell (Ed.), The Long Road to Recovery: Community Responses to Industrial Disaster. (New York: United Nations University Press), pp. 183–230.

Maxwell, J., L. Matysiak, J. Nash, & J. Ehrenfeld (1993, Summer). "Preventing waste beyond the company walls: P&G's response to the need for environmental quality." Pollution Prevention Review, 3, 317–333.

Maxwell, J., & S. Weiner (1993, Winter). "Green consciousness or dollar diplomacy? The British response to the threat of ozone depletion." International Environmental Affairs, pp. 19–41.

"Men of the Year." (1961, January 2). Time, pp. 40–46.

Meyer, A. (1982). "Adapting to environmental jolts." Administrative Science Quarterly, 27, 515–537.

Meyer, J., J. Boli, & G. Thomas (1987). "Ontology and rationalization in Western cultural account." In Thomas and others (Eds.), Institutional Structure: Constituting State, Society, and the Individual. (Thousand Oaks, CA: Sage), pp. 12–38.

Meyer, J., & W. R. Scott (1992). Organizational Environments: Ritual and Rationality. (Thousand Oaks, CA: Sage).

Michels, R. (1962). Political Parties. (New York: Free Press).

Miller, R. (1989, January 2). "Earth is chosen as Time's planet of the year." Time, p. 3.

Molotch, H. (1970). "Oil in Santa Barbara and power in America." Sociological Inquiry, 40, 131–144.

Morgan, G. (1986). Images of Organization. (Thousand Oaks, CA: Sage).

Morrison, C. (1991). Managing Environmental Affairs: Corporate Practices in the U.S., Canada and Europe. (New York: Conference Board).

Myers, P. (1990). "The road we've traveled." EPA Journal, 16(5), 57–60.

North, D. (1990). *Institutions, Institutional Change and Economic Performance.* (New York: Cambridge University Press), p. 107.

Novick, S. (1986, January). "The 20 year evolution of pollution law: A look back." *Environmental Forum,* pp. 12–18.

Ocasio, W. (1994). "Political dynamics and the circulation of power: CEO succession in U.S. industrial corporations, 1960–1990." *Administrative Science Quarterly, 39,* 285–312.

Oliver, C. (1991). "Strategic responses to institutional processes." *Academy of Management Review, 16,* 145–179

Olson, M. (1965). *The Logic of Collective Action: Public Goods and the Theory of Groups.* (Cambridge, MA: Harvard University Press).

Opheim, T. (1993). "Fire on the Cuyahoga." *EPA Journal, 19*(2), 44.

Orru, M., N. Biggart, & G. Hamilton (1991). "Organizational isomorphism in East Asia." In Powell & DiMaggio (Eds.), *The New Institutionalism in Organizational Analysis.* (Chicago: University of Chicago Press), pp. 361–389.

Orti, L. (1995). *Environmental Alliances: Critical Factors for Success.* (New York: Conference Board).

Palmer, K., W. Oates, & P. Portney (1995). "Tightening environmental standards: The benefit-cost or the no-cost paradigm?" *Journal of Economic Perspectives, 9*(4), 119–132.

Perrow, C. (1970). "Departmental power and perspectives in industrial firms." In Meyer and Zald (Ed.), *Power in Organizations.* (Nashville, TN: Vanderbilt University Press).

Pfeffer, J. (1981). *Power in Organizations.* (Boston: Pitman).

Pfeffer, J. (1982). "The external control of the organization." In J. Pfeffer (Ed.), *Organizations and Organization Theory* (Boston: Pitman).

Pham, A. (1994, June 28). "Business schools see green." *Boston Globe,* p. 35.

Pillar, C. (1991). *The Fail-Safe Society: Community Defiance and the End of American Technological Optimism.* (Berkeley: University of California Press), p. 5.

Popoff, F. (1991). "Pollution prevention: No longer a pipe dream." *Business Week, 30,* 90.

Porter, M., & C. van der Linde (1995, September-October). "Green and competitive: Ending the stalemate." *Harvard Business Review,* pp. 120–134.

Portnoy, P. (1990). *Public Policies for Environmental Protection.* (Baltimore: Johns Hopkins University Press).

Powell, W. (1991). "Expanding the scope of institutional analysis." In Powell & DiMaggio (Eds.), *The New Institutionalism in Organizational Analysis.* (Chicago: University of Chicago Press), pp. 183–203.

Powell, W., & P. DiMaggio (1991). *The New Institutionalism in Organizational Analysis.* (Chicago: University of Chicago Press).

"Presbyterians ratify teaching on sex, ecology." (1991, June 9). *Boston Globe,* p. 4.

"Product stewardship: Responsibility never ends." (1973, October 3). *Chemical Week,* p. 45.

Protess, D., and others. (1987). "The impact of investigative reporting on public opinion and policy-making: Targeting toxic waste." *Public Opinion Quarterly, 51,* 166–185.

Rathje, W., & C. Murphy (1992, August 22). "Poor, misunderstood garbage." *New York Times,* p. 21.

"Real property." (1987, November 1). *ABA Journal,* p. 67.

Rice, F. (1993, July 26). "Who scores best on the environment?" *Fortune,* pp. 114–122.

Russell, M., W. Colglazier, & B. Tonn (1992). "The U.S. hazardous waste legacy." *Environment, 34*(3), 12–15, 34–39.

Russo, J., & P. Shoemaker (1989). *Decision Traps.* (New York: Doubleday).

Sarokin, D., and others (1985). *Cutting Chemical Wastes.* (New York: Inform, Inc.).

Scheffer, V. (1991). *The Shaping of Environmentalism in America.* (Seattle: University of Washington Press).

Schein, E. (1985). *Organizational Culture and Leadership.* (San Francisco: Jossey-Bass).

Schein, E. (1990). "Organizational culture." *American Psychologist, 45,* 109–119.

Schmidheiny, S. (1992). *Changing Course.* (Cambridge, MA: MIT Press).

Schmidheiny, S. (1996). *Financing Change.* (Cambridge, MA: MIT Press).

Schwartz, I. (1973, February 14). "More of management moves into the environment picture." *Chemical Week,* p. 59.

Scott, W. R. (1991). "Unpacking institutional arguments." In Powell & DiMaggio (Eds.), *The New Institutionalism in Organizational Analysis.* (Chicago: University of Chicago Press), pp. 164–182.

Scott, W. R. (1995). *Institutions and Organizations.* (Thousand Oaks, CA: Sage).

Scott, W. R., & J. Meyer (1991). "The Organization of societal sectors: Propositions and early evidence." In Powell & DiMaggio (Eds.), *The New Institutionalism in Organizational Analysis.* (Chicago: University of Chicago Press), pp. 108–140.

Scott, W. R., & J. Meyer (1992). "The organization of societal sectors." In Meyer & Scott (Eds.), *Organizational Environments: Ritual and Rationality.* (Thousand Oaks, CA: Sage), pp. 129–154.

Selznick, P. (1949). *TVA and the Grass Roots.* (Berkeley: University of California Press).

Selznick, P. (1957). *Leadership in Administration: A Sociological Interpretation.* (Berkeley: University of California Press).

Shrivastava, P. (1992). *Bhopal: Anatomy of a Crisis.* (London: Chapman & Hall).

Shrivastava, P. (1996). "Long-term recovery from the Bhopal crisis." In Mitchell (Ed.), *The Long Road to Recovery: Community Responses to Industrial Disaster.* (New York: United Nations University Press), pp. 121–147.

Smart, B. (1992). *Beyond Compliance.* (Washington, DC: World Resources Institute).

Smith, T. (1987, September 16). "If you tread on me, let's talk about it." *Chemical Week,* p. 3.

Stavins, R. (1988). *Project 88: Harnessing Market Forces to Protect Our Environment.* Public policy study sponsored by Senators Timothy Wirth and John Heinz, Washington, DC.

Stern, R., & S. Barley (1996). "Organizations and social systems: Organization theory's neglected mandate." *Administrative Science Quarterly, 41*(1), 146–162.

Stone, P., and others (1968). *The General Inquirer: A Computer Approach to Content Analysis* (Cambridge, MA: MIT Press).

Thomas, G., J. Meyer, F. Ramirez, & J. Boli (1987). *Institutional Structure: Constituting State, Society, and the Individual.* (Thousand Oaks, CA: Sage).

Thomas, R. (1994). *What Machines Can't Do: Politics and Technology in the Industrial Enterprise.* (Berkeley: University of California Press).

Tolbert, P., & L. Zucker (1983). "Institutional sources of change in the formal structure of organizations: The diffusion of civil service reform, 1880–1935." *Administrative Science Quarterly, 28,* 22–39.

"Training post for DuPont top brass." (1982, June 16). *Chemical Week,* p. 40.

U.S. Census Bureau (1980–1993). *Statistical Abstracts of the United States.* (Washington, DC: U.S. Government Printing Office).

U.S. Council of Economic Advisors (1994). *The Economic Report of the President.* (Washington, DC: U.S. Government Printing Office).

U.S. Department of Commerce (1973–1992). *Current Industrial Reports: Abatement Costs and Expenditures.* Report Nos. MA200(73)-1 through MA200(92)-1, Economics and Statistics Administration. (Washington, D.C.: U.S. Government Printing Office).

U.S. Environmental Protection Agency (1990). *Superfund: Environmental Progress.* (Washington, DC: U.S. Government Printing Office).

U.S. Environmental Protection Agency (1991). *Industrial Pollution Prevention Opportunities for the 1990s.* Report No. 600-8-91-052. (Washington, DC: U.S. Government Printing Office).

U.S. Environmental Protection Agency (1992). *The Guardian: Origins of the EPA.* (Washington, DC: U.S. Government Printing Office).

U.S. Environmental Protection Agency (1992). *1990 Toxic Release Inventory.* Report No. 700-S-92–002. (Washington, DC: U.S. Government Printing Office).

U.S. Environmental Protection Agency (1993). *U.S. EPA Oral History Interview #1: William D. Ruckelshaus.* (Washington, DC: U.S. Government Printing Office).

U.S. Environmental Protection Agency (1994). *Enforcement Accomplishments Report, FY 1993.* Report No. 300-R94–003. (Washington, DC: U.S. Government Printing Office).

U.S. General Accounting Office (1988). *Hazardous Waste: The Cost and Availability of Pollution Insurance.* (Washington, DC: U.S. Government Printing Office).

U.S. Office of Technology Assessment (1986). *Serious Reduction of Hazardous Waste.* Report No. OTA-ITE-317. (Washington, DC: U.S. Congress, Office of Technology Assessment).

Veasey, D. (1992, August 16). "By land, sea and air, at war with pollution." *New York Times,* p. 1.

Wagner, B. (1994, March 21). "The greening of the engineer." *U.S. News & World Report,* pp. 90–91.

Walley , N., & B. Whitehead (1994, May-June). "It's not easy being green." *Harvard Business Review,* pp. 46–51.

Weber, R. (1985). *Basic Content Analysis.* (Thousand Oaks, CA: Sage).

Weick, C. (1979). *The Social Psychology of Organizing.* (New York: Random House).

White, H. (1992). *Identity and Control: A Structural Theory of Social Interaction.* (Princeton, NJ: Princeton University Press).

Woodward, K., & R. Nordland (1992, November 30). "New rules for an old faith." *Newsweek,* p. 71.

Woolard, E. (1992, Spring). "An industry approach to sustainable development." *Issues in Science and Technology,* pp. 29–33.

World Commission on Environment and Development (1987). *Our Common Future.* (New York: Oxford University Press).

Yergin, D. (1991). *The Prize.* (New York: Touchstone).

Zucker, L. (1987). "Normal change or risky business: Institutional effects on the 'hazard' of change in hospital organizations, 1959–79." *Journal of Management Studies,* 24, 671–701.

Zucker, L. (1988). *Institutional Patterns and Organizations.* (New York: Ballinger).

INDEX

A

Accounting field, 181

Acid rain issues, 91, 107, 122–123, 168

Action, organizational and institutional, 174. *See also* Environmental activists

Adoption, timing of, 158–159

Aegean Captain oil spill, 164

Agency, and change, 9–10, 173–175

Agent orange, 53, 188

Alaska, University of, Earth Day at, 59

Alliance for Environmental Innovation, 181

Alliances: in future, 180–181; and strategic environmentalism, 108, 111, 125, 133

Allied Chemical Corporation: and industrial environmentalism, 53; and regulatory environmentalism, 75, 80

Allied Signal: AP program at, 42; and strategic environmentalism, 110, 124

Allison, G., 207

American Cyanamid Company: and industrial environmentalism, 51, 53; and strategic environmentalism, 110, 124

American Oil Company, 60

American Petroleum Institute (API), 77, 95, 146, 219; Strategies for Today's Environmental Partnerships of, 118, 126, 133

Amoco Cadiz, 20, 78, 99–100, 162, 163, 164

Amoco Corporation: case study of, 43, 203–204; external relations at, 132–133; function at, 60, 82–84, 102–104, 129–132; history of, 17–22; implications for, 186–189; organizational change at, 99–101, 125–126; and strategic environmentalism, 110, 124; structure at, 60, 81–82, 101–102, 126–129

ARCO: and benchmarking, 187; and strategic environmentalism, 110, 124, 125

Arrow oil spill, 56

Arthur Anderson, 139

Artifacts, as level of culture, 41

Ashland Oil, 124, 125

Assisi Accord, 139

Assumptions, underlying, and culture, 42

AT&T: and benchmarking, 187; and strategic environmentalism, 125

Atlantic Empress oil spill, 164

Audubon Society, 59

Auerbach, R., 47

Ausubel, J., 209

Automobile industry: and compression rates, 54; environmental program in, 126; oil companies and, 77

Automobile Pollution Prevention Project, 126

B

Bailey, J., 226

Bank of America, 122

Barley, S., 207